MULTIPLE REALITIES

A Study of 13 American High Schools

Barbara Benham Tye

UNIVERSITY
PRESS OF
AMERICA

LANHAM • NEW YORK • LONDON

D1446842

Copyright © 1985 by

University Press of America,™ Inc.

4720 Boston Way
Lanham, MD 20706

3 Henrietta Street
London WC2E 8LU England

Library of Congress Cataloging in Publication Data

Tye, Barbara Benham, 1942-
   Multiple realities.

   1. High schools—United States.   2. High school
teaching—United States. I. Title.
LA222.T94   1985   373.73   84-22108
ISBN 0-8191-4462-2 (alk. paper)
ISBN 0-8191-4463-0 (pbk. :   alk. paper)

All University Press of America books are produced on acid-free
paper which exceeds the minimum standards set by the National
Historical Publications and Records Commission.

THIS BOOK IS DEDICATED TO MY HUSBAND, KEN,
AND TO MY PARENTS, SYLVIA AND HARVEY BENHAM.

ACKNOWLEDGMENTS

Three groups of people made this book possible. First, of course, are the students, teachers, administrators, parents, and others in the thirteen high schools which participated in the Study.

Second are the agencies which provided funding for A Study of Schooling:

The Danforth Foundation
The Ford Foundation
International Paper Company Foundation
The JDR 3rd Fund
Martha Holden Jennings Foundation
Charles F. Kettering Foundation
Lilly Endowment, Inc.
Charles Stewart Mott Foundation
National Institute of Education
The Needmor Fund
Pedamorphosis, Inc.
The Rockefeller Foundation
The Spencer Foundation
U.S. Office of Education

Third are the staff of A Study of Schooling--those who shaped the project in its early stages, those who participated in instrument development, pilot testing, and the final data collection, and those who eventually grappled with data analysis and preparation of the technical reports upon which much of this book is based.

I extend special thanks to several colleagues who gave me unfailing support and help: /I/D/E/A/-Research Director John I. Goodlad, who invited me to join the Study staff in 1977; Ken Tye, Program Officer, who oversaw the day-to-day operation of the project and created the healthiest, most enjoyable work environment I have ever encountered; and Joyce Wright, office mate, friend, and a great source of professional help and encouragement.

The data analysis phase of the project ended and /I/D/E/A/-Research closed its doors in June, 1980. The following month Ken Tye and I were married and left for

v

a two-year period of work overseas. During those two years, we carried masses of computer printouts and data reports around the world, working on the junior high and high school books in every spare moment. We spent countless hours discussing, analyzing, and reviewing each other's work: my deepest gratitude to Ken, my best friend, respected co-worker, most rigorous critic, and dear husband.

TABLE OF CONTENTS

PREFACE

This book grew out of A Study of Schooling, a comprehensive inquiry into elementary and secondary education that spanned in its duration the concluding years of the 1970's and the early years of the 1980's. Schools in seven regions of the United States were studied in triples: elementary schools passing their students into middle schools from which they progressed to senior high schools. The 38 schools comprising the sample were selected so as to be as representative as possible of the nation's schools--in diversity of location, size, socio-economic status of students' families, and so on. They were studied in depth and breadth from the perspective of students enrolled, their teachers, their parents, the principals, and others. The data encompassed nearly 18,000 students, approximately 1,350 teachers, and some 8,600 parents. In addition, carefully trained observers recorded human interactions, pedagogical procedures, curricular content, and instructional materials in 1,016 classrooms.

Overall findings, as well as personal observations on the data and dozens of recommendations for improvement are reported in my book, A Place Called School (McGraw-Hill, 1984). But the data bank is so enormous and the ways of coming to grips with the information so varied that one book simply does not do justice to what many reviewers have described as the most comprehensive study of schooling ever conducted. Consequently, three additional books, including this one, are going to press almost simultaneously and another is in preparation. All four of these manuscripts represent the work of senior members of the research staff of A Study of Schooling whose long and deep involvement in conceptualization, data gathering, and data analysis lend authority to their conclusions and interpretations.

These authors benefitted also from having the opportunity to note the emphases and omissions in my book, as well as from having available nearly all of the technical reports on segments of A Study of Schooling. They both expand on topics and themes addressed by me and introduce new ones. The result is a more

ix

exhaustive treatment of what they chose to focus upon and, overall, a more comprehensive understanding of schooling at each level. Without this understanding, recommendations for reform tend to fall short of what is required.

As the Study drew to a close, I asked Dr. Barbara Benham Tye to focus on the 13 senior high schools in our 38-school sample. Interest in and concern for the high school has reached a high peak following the publication in 1983 of A Nation at Risk, the report of the National Commission on Excellence in Education appointed two years earlier by Education Secretary Terrell Bell. The opening pages of this report, prelude to a long list of specific recommendations, carried with them a rather breathless urgency, as if some pestilence such as the fruit fly had descended upon us and had to be stamped out quickly.

This urgency in tone grew out of the eye-opening experiences of the Commission's members, not out of crises suddenly upon us, however. Many of the conditions and problems identified by the Commission have been with our high schools from the time they expanded from admitting one child in eight early in this century to the present, when virtually the entire student population of elementary and junior high schools moves on into senior highs.

Barbara Tye addresses a series of questions that arise out of this shift and other changes in the context and circumstances of schooling. Clearly, teachers today confront greater student variability than once was the case. Home and school no longer have the mutually supportive relationship they once ejoyed. The status of teachers has diminished; teachers' salaries have not kept pace with incomes in occupations requiring less preparation and receiving less public scrutiny. All of these conditions have an impact on teachers' satisfaction and frustration.

In most human endeavors, increasing complexity has been met with relatively rapid evolution of correspondingly sophisticated techniques for dealing with it. The data presented by Dr. Tye lead to the conclusion, however, that today's teachers teach very much as did yesterday's: they lecture, talk, and question the total class; they use textbooks and workbooks commonly and regularly, and they assign desk work. These procedures conspire to keep students passive; teachers do most of the talking and make almost all of the decisions regarding what transpires in classrooms. Our goals for schooling conjure up a vision of students engaged in problem-solving, decision-making, creativity, collaborative activities with fellow students, and the like. But very little of these sorts of things were observed in the rather large number of classrooms constituting the sample. The high schools differed from each other in significant ways, but they were surprisingly alike in the form of the curriculum (for example, the succession of specific topics covered), the materials in use, and the mechanics of pedagogy.

Preparing teachers to behave differently and creating school settings to support alternative models of teaching and learning will not be easy. Yet, the diversity of the high school student population and the wide range of skills and understandings we expect these students to possess call out for teachers whose pedagogical repertoire is equally rich and diverse. Dr. Tye discusses these challenges to both the pre-service and in-service education of teachers.

Many of the practices described by the author are conditioned and even reinforced by the circumstances of schooling. Our data show that many teachers are at least aware of practices other than those they consistently use; indeed, they endorse alternatives as desirable. But the circumstances of seeking to control two dozen or more energetic young human beings in a small box of a room causes teachers to be leery of teaching procedures calling for movement and noise. Teachers teach the way they were taught and the circumstances of teaching tend to reinforce these ways.

A major implication of Barbara Tye's concluding chapter is that change processes focused exclusively on individuals are not sufficient. The "deep structure" of schooling must be addressed. Schools are cultures. They are made up of complex relationships that must be understood, or policies directed to their improvement almost always will fall short of their mark. Her analysis of this representative sample of high schools is a useful contribution to the necessary understanding.

Our initial analyses of data collected in A Study of Schooling remained within the framework used for gathering them, virtually of necessity. Members of the research staff took responsibility for collating and analyzing, for example, all of the data on students, or teachers, or parents, or the subject fields, producing meaty source books designed to facilitate the study of relationships among the components of schooling. Dr. Tye was an active participant in all of this work. Consequently, the volume she has written reflects this intimate involvement with the data.

Before I asked her, in 1977, to join the research staff of A Study of Schooling, Barbara had already accumulated an impressive background of experience with high schools. After five years of teaching, she became involved in the original development of the IGE High School Model at I/D/E/A's home office in Dayton, Ohio. Following this, she accepted the challenge of helping teachers at Greer High School, in South Carolina, as they worked to transform their school into an IGE high school. Concurrently, she taught in the Teacher Preparation program at Furman University, and also supervised junior high and high school student teachers. These field experiences in pre-service teacher education and in-service staff development combined with her doctoral work in curriculum theory to give Barbara a rare understanding of the real world of secondary schooling. Her speculations about high schools and the recommendations she puts forward arise out of this knowledge and, as a result, carry with them the attributes of credibility and practicability.

All of us who worked on A Study of Schooling are grateful to the 12 philanthropic foundations and two agencies of the federal government that supported our work over a period of approximately six years. We appreciate particularly the role of the Institute for Development of Educational Activities, Inc., then the educational arm of the Charles F. Kettering Foundation (a major source of financial support), for managing the funds gathered and for assisting with the process of reporting regularly on their use and on our progress. Publication of this book represents still another outcome from the funds contributed to support our work.

John I. Goodlad
October, 1984

CHAPTER I

CONTEXT AND QUESTIONS

Prologue: Flashbacks

From a Student's Desk

Because my name began with B, I was usually assigned a desk toward the front of the room and on the side, either along the windows or along the bulletin board. Typically, Joey Baker sat in front of me and Lynette Curreri sat behind--he was ears and neck, she was a whisper and sometimes a giggle. My best friend Carol Stanziola was always on the far side of the room, which made it rather difficult to get notes to her.

The high school I attended for 9th grade was large and old and located in a city. My friends and I were bused in from a suburb which did not yet have a high school of its own; waiting for the school bus is one of the memories I share with millions of Americans who did not live close enough to walk to school. The desks in that old school were all well worn. They were also bolted to the floor. I particularly remember the desk I had in History class; it had many names and doodles scratched into its top, and the word WHY was carved deeply into the lower left-hand corner. I always wondered about that.

To us freshmen, the seniors looked unbelievably old and mature. We were very much in awe of them. Three years later, we had forgotten that 13-year-old perspective, and didn't stop to reflect upon how we must seem to the newest batch of 9th graders.

While my friends and I were learning to cope with the expectations of high school, our village was building its own school, in cooperation with two other outlying townships: the resulting regional high school opened in 1957, and we were its first 10th graders. The new school was small, clean, and rural/suburban. We still had to ride a bus to get to school, but a lot of other things were different.

1

I particularly recall the desks. First of all, of
course, they were brand-new. Then too, they weren't
bolted to the floor. And in some classes we didn't
even have desks at all, but were--still alphabetical-
ly--assigned to seats at tables instead. The chalkboards were brown or green, instead of the old black
slate boards we were used to, and the walls were tan or
cream or light blue or apricot instead of the familiar
pale green.

The world looked awesome from where I sat. My
personal reality, as I recall, seemed to be a mishmash
of impressions; thinking back, I recognize that it was
like watching the shadows on the cave wall and, not
knowing any better, assuming them to be real-life. For
example, since I was in a college-prep track, I didn't
have much contact with students whose plans did not
include college. It wasn't until many years later that
I understood how this segregation had narrowed my world
and left me shortchanged.

Another impression: real life was always something
that one was getting ready for, not something being
experienced every day. And another: we students were
accustomed to a confined, restrictive atmosphere. The
world of school was a place of "thou shalt not's," and
we were used to having our lives between 8:00 and 3:00
all planned for us by adults. We were learning to
assume that "learning" meant mostly listening plus some
writing and test-taking. Some learned to play the game
successfully, while others learned to hate school.

For most of us, the social life at school was the
best part of all. Seeing our friends was what we
really looked forward to each day when we got on that
school bus, and this meant that the time before and
after school and between classes was, in a very real
way, far more important to us than any other time of
the day. Certainly it was more important than what
happened in our classes.

A lot of questions occur to me when I think about
what goes on in high schools now, 25 years later, and
inevitably many of these questions have roots in my own
experience. Has life in high schools changed much
since the 1950's? How do students spend their time in
school? What do they regard as important? How do the
structures of schooling shape students' behavior?

2

From a Teacher's Desk

Mark and Rose wrote heart-wrenching poems about the city life around them. Rachel appeared at my home one night, running away. Michael and his brother started a club, which grew into the national campaign against pay toilets. At school dances, Marcus gallantly danced with every girl who didn't have a date, and made everyone around him feel happy--where did a 15-year old get such exuberant generosity? Shy Kathy spoke up one day and said something that made the whole class sit up and take notice.

Of the hundreds, I remember only a few. One of the realities of high school teaching is that it simply is not possible to get to know 150 different students each semester, let alone to touch each one's life in a significant way. Teachers rarely know if, or how, they have made a difference to students.

I remember wondering about what seemed to me to be a huge gulf between our rhetoric and our reality--for instance, our school system maintained that its policy of homogeneous grouping made it possible for teachers to teach more effectively and efficiently to the whole class. In fact, however, whether I was assigned high, average, or low track classes I always found a tremendous range of abilities within each class. Deciding whether to teach to the whole group or to ability-group within each class was part of the never-ending pressure of teaching. And if I opted for within-class grouping, where could I find the help, the support, and the materials I needed? Moving the whole class systematically through the textbook was considered the proper way to proceed. But it left so many kids floundering--unnecessarily, I thought.

When I taught low-track classes I could almost feel the hopelessness of young people who had learned to expect little of themselves. Working to generate enthusiasm and curiosity in such an atmosphere took every ounce of energy I had. In the face of these persistent realities I began to question the justification for tracking.

My classroom was my domain and my desk was my special place within that domain. It was, come to think of it, one of the "tools of the trade" of teaching--it gave me storage space, work space, and a home

3

base within the room. I could sit at it, or on it; I could pound it for emphasis or even jump up onto it. And in the bottom drawer I kept my copies of the school handbook and the state and district curriculum guides we were issued each September.

Because I spent most of my time in that room, I spruced it up as best I could with a few posters and potted plants. Somehow I never found time to change my bulletin boards very often, though, so the appearance of the room didn't alter much from September to June. One year, I decided on a radical change and requested two couches, three round tables and twelve chairs, and extra bookshelf units. I asked that fifteen of the twenty-seven desks in my room be removed. My plan was to set up three distinct areas within the room and to go all-out for small group teaching. I was politely but firmly told that what I asked was not possible: there were no couches or extra bookshelves, and the round tables were needed in the library, and what would happen anyway if every teacher decided to get rid of fifteen desks?

The view from the teacher's desk is mostly of students. Interaction with students is the dominant fact of life for a teacher. But it isn't the only fact of life; there's also interaction with other teachers, and with the administration.

The teacher's lounge was fairly bleak, and far too small. It needed a new coat of paint and new furniture (I don't think it ever occurred to the principal that he could have boosted his staff morale and won points with his teachers just by authorizing a new coat of paint for the teacher's room), but we went there, anyway, to put our feet up and let our hair (and our guard) down for a few minutes during our one "free" period. Conversation in the teacher's lounge was usually on the light side--there simply wasn't enough energy left over from teaching to deal with anything too serious.

Faculty meetings turned the tables on us: like students, we sat and listened as the principal, like a teacher, told us what he thought we needed to know. Departmental meetings and committee meetings were more fun, mainly because they were usually directed towards a task or goal that made sense to us and we could get some satisfaction out of making real decisions. Other

4

duties, like being the student council advisor or chaperoning dances, caused some friction among the faculty, though we never talked about it: those who took on these duties felt overworked (even though they seemed to enjoy the extra contact with kids), and those who refused extra duties felt guilty and were sometimes defensive. Such unspoken feelings fed the ever-present undercurrent of staff competitiveness, reducing the chances of cooperation and cohesion and keeping morale lower than it could have been.

When I think about what goes on in high schools, I have a lot of questions about what it feels like to be a teacher. I know what it felt like to me. But how common is my experience? Do most teachers today feel as powerful--and as isolated--in their classrooms as I did? How do they perceive their relationships with their colleagues? What kind of interaction do they have with their principals? What problems do they think their schools have? What kind of decisions can they make about what activities and materials to use and how to organize their teaching? What are the sources of job satisfaction for high school teachers?

The Multiple Perspectives of Schooling

The view looks different from the principal's desk, too, and from the librarian's, and the guidance counselor's. Within every high school there are many realities and it is as difficult to capture a description of the American high school as it is to freeze a kaleidoscope in one pattern: the pieces keep falling into new positions.

I have titled this book Multiple Realities because if there is one thing I have learned both from my experiences in schools and from my work with the Study of Schooling findings, it is that there is no single vision either of what American high schools are or of what they should be.

A Study of Schooling was intended to be, first, a descriptive effort; that is, an attempt to paint a picture of 13 high schools as we found them. It was expected that out of this description, questions would emerge about whether schools as we found them were adequate to a vision of what they should or could be and, if not, what it would take to improve them.

5

Questions can come from other sources as well, of course. Though a major portion of this book is devoted to the actual findings of the Study, two other sources of questions about schooling play an important role as well. One of these is my own experience, which inevitably shapes my attitudes towards schools and determines the kinds of issues that will be of interest to me. I have already tried to give the reader a general idea of what some of these issues are. No one, I think, can entirely avoid making comparisons with their own experience when they study schools.

The other source of questions about schooling is history. As we shall see, decisions made between about 1830 and 1950 shaped the American high school as we know it today, and the resulting patterns of assumptions and practices which now seem so familiar may change as decisions made today shape the secondary schools of the coming century.

In the rest of this chapter, I intend to do three things. First of all we will take a brief look at the history of the American high school. This is a useful preliminary to our later exploration of the Study findings, for it sets our 13 schools within a social and historical context and will suggest questions for which the findings presented in later chapters may be able to provide some insights.

Secondly, I will describe the Study itself--how it came about and how it was conducted. Finally, I will summarize the major questions about high schools which will be addressed in the remainder of this book and describe the way the book will be organized.

Historical Context: the American Public High School in Retrospect

History and hindsight combined enable us to perceive a certain logic in the way the American high school developed. There were undoubtedly periods during which different decisions might have been made, times when popular sentiment might have swung in a direction other than it did, or when the presence--or absence--of charismatic leadership might have tipped the balance differently. But all that is just speculation; in fact, events unfolded as they did and, without

6

being overly deterministic, it is possible to see a certain inevitability in that process.

A Brief Review

The Latin grammar schools set an early precedent for secondary education and established preparation for college firmly in the minds of Americans as a primary purpose of secondary schooling. This purpose was insufficiently expansive, however, to accommodate the new American spirit of resourcefulness and practicality. The academies which flourished from the late 1700s to the late 1800s broadened the scope of secondary education to include modern languages, mathematics, and "natural and mechanic philosophy" (sciences) as well as the classics.[1] Before long, however, even the curriculum of the academy was seen as being too narrow for the expanding needs of the nation. The publicly financed secondary school made its first appearance in Boston in 1821. Boys of twelve were eligible to sit for an entrance examination and, if admitted, undertook a three-year course of study in English, math, social studies, and sciences.* A few years later, the state of Massachusetts required a high school curriculum of eight subjects, and by 1857, twenty subjects were required in the Massachusetts high school.[2] Expansion of the curriculum, clearly, has been both a trend and an issue since the earliest days of public high schools in this country.

The first real comprehensive high school opened in Philadelphia in 1838. From the beginning, it offered three different curricula: the "principal" course, a classical course, and an "English" course. The principal course included modern languages, English, mathematics, social studies, sciences, drawing, and religion; the classical course was similar but stressed the classical instead of modern languages. The "English" course was just two, instead of four, years, and included no foreign languages at all. In theory, then, the Central High School in Philadelphia could provide for students who wished to prepare for college (the

---

* A high school for girls opened in Boston in 1826 but closed two years later amidst controversy: more students wished to enroll than the city was willing to pay for. Educating girls was not yet seen as a worthwhile civic investment.

7

classical curriculum), to enter the world of work (the principal curriculum), or who wanted only two years of secondary schooling (the English curriculum). In fact, however, two-thirds of the students chose the principal curriculum, and after a few years the two-year curriculum was dropped altogether. When colleges and universities began to accept modern languages instead of classical languages as appropriate preparation for college entrance, the classical curriculum declined rapidly. What had been known as the "principal" curriculum became, in reality, the principal general education curriculum found in most high schools by the late 1800s. With the exception of religion, no longer taught in our public schools, the principal curriculum offered in 1839 bears a striking resemblance to the general education courses which still, in the late 1900s, form the core of American high school education.

Secondary education expanded rapidly in the years following the Civil War, particularly in the newer states. Whereas the establishment of a public school system had taken almost 50 years in Ohio after that state entered the Union, Iowa had a public school system within ten years of becoming a state. Some of the territories in the Far West didn't even wait to be admitted into the Union before opening public elementary and secondary schools, developing state education agencies, and even establishing universities.[3]

According to Cremin, the "most vigorous pedagogical battle of the 1880s" was fought over the issue of manual training and the question, what should be the purposes of the publicly-financed secondary school? The tradition of classical intellectual education gave way to a new conception of the high school as a place where young people would develop their hands as well as their heads. A survey conducted in 1890 found "thousands of boys and girls studying carpentry, metal and machine work, sewing, cooking, and drawing in 36 cities representing fifteen states and the District of Columbia."[4]

Baltimore opened the nation's first manual arts high school in 1883 and seven years later there were nearly 100 such technical high schools in the country. The stronger trend, however, was toward the comprehensive high school which could offer college preparatory courses, "principal" or general education courses, and

8

manual training courses under one roof. Even the
Report of the Committee of Ten, published in 1893 and
emphasizing the paramount importance of intellectual
development, failed to de-fuse the manual training
movement or the rapid spread of the comprehensive high
school idea. Indeed, even within the Committee itself
there was such disagreement as to the purposes of
secondary schooling that a minority report emphasizing
activity subjects and general education for "the 90%
who would not go on to college" was published.

                    *   *   *

A number of important things happened around the
turn of the century. Increasingly, schools were being
looked upon as the primary institution charged with
educating young people. Previously, schools had been
considered one of many educating institutions. Furthermore, many people were coming to regard the school
as an agency of social reform. This is the legacy of
the progressive era: not only was the school to trans-
mit the culture and prepare well-rounded, literate
citizens, it also was expected to instill a certain
social consciousness and desire to contribute to the
improvement of society. Unfortunately, American
measures of both personal worth and societal improvement were basically economic; there was little genuine
altruism involved. This economic orientation has led
Americans to look upon years of schooling as an economic investment likely to pay off in dollars and cents,
rather than as personal self-development likely to pay
off in increased wisdom and understanding. In Chapter
4 of this book we will examine the data in order to
determine the degree to which this was true of the
students we sampled.

Another thing that happened around the turn of the
century was the formation of regional accrediting
associations. Formed by and for colleges and universities, these agencies soon had the power to determine
the high school curriculum, at least for those students
who were preparing for college: they set college
entrance requirements.

Finally, for those who were not planning on going
to college, the vocational guidance movement emerged in
the early years of the 20th century. As originally
conceived by Frank Parsons, vocational guidance was to
have three components: self-analysis, occupational

knowledge, and expert advice as to the type of preparation necessary. Theoretically, this sort of self- and career-awareness would be suitable for any young person. In practice, however, it tended to focus on the students who were not college bound and in fact has deteriorated into one facet of the sorting and sifting process (curriculum tracking is another facet of this process), which all too often pigeonholes students early in their secondary school life and leaves them little voice in their own future. In Chapter 6, we will be taking a close look at tracking effects as revealed by A Study of Schooling findings.

*   *   *

The high school was still taking shape in the second and third decades of the 20th century. Although the foundations of the comprehensive school idea had been laid long before, as we have seen, the issue was still being debated during World War I. At that time, several states were considering legislation which would have created a European-style dual system of schooling.[5] Had that pattern been established, today we would have separate schools for college and non-college bound students.

In 1917 the National Association of Secondary School Principals was formed. The issue which was of immediate concern to its members at that time was the question of how the high school could best function as a "higher common school." One answer to this question came a year later, when the report of the NEA's Commission on the Reorganization of Secondary Education was published. This report helped to "fix" certain patterns which until then had been variable. For example, it approved of the establishment of the junior high school; henceforth the dominant pattern of schooling in America would be 6-2-4 or 6-3-3 instead of the 8-4 pattern which had been common until then. The report put the seal of approval, once and for all, on the comprehensive high school idea and marked the final defeat of the dual system movement. It proposed a balance between courses which would be required of all students--the "common school" idea at the secondary level--and courses which would be optional, leaving room for the variety of programs characteristic of the comprehensive school.

The NEA report also affirmed that the primary purpose of the high school was to prepare young people for life. This was quite a shift from earlier ideas, and underlines the degree to which the high school as a social institution was still being shaped. This "life preparation" ideal was set forth as a set of seven principles which, in effect, became guidelines for the comprehensive high school curriculum from then until now. The secondary school should help students in the following seven areas: health, command of fundamental processes, worthy home membership, vocation, civic education, worthy use of leisure time, and ethical character. In other words, high schools should prepare students to lead physically healthful lives; to master basic intellectual skills; to be good children and, eventually, good parents; to select a career wisely and prepare for it appropriately; to be good citizens; to use leisure time constructively; and to behave according to the accepted ethical norms of our society. A tall order, indeed. These goals are still part of our national assumptions about what high schools are for.

                    *   *   *

The period of national optimism which had lasted so long finally came to an end during the 1930s, and the spirit which had driven the progressive era gave way to the sense of impotence that is still with us. The Depression years and the rise of world totalitarianism combined to deal nearly fatal blows to the American faith in the improvement of human institutions. The emergence of mass media put terrible news at everyone's ear and, before long, in front of their eyes, at the turn of a switch. Powerful tools for influencing people's thoughts and beliefs became part of our lives almost overnight, and did their part to contribute to the uneasy feeling that someone else was in control of our lives.

Interestingly, it was during that troubled decade of the 1930s that the greatest surge in high school attendance took place. High unemployment was undoubtedly a factor: young people who might otherwise have been working stayed in school longer; schooling came to be seen as the best possible investment in future earning power.

As the age of optimism gave way to the decades of despair, the American high school was nearly "finished." In the absence of faith in perfectability, no further major changes would be tried. One last effort to keep the high school curriculum flexible, the Eight-Year Study, failed to make a significant impact; the structures which would endure were already firmly in place. When the results of the Study were published in 1941, everyone's attention was on the war.

Table 1.1

Percentages of high school age population enrolled in secondary school at ten-year intervals from 1890 to 1981.[6]

enrolled in secondary school
(ages 14-17)

1890	6.7%
1900	11.4
1910	15.4
1920	32.3
1930	51.4
1940	73.3
1950	76.8
1960	86.1
1971	93.3
1981	92.3

And as the war ended, the pace of life seemed quicker. New developments in technology brought new social pressures as well as changes in life styles. The world was getting smaller and more interdependent. Old structures--colonialism, for instance--were toppling and new ones--such as communism--seemed to be gaining strength.

All of a sudden, life seemed to be full of anxieties. Some of these found an outlet in Cold War hysteria. Others were expressed in a wave of criticism of the schools. Schools were too lenient; "progressive" education had failed; students were not getting enough discipline, or enough science; the basics were

being neglected.* In the absence of a national consensus on the purposes of schooling, these pendulum-swings
of public sentiment are probably unavoidable. I tend
to agree with Downey that:

> ...the important conflict over education
> is not a controversy between the school-
> men and the people. Rather it is a
> matter of fundamental differences in
> attitudes and values of subgroups of
> citizens...there is no such thing as a
> general philosophy of secondary education
> that earns the support of a majority of
> the people.[8]

No wonder, then, that first one philosophy, then
another should dominate the debate. And if the conservative critics of the 1950s managed to spark dialogue
about the proper role of the schools, so much the
better. The pendulum swung back towards liberalism in
the 1960s--a nation that had listened to Bestor and
Rickover was listening to Illich and Kozol ten years
later. The schools as they are probably represent some
kind of a synthesis of the two extremes, but it's an
unstable synthesis at best, as the schools continue to
be buffeted this way and that. Perhaps the lack of
real change since World War II is as much a defense
mechanism as it is a consequence of the institution's
having developed, from 1840 to 1940, a form which
seemed to work in terms of our society's needs and
values.

*   *   *

The late '50s marked the beginning of a period of
experimenting with alternative organizational patterns
and instructional technologies such as team teaching,
differentiated staffing, modular scheduling, instructional television, and programmed instruction. These
efforts originated as a response to the critics of the
1950s and to a national feeling that schools were not
doing a good job to prepare students for modern life.

---

* Feinberg has suggested that "tough," back-to-basics rhetoric
has, historically, been characteristic of times when the nation is
perceived to be threatened by external forces, while "tender,"
child-centered rhetoric has been characteristic of times when the
national stresses are primarily domestic.[7]

These were also the baby boom years; more children in school meant more adults directly concerned with the quality of those schools. As the 1960s began and the political calm of the Eisenhower years yielded to the activism and energy of the Kennedy and Johnson administrations, for a while our culture seemed to catch a glimpse of its earlier optimism. The possibility of change for the better fueled the curriculum improvement movement, into which so many private and public dollars were poured between 1960 and 1970. Organizational reforms, curriculum development, and student participation characterized education in these ten hopeful years. School desegregation was also taking place, as the Supreme Court's 1954 ruling against "separate but equal" schools was acted upon, and the continuing explosion of knowledge created pressure for specialization which led to a new round of curriculum expansion leaving secondary schools, by the later 70s, seriously overextended.

On the whole, it was an exciting and hopeful, if fragmented, time--but it didn't last. By the early '70s, research was raising questions about the ability of the schools to solve problems whose origins could be traced to the basic economic inequities of our society. Foundations were evaluating their investments in educational programs, and finding that all that money seemed to have made little lasting impact. The baby boom was over, the nation's psyche was exhausted by the Viet Nam war and then by the revelations of Watergate, and the country's economy was headed into a recession.

The Study of Schooling: Background and Rationale

As the excitement of the 1960s subsided and educators began to take stock of the situation, it became clear that some changes attempted by schools in the previous decade had "stuck," while others--by far the majority, it seemed--had vanished into thin air. Billions of dollars had been spent, with little visible result. No one knew just where to place the blame, and the frustration this caused is still feeding public mistrust of the education establishment.

Many teachers, too, were left feeling frustrated and let down, and returned--some reluctantly, some gladly--to doing things the old way. Innovative grouping/scheduling and curriculum projects were

14

abandoned with varying degrees of relief and regret. The old ways, however, did not always work, because students had changed. They seemed, on the whole, much harder to manage; often disobedient and disrespectful of teachers and--what was even worse--uninterested in learning. This added immensely to teachers' frustration; some blamed the reform efforts and declared that, in the future, they would be much more wary of proposals for change.

As educators surveyed the gains and losses of the '60s, it began to dawn on some of the more thoughtful that they themselves might be at least partly to blame. Perhaps they had promoted school reforms without first having a thorough understanding of what schools were really like. They had "laid on" changes without real comprehension of the complex dynamics of schools.

This realization prompted John Goodlad and his associates at the Research Division of IDEA to propose, in 1972, a major study of schools which would proceed from a humble premise: we don't really understand schools well enough. Let's study schools, and educate ourselves. And let's not assume that we know what we're going to find. We do begin to realize that schools are very complex organisms. Maybe we'll learn enough to begin to know what questions to ask and perhaps--in time--we'll discover some answers.

A Study of Schooling was therefore designed as a research effort which would not attempt to test preconceived hypotheses, but rather would attempt to describe the schools studied in such a way that some hypotheses about significant features of schooling might be generated. In a very real way, then, A Study of Schooling has been an effort to provide a descriptive data base for future research by others.

Its findings should be useful for practitioners, as well; they may provide insights into specific local problems or conditions which can then lead to local improvements on a scale which is realistic and manageable in the judgment of those involved.

The instruments developed for A Study of Schooling can be adapted for use by any school or school

15

district.* They are potentially helpful tools for school self-study leading to school-based problem solving or change efforts.

Since the publication of the Study of Educational Change and School Improvement,[9] it has been a consistent position of the IDEA staff that the most effective unit for successful and appropriate change is the single school, its teachers and administrative team (and sometimes students and parents) supported by the district, working together to identify and solve problems of concern to all. This philosophy also guided A Study of Schooling. Data from the Study were returned to the participating schools to use, as they saw fit, for their own improvement efforts.[10]

Although it was assumed that each school studied would be unique in many ways, it was also felt that the schools would probably share a great many common characteristics. Points of consistent similarity suggest aspects of schooling which may be common beyond our sample, in many other schools throughout the nation. Points of difference serve as a constant reminder that every school in the United States is unique in its particular combination of circumstances, and that educators and policymakers should not be too hasty in mandating across-the-board changes without allowing latitude for these differences.[11]

An expectation that each school would be unique and, at the same time, very similar to other schools, then, led to the decision to select schools for study which would be fairly typical of most schools in the nation,[12] and yet would be distinctly different from each other. The findings which will be presented in Chapters 3-6 reflect this duality.

Sample and methodology

Schools were studied in sets of three: first a high school was chosen, followed by one of its feeder junior highs, and a feeder elementary school. This permitted

---

* Note: These may be obtained from the Laboratory in School and Community Education, University of California, Los Angeles, California 90024.

16

a grade 1-12 perspective. The community in which each
"triple" was located was also part of the Study.

Of the thirteen high schools studied, four were
large, five were medium-sized, and four were small.[13]
Four were urban, four were rural, and five were suburban. As to socioeconomic status (SES), seven were
middle, two were low, three were mid/low and one was a
mid/high combination.[14] Ethnically, seven were virtually all white, one was 99% black, one was 100%
Hispanic and four were ethnically heterogeneous, with
nonwhite populations ranging from 20% to 53%. At
several schools, languages other than English were
spoken; the Study instruments for parents and community
were produced in Spanish, and were translated into
Korean, Armenian and Spanish for use by those adminis-
tering classroom questionnaires.

Each of the thirteen high schools and its community
reflect a combination of the four demographic factors
just listed: size, location, SES, and ethnicity. In
addition, the thirteen communities in which these high
schools were situated are spread all over the United
States; the only major geographic region not represented was the Northeastern United States.[15]

The intent of the Study was to examine the participating schools in far greater detail than had been done
before in a study of comparable size. Rather than
examine a few aspects of a great many schools, the IDEA
staff chose to study a great many aspects of just a few
schools. While its purpose was descriptive and its
methodology that of one-time survey and observational
research, the richness of the data which were accumulated places this Study in rather a unique category--
beyond conventional survey research, but stopping short
of ethnography.

Intermediate agencies in twelve of the thirteen
communities worked with IDEA staff to select the
schools to be included in the Study. In several cases
these intermediate agencies were the county or district
offices, and in other cases they were regional service
centers. In one location, the cooperation of the local
AFT chapter was required--and received.

Each triple was studied for one month during 1977
by a team of approximately 24 locally-recruited data

17

collectors, trained and directed by IDEA staff and specially-selected Site Managers.[16]

Overall, 11,051 questionnaires were received from 7,677 high school students.[17] 716 questionnaires were received from 664 high school teachers; of these 479 were also interviewed and 525 had their classes observed.[18] 599 teachers provided the Study with packages of curriculum materials which included lists of topics and skills taught, of books and other materials used, and samples of tests, quizzes, and worksheets used.[19] Sampled classes were identified as to track level: low, average, or high ability tracks, or heterogeneous grouping.[20]

Questionnaires were received from all thirteen of the principals, and twelve of the thirteen also agreed to be interviewed. Most of the vice-principals, counselors, librarians, and other non-teaching staff also completed questionnaires, and many of these were interviewed as well.

In each school district, information was gathered from the business division, adult and pupil personnel service offices, curriculum specialists and superintendents. Members of the Board of Education were interviewed and completed questionnaires. 4,212 parent questionnaires were received. Master schedules and course listings were provided by all schools, and many also provided student and teacher handbooks, records of school publicity, school newspapers, and anecdotal data (often in the form of unsolicited notes or letters) from students and teachers. State and district curriculum guides and goal statements were also collected. Finally, data collectors kept daily logs of their experiences, and Site Managers recorded their impressions of the experience in taped interviews after the data collection phase was over.

The remainder of this book will draw from all of these data sources as appropriate, focusing sometimes on one group (for instance on teachers, in Chapter 3), and at other times on comparing the perceptions of several groups (many teacher, student, and parent perceptions will be compared in Chapter 6), or data sources (teachers' and students' perceptions of the classroom encounter will be compared with those of trained observers in Chapter 5).

Limitations and Strengths of the Study

The findings which follow are based on the study of just thirteen high schools, and are reported as such. They are not generalized beyond this sample; therefore no probability statistics are given. In the final chapters, however, these data will be used as a basis for speculation about the state of secondary education. Particularly important are observations about consistencies and inconsistencies from school to school. Questions will be raised and hypotheses proposed, in keeping with the original purposes of A Study of Schooling.

Secondly, the reader should keep in mind that this was not a longitudinal study. Each school was observed for one month, and each classroom for three days within that month. The result, however, is probably one of the richest research data banks ever generated in a study of schools.

A third limitation of A Study of Schooling is inherent in the decision to rely primarily on survey methodology. The nature of closed-format questions forces respondents to select one of several possible given answers--none of which, perhaps, would have been the answer the person would have given had the questions been open-ended. The advantage of closed questions is, of course, that they are easily quantified. Every research project is faced with this choice at some time or another and the dilemma, which is philosophical, financial, mechanical, and political, must be resolved somehow. In the case of the Study of Schooling, survey research was felt to be the best use of the time and resources which were available. As I have already indicated, however, we did not rely on survey data alone. One of the major strengths of A Study of Schooling was its use of observation data. At the 13 high schools, 525 classrooms were observed for three days each, by carefully trained observers using an extremely detailed observation instrument.[21]

Since A Study of Schooling was designed in an attempt to understand the internal dynamics of schools no student achievement data were collected. Instead, the Study focused on processes, relationships, and attitudes towards the daily experiences of schooling.

19

One of the major strengths of A Study of Schooling suggested the title of this book. The staff deliberately set out to collect data on schools from a variety of viewpoints. This gives us a unique capability to make comparisons across data sources. For example, we can compare the principals' views of problems at their schools with the views of their teachers, the students, and the parents. We can compare what teachers say about their own teaching with the perceptions of their students and of trained observers. No other high school study to date has done a more thorough job of gathering data from a variety of perspectives on such a vast range of variables.

The reader is asked to bear in mind that the interpretations of Study data presented in this book are those of the author. Alternative explanations and hypotheses will occur to every reader who is closely involved with the day-to-day business of schooling, as well as to researchers who operate at a more theoretical level. The technical reports upon which this book is based, as well as the original data bank itself, are available from the ERIC Document Reproduction Service, P.O. Box 190, Arlington, VA 22210.

Into the Forest: a Personal Note

I have referred briefly to the richness of the data that were collected and to the decision of the Study staff to examine a handful of schools in depth rather than go for a larger sample but a smaller number of variables. In fact, A Study of Schooling differed dramatically from much educational research in this respect, and the conceptual challenges involved in organizing the data and presenting the findings were formidable.

It was a little bit like standing on the edge of a huge forest. No path exists; yet one wants to enter and explore, and to learn as much as one can about that forest. But where should I enter? To my right, the undergrowth is thick and tangled. Straight ahead, the trees are young and not too tall; visibility might be good there. To my left, the ground looks rocky but I can hear a brook gurgling. There are so many possibilities, but sooner or later I will have to decide: I will enter between this oak tree and that rock. And, having entered, I must continue to make choices as I work my way deeper into the forest. Some attractive paths must wait for another time. Eventually, I will find my way out, on the other side of the forest. Then, I should know something about the place--but not yet everything. It would take a long time to know that forest through and through.

How shall I organize and present A Study of Schooling findings? My book can't be more than a few hundred pages; what should I leave out--and why? What do I feel it is important to include, and what are the personal values and biases which shape my choices?

Shall I focus on the student data? How much space should I give to presenting the results of interviews with the principals? Should I devote a separate chapter to the parent data, or compare parent, teacher, and student data on specific topics? Are there any conceptual frameworks in the literature on high schools that might provide some appropriate organizational guidelines? These are the kinds of questions we all faced when, in early 1978, the data were all gathered and we had to begin to analyze it (entering the forest) and to present the findings (describe what we found there).

Questions to be Explored

As I worked with the high school data from 1980 through 1983, it seemed to me that about six or maybe seven large questions were emerging as focal points. The first of these was: What are the frustrations and satisfactions of teaching as a career? This question became the basis of Chapter 3, which presents the findings from the approximately 660 high school teachers in our sample. The next question, How do schools shape students' behavior? emerged from the massive amount of data we gathered from students. Student data are the primary focus of Chapter 4, but this question recurs in later chapters as well.

Chapters 5 and 6 present findings which address the third major question, What goes on in classrooms? These are drawn from our observations of 525 high school classrooms, from student and teacher perceptions about materials and activities, and from student perceptions of teacher behavior.

The remaining questions are of a slightly different type. They reflect the cumulative and overlapping nature of much of the data. Complexity has always been a distinctive feature of A Study of Schooling--one finding leads to another, or to a new question, and before long one has a many-layered, many-faceted description. One which, moreover, raises normative questions such as those addressed in Chapter 7: How could teachers be better prepared? Are all schools basically alike? And then, finally, we cannot escape the responsibility for asking two more questions: what are the chances of improving high schools? And what policy changes would help make such improvement possible? To the extent that the findings of A Study of Schooling provide some answers to these questions, they will be discussed in Chapter 7.

First, however, it will be important for the reader to have an impression of the thirteen schools in our high school sample. The thumbnail sketches presented in Chapter 2 are intended to serve this purpose, introducing the reader to each school almost as if it were a character in a novel. The findings presented in later chapters will add depth to these "characters" until, by the end of the book, what I will come to refer to as each school's "unique personality" is fully appreciated.

1. Proposals Relating to the Education of Youth in Pensilvania, Benjamin Franklin, 1749.

2. The Shape of American Education, by Geraldine J. Clifford (Englewood Cliffs: Prentice-Hall, 1975) p. 136.

3. A History of Western Education, 2nd edition, by H.G. Good (New York: Macmillan, 1960) p. 498.

4. The Transformation of the School, by Lawrence A. Cremin (New York: Vintage, 1961) p. 32.

5. "Splitting Up The School System: Are Comprehensive High Schools Doomed?" by Daniel Tanner, Phi Delta Kappan (October, 1979)

6. U.S. Department of Education, National Center for Education Statistics. Table 38, 1983-84 Report (in press).

7. Reason and Rhetoric, by Walter Feinberg (New York: Wiley, 1975) p. 142.

8. The Secondary Phase of Education, by Lawrence W. Downey (New York: Blaisdell/Ginn, 1965) pp. 48-49.

9. The "SECSI" Study involved the formation of a League of Cooperating Schools and led to the development of the DDAE Model of school-based problem-solving: Dialogue, Decision-Making, Action, and Evaluation. The books published as a result of the SECSI Study were:
   The Dynamics of Educational Change -- John I. Goodlad
   Schools in Transition -- Kenneth A. Tye and Jerrold Novotney
   The Magic Feather Principle -- Mary Bentzen
   The Power to Change -- Carmen Culver and Gary Hoban
   Organizational Renewal -- Richard C. Williams, Charles Wall, W.M. Martin, and Arthur Berchin

10. Feedback packages returned to each participating school contained only the data from that school.

11. In an era when control of schools is rapidly passing from local to state and federal levels--helped along by tax reforms which place the responsibility for financing schools at the state level--it is even more important for policymakers at

23

these higher levels to recognize the principle of the single school. Regulations and legislation must allow for exceptions, and guidelines must contain legitimate loopholes so that schools engaged in special improvement efforts can have the latitude they need for experimentation.

12. Bette Overman, A Study of Schooling: Methodology (Technical Report No. 2, 1979).

13. Large = student population over 2,000; Medium = 500 to 1,500; Small = under 500.

14. SES of the community was defined by the local school district.

15. Budget constraints forced a cutback from the original plan to study 72 schools in 24 communities. The final sample of 38 schools came from 13 communities located in seven states.

16. For a full description of the logistics of selection and training, see Overman, op. cit.

17. Due to sample design, which involved questionnairing and observing in a cross-section of classes in every subject area, some students were sampled more than once.

18. Each class was observed three times. The subject area distribution of observed classes was as follows: English - 83, Math - 72, Social Studies - 76, Science - 65, Fine Arts - 65, Foreign Language - 27, Vocational Education - 105, Physical Education - 33.

19. Teacher reactions to participation in the Study were positive. Each received $20, but that was hardly adequate to compensate for 5-10 hours of work, which included responding to questionnaires, providing materials, being interviewed and/or being observed while teaching. Four factors seemed to account for the generally favorable response from teachers. First, they received both school-general and class-specific feedback. Second, they had been well oriented to the purposes and procedures of the Study. Third, the Study staff, including intermediate agency and district office personnel, and particularly site coordinators, were quite sensitive to the particular needs of each school. Finally, the teachers themselves were basically open, cooperative and curious people who saw participation as a professionally responsibility.

20. Jeannie Oakes. Tracking Policies and Practices: School Summaries. (Technical Report No. 25, 1981).

21. Philip Giesen and Kenneth A. Sirotnik, The Methodology of Classroom Observations in A Study of Schooling (Technical Report No. 5, 1980).

CHAPTER II

THE THIRTEEN SCHOOLS

The thirteen high schools which participated in the
Study of Schooling differed on a variety of demographic
dimensions: size, location, socio-economic level, and
ethnicity. These differences are summarized below:

	size*	location	SES	ethnicity
Dennison	61	rural	mid	97% white
Euclid	262	rural	mid	100% white
Laurel	271	rural	low	52% white/48% black
Atwater	450	suburban	mid	96% white
Crestview	1091	suburban	mid/lo	99% white
Fairfield	1137	rural	mid/lo	53% white/42% Hispanic
Woodlake	1202	suburban	mid	80% white/10% Asian
Bradford	1350	suburban	mid/lo	90% white/8% black
Palisades	1402	urban	hi/mid	50% white/50% black
Vista	2312	suburban	mid	98% white
Newport	2508	urban	mid	47% white/18% Hispanic
				17% Asian/9% black
Rosemont	2702	urban	low	100% Hispanic
Manchester	3006	urban	mid	99% black

The descriptions which follow provide more detail
about each of the schools. Information is given in six
areas: the community, the parents, the school, the
teachers, the students, and the curriculum. Each
description contains only a small amount of the total
which is available, however. The intention at this
stage is to provide the reader with a thumbnail sketch
of each school to which other data will later be added.

---

* size of student body in 1977

27

Dennison

The Community

Dennison is a small rural farming community with a total population of 350. It is rather isolated; the nearest really large town is 70 miles away, and other communities closer to Dennison also are small. The village, therefore, is fairly self-sufficient, and everybody knows everybody else.

All homes are single-family dwellings; property values range from a low of $3,500 to a high of $50,000, with a median of about $20,000. Economically, Dennison is a middle-class community. There is not a great deal of poverty, although several families were reported to earn less than $5,000 annually.

The Parents

Of the 32 parents who had children enrolled in Dennison Secondary School (grades 7-12), fifteen (47%) participated in the Study. Of these, only thirteen reported their annual income range--for most, it was between $10,000 and $20,000 a year, though one parent reported earning less than $5,000 and two reported earning more than $25,000.

One of the Dennison Secondary parents was Mexican-American; the rest were white.

Higher education was not a common experience for most Dennison parents--only two out of the fifteen parents who participated in the Study were college graduates, and another had completed a postgraduate program. Of the remaining twelve, three had attended college for awhile but had dropped out without graduating, one had attended a trade school, six had graduated from high school but had gone no further, one had dropped out before finishing high school, and one had not completed the eighth grade.

Dennison parents were politically moderate to conservative; the streak of populism sometimes found in farming communities seems to have aligned itself in recent years with a more conservative ideology, despite its liberal origins. Only one of the fifteen Dennison

28

parents identified himself or herself as liberal; seven said they were moderate, six were conservative, and one was "very" conservative.

Several of the fifteen Dennison parents in our sample had more than one child enrolled in Dennison Secondary School. The effect of this on the school's ambience cannot be overemphasized--this was, actually, a <u>family</u> school--almost, but not quite, a "one-room schoolhouse."*

Not only were the school and its community both very small, they were also very stable. There was, and is, very little mobility out of or into the Dennison community; when families own farms they tend to remain on them for generations, barring unusual reasons for displacement. Most Dennison Secondary students graduate with friends they have known since kindergarten. Twelve out of fourteen Dennison Secondary parents (86%) had lived in the Dennison community for fifteen years or longer. One had been there for more than nine years and the other, a relative newcomer, had moved in within the previous three years.

Dennison Secondary parents had quite a lot of contact with the school. For one thing, <u>all</u> of them reported having parent-teacher conferences about their children's progress. For another thing, larger percentages of parents reported being involved in more kinds of school-related activities at Dennison than at any other high school in the Study: over one-third had worked as classroom aides at one time or another; almost half said they had taken adult education classes at the school; well over half said they had attended meetings held at the school to discuss community problems, and almost all (93%) said they attended special school events.

Not surprisingly, Dennison parents felt they knew their school very well, and they seemed proud of it: they gave it a higher grade than that given by parents at any other high school in the Study.

---

* In fact, with just 61 students in grades 7-12, it <u>could</u> have been a conventional small rural school. That it was far more was due to teacher dedication, principal leadership, and community support.

The School

Dennison Elementary and High Schools are housed in
a single building located in the village of Dennison.
It was built in 1920 and was the oldest school building
in the Study. The school grounds, with their play-
ground and playing fields, are adjacent to a city park,
which has a tennis court.

In the fall of 1977, 61 students were enrolled in
Dennison Secondary school, grades 7-12. Of these, 59
participated in the Study. There were eleven teachers
and ten participated in the Study (the eleventh was the
principal, who responded to the Study as an administrator rather than as a teacher). Basically, the entire
school was involved.

At the time of the Study, Dennison Secondary was in
the second year of an innovative modular quarter-course
schedule which had been suggested by the Superintendent
and the counselor, and developed by the teachers with
the agreement of pupils and parents three years earlier. The principal was also in his second year, and had
come on board as principal just as the new plan was
getting started. Everyone seemed very enthusiastic
about the innovative schedule and the curricular
variety which it made possible.

The administrative structure of Dennison Secondary
was minimal: the principal also taught classes, did
some student counseling, coached all boys' sports, and
functioned as athletic director.

There was one counselor, who also served as librarian part-time. One psychologist, one Learning Disabilities teacher, and one nurse served the Dennison
schools part-time.

The Superintendent also functioned as principal of
the Elementary School, located in the same building as
the Secondary School.

The Teachers

Five of the ten Dennison Secondary teachers were
new in the fall of 1977, which meant a turnover rate of
50% for the previous year. Several teachers, when
interviewed, mentioned that the community's isolation

and lack of social facilities caused some teachers to look for work elsewhere, and one teacher mentioned low salaries as a reason why some teachers leave Dennison each year.

Half of the Dennison Secondary teachers were male. Nine of the ten who participated in the Study were under 40 years of age; all were white.

Due to the small size of the group involved, no data on salaries were provided. However, teacher salaries were evidently not too high: half of the teachers indicated that if they were to leave their present position, it would be because of money.

Aside from this, Dennison Secondary teachers seemed quite happy with their work situation.*

All but one of the Dennison Secondary teachers lived in the Dennison community, including those who had just joined the faculty. In such a small town, this might have been confining for teachers with no family ties in Dennison (or who had not grown up in similar, isolated villages), and in fact several did mention the lack of any recreation facilities within 60-70 miles.

Because of the unusual modular schedule, teacher schedules varied somewhat, but all teachers at Dennison Secondary worked very hard. All had a work day of six hours and forty minutes, from 8:00 a.m. to 2:40 p.m. This included five hours and twenty minutes of actual class time, during which most taught six to eight different modules, plus one hour of planning time and a twenty-minute lunch break.

This demanding schedule, moreover, changed every nine weeks for many (though not all) courses. The teacher work load for a full year, therefore, may have

---

* On the Wright Satisfaction Index, which is based on questions about various school facilities, on a scale from 0 to 7, Dennison Secondary teachers gave their school a 6. On the Adult Climate Inventory Job Satisfaction subscale, the mean score for Dennison Secondary teachers was higher than that of any other high school faculty in the Study. Group means on the Principal Leadership and Staff Cohesiveness Composite scales were also highest in the Study.

31

included as many as twenty different course preparations. While this was hard work for the teachers, and
required that they put in many hours of curriculum
planning and preparation time beyond their regular
daily teaching hours, it maximized the curricular
diversity possible in such a small school, and gave the
students a real opportunity to make some choices.

At no other school in the Study, regardless of
size, were the teachers as involved in curriculum
development as they were as Dennison Secondary School.
We found no evidence that actual teaching practices at
Dennison were comparably innovative, however.

The Students

Of the 61 students enrolled in grades 7-12 at
Dennison Secondary during the fall of 1977, 59 participated in the Study. Absenteeism, reported by the
principal as 2% on an average day, may have accounted
for the non-participation of the other two students.

No one drops out of Dennison Secondary, and almost
no one wants to. Two students said they'd like to
quit, but "probably wouldn't." One out of every four
students wanted to graduate and go right to work.
Another one in four planned to attend a trade school.
Of the remaining twenty-eight students, six said they
would probably go to junior college, seventeen wanted
to go to a four-year college or university, and three
wanted to continue on to postgraduate work. Two didn't
know what they would do.

Dennison Secondary students seemed proud of and
interested in their school. They gave it a higher
grade than did students at any other school in the
Study. On the whole, they felt good about their own
academic performance, and all but two (perhaps the same
two that said they would like to quit) agreed that
"this school gives students a good education."

Student participation in extracurricular activities
was extraordinarily high at Dennison Secondary, largely
due to the isolation of the community and the lack of
other things to do. Out of 55 students responding to a
question about extracurricular activities, 50 said they
participated in sports teams, 41 said they were active
in school or community service activities, 32 said they

32

belonged to music or drama groups, 31 were in special-interest clubs such as FFA and 4-H, and 23 said they were involved in student government. No other high school in the Study had a comparably high level of student participation in extracurricular activities. As we shall see in Chapter 4, schools where many students participate in extracurricular activities seem to be healthier places--that is, to have fewer serious problems--than schools where students are not much involved in extracurricular activities.

The Curriculum

Dennison Secondary's unusual curriculum has already been mentioned in general terms. Ten teachers and a teaching principal provided a varied program of course offerings for the 61 students in their charge, maintaining a healthy balance between basic requirements and interesting-sounding electives. The overall impression is of a truly exemplary program for a small school. The teachers all obviously worked very hard and put a great deal of individual and collective effort into curriculum planning. The principal also taught in the minicourse format, thereby both supporting and modeling this type of master schedule and teaching approach.

The student/teacher ratio in our sampled classes ranged from 4:1 to 23:1 with an average, in the academic courses, of about 10:1. There were no interdisciplinary or team-taught courses.

The curriculum seemed quite cosmopolitan for such a small and isolated school. The decision to offer a nine-week minicourse in the problems of minorities, for example, in a community where there were only a handful of minority families, represents an interesting value position.

From the data, Dennison Secondary seems as though it would be a nice place to work. Teacher morale is high, and within familiar and secure surroundings, teachers are encouraged to "stretch" themselves professionally.

Euclid

The Community

The Euclid school district is a large, sparsely populated farming and ranching area in the Great Plains, west of the Mississippi and east of the Rockies. The total population in 1977 was 4,932. All of the students but a handful--those very few who lived in the town itself--were bused to school.

Property values at the time of the Study ranged from a low of around $8,000 to a high of about $60,000, with a median of approximately $22,000. Virtually all homes were single-family dwellings and most were owner-occupied.

The Parents

219 Euclid families had children enrolled in Euclid High at the time of the Study. Of these, 81 parents responded to the Study questionnaire. The median income of this group was $14,000 a year, although one out of every four reported earning less than $10,000.

Almost half of the Euclid High parent sample said that they had graduated from high school themselves but had gone no farther. Another one-fourth went to college, but dropped out before graduating. The pattern in most cases was to remain on--and eventually take over--the family farm or ranch. 74% of the parent sample told us that they had lived in the Euclid area for over fifteen years. In all likelihood, they themselves had attended the Euclid schools. Over one-fourth felt that they knew a great deal about the high school, and 60% said they knew a moderate amount. As is frequently the case in small, isolated communities, the school sometimes functions as a community center: almost one-fourth of the Euclid High parent sample said that they go there for adult education classes, 42% had met there for discussions of community problems, and over two-thirds said that they attend special school events. It was the principal's feeling that parental support for the school was very good.

The School

The high school and the junior high share the same building. Of the 395 students enrolled in 1977-78, 133 were in grades seven and eight, and 262 were in grades nine through twelve. Twenty-four teachers taught the high school courses, but six of these taught some junior high courses as well. The sample populations at Euclid High consisted of 246 (94%) of the students and 23 of the 24 teachers.

The secondary school building itself was rather old. (The oldest part dated from 1937), although a new Agriculture building had been completed just a few months before the Study.

The principal was the only administrator at Euclid High School. At the time of the Study, he had been there for ten years. There was one full-time counselor, and one librarian. One full-time psychologist served both the elementary and secondary schools.

Euclid High had a seven-period day; each period was 52 minutes long.

The estimated annual per pupil expenditure of $1,947.47 at Euclid High was the highest in the Study.

The Teachers

Beginning teachers at Euclid High were paid $9,000 a year in 1977-78. The median salary for the faculty as a whole was $11,841. Teacher turnover was estimated by school officials at about nine per cent annually, which means that for Euclid High, two or three teachers of the 24-person faculty leave and are replaced each year. In 1977-78, 65% of the Euclid High teachers were male. 70% were married. It was a fairly young faculty--20 of the 23 who participated in the Study were under 40 years of age. All were white.

The daily teacher work load at Euclid High included six classes and one planning period, or five classes, one study hall duty, and one planning period. The school day was a long one--from 8:30 a.m. to 4:00 p.m. Most of the teachers had three or more preparations, and the school was on a quarter-course schedule. So all in all the work load was fairly heavy. On the whole, however, Euclid High teachers seemed quite satisfied with their working conditions. When asked to give Euclid High a "grade," they gave it a high B+--no other high school faculty gave their school a higher grade. The teachers seemed to get along well with the principal and he, in turn, thought very highly of his staff.

The Students

246 of the 262 students at Euclid High participated in the Study. School officials estimated that about 35% of the school's graduates went on to four-year colleges or universities, and in fact 30% of our student sample did expect to do so. (Another 4% expected to go on to postgraduate work as well). About the same percentage said they planned to go to either trade school or junior college; approximately one in every four responding students said they would finish high school but go no further. And 12% said that they simply didn't know what they would do--at no other high school in the Study did such a high percentage of students admit that they didn't know what they would do in the future.

Almost no one drops out of Euclid High, though. Only two students out of 239 said that they would probably quit, and school officials estimated the average annual dropout rate at only .8%--97% of the students who entered Euclid High in 9th grade completed all four grades and graduated.*

The Curriculum

Euclid High had a fairly standard curriculum, unusual only in that it was evenly balanced between academic and vocational emphases. Allocation of FTEs was 41% academic, 41% vocational. This even balance was uncommon--at the other high schools in the Study, academic subjects had a higher (sometimes a much higher) percentage of FTEs than did the vocational

---

* These estimates throughout this chapter have been calculated independent of the transiency rate. Transiency varies from a low of two percent at Euclid to a high of eleven percent at Crestview and Fairfield.

subjects. The reason for this unusual balance is the
curricular emphasis on agriculture courses found at
Euclid High. Whereas at most high schools one expects
to find programs in office practices, home economics
and industrial arts, it is less common to find a full
range of agricultural courses. This curricular emphasis is clearly a school response to the needs of the
farming community.

The quarter-course schedule and the large number of
preparations taught by each teacher at Euclid High
meant that a wider range of courses was available to
students than would have been possible with a year-long
or semester-long course schedule and/or fewer preparations per teacher.

Laurel

The Community

The rural town of Laurel is located about an hour's
drive from a major city in the South. Small farms of
from 50 to 300 acres comprise most of the the 400
square miles of the Laurel school district, and many
students come to school by bus. In addition to farming, several local industries provide employment for
Laurel residents.

The total population of the Laurel district at the
time of the Study was 3,000 people, just about evenly
divided between whites and blacks. The schools had
been segregated prior to 1972, and in 1977 many whites
were still rather uneasy about the unified system.
Many told Study researchers that they felt the quality
of educational programs had deteriorated and that they
themselves were no longer as interested in supporting
the schools as they had been previously.

Property values in the Laurel district ranged from
$5,000 to $400,000--the shacks of tenant farmers and
the large, stately old homes of the landed gentry represented these extremes. The typical house of the
average Laurel family, however (valued at about
$20,000) was a modern brick ranch house on the out-
skirts of town, or a slightly older frame house in the

37

town itself. Almost all homes in Laurel were single-family units.

The Parents

218 Laurel residents had children attending Laurel High during the 1977-78 school year. Of these, 81 (37%) responded to the Study questionnaire. Black parents were under-represented in our sample relative to their actual numbers in the total population: 27% of responding Laurel parents were black, and 72% were white.

The estimated median income of the Laurel High parent sample was $13,500 at the time of the Study. However, over one-third of the responding parents reported earning less than $10,000 a year.

As might be expected in a community which offers very little in the way of white-collar managerial or professional employment, the educational level of Laurel High parents was not particularly high. 35% of the sample said that they had never finished high school themselves; another 33% said they had graduated from high school but had gone no further. Only a handful (5%) reported graduating from a four-year college or completing a postgraduate degree. The Laurel High parents were moderate to very conservative in their political beliefs.

Laurel is an old and a fairly stable community; over half of the Laurel High parent sample had lived in the Laurel area for fifteen years or longer, and only ten per cent reported moving there within the previous three years.

Parent participation in many kinds of school-related activities was low at Laurel, as it was at most of the other high schools we studied, but Laurel (unlike many of the other twelve schools) had quite an active PTA (65% of the Laurel High parent sample reported participating in PTA, and 15% of them said that they had served on the PTA Board). Also, one out of every five responding parents said that they had worked in the high school as a classroom aide. Finally, over half said that they did attend special events at the school--this was a finding common to all four of the small high schools we studied.*

The School

Laurel High had 18 teachers and 271 students in grades 9-12 during the fall of 1977. The Study sample included all but one of the teachers and 238 (88%) of the students.

The school is located near the center of town, on an attractive, tree-shaded 15-acre lot which it shares with the immediately adjacent middle school. The two schools are connected by a covered walkway and because grades 6-12 are in such close proximity, each school seems larger than it really is: 550 students are in evidence between classes, but half of them are in the middle school.

The Superintendent's office is located in the high school building, just down the hall from the office of the high school principal. Each had a secretary; there were no other office personnel.

The principal was also the high school's only guidance counselor. Other support staff included one full-time curriculum specialist, one full-time Special Education teacher, and one full-time librarian.

Laurel School District was very proud of its independence--in 1977 it was one of the very few school districts in the state that had not been absorbed by a larger city or county district. In practice, this meant less money for the Laurel schools, but the feeling seemed to be that it was better to have less money than it would be to have more money with county, city, or state strings attached. Per pupil expenditure at Laurel High was much lower than at any other high school in the Study.

---

* Conversely, at our three largest high schools, only about one-fourth of the responding parents reported attending special school events. At the medium-sized schools, parent attendance at special events ranged from one-third to just under one-half.

Laurel High had a conventional six-period day in the fall of 1977.

The Teachers

Of the 17 Laurel High teachers sampled, only eight taught exclusively at the high school. Nine divided their time between the high school and the middle school. The daily work load consisted of five classes and one planning period.

At Laurel High, about two-thirds of the teachers were female. All but a few were married, and of the 17 who responded to the Study questionnaire, 14 were under the age of 40. Thirteen were white, three were black, and one was Mexican-American.

The salary for a beginning teacher at Laurel High School in 1977-78 was $8,391, and the median teacher salary that year was $9,590--lower than that at any other high school in the Study. Low salaries were both a cause and an effect of the extraordinarily high teacher turnover of 40% annually. The high rate of teacher turnover was also caused partly by the size and location of the town: the Laurel community itself did not have enough teachers for its schools, so many teachers had to be hired who did not live in Laurel themselves, but who commuted from as far away as 50 miles. Traveling that far to work each day was an unpopular aspect of teaching in Laurel, and many teachers left as soon as they were able to find work closer to their own homes. The community, in turn, suffered from having teachers who not only were less than happy with their teaching situation but who could not participate fully in the life of the school and the town.

Low salaries and a long commute weren't the only aspects of teaching at Laurel High that made the teachers unhappy, however. Many of them were disillusioned with teaching itself: over half admitted that, given the choice, they would not choose education again as a career. This was a higher figure than at any other high school in the Study.

The Students

238 of Laurel High's 271 students participated in the Study. Of these, just over half were white and the rest were black. The Laurel schools had been integrated when the 1977-78 seniors were in 7th grade and the 1977-78 freshmen were in 4th grade, so all of the Laurel High students at the time of the Study had experienced the dual system and had been part of the changeover to a unified system. While racial conflict was not seen by many students as the biggest problem at Laurel High, 70% of them did agree that "lots of students in this school don't like other students because of their race or color," and 50% of the student sample felt that teachers were similarly biased.

Only 15% of the responding students at Laurel High said that they expected to go on to a four-year college --a very low figure compared to student responses at the other high schools. Conversely, a much larger percentage--42%--said they would just finish high school and go no further. Some had work waiting for them on the family farm, and others would go directly to work in the mill, the plastics factory, or one of the other two small local industries.

Laurel High had the highest estimated dropout rate of the Study--13.5% annually, averaged across the four grade levels--and the lowest number of graduating students: only about 56% of the students who entered Laurel High in 9th grade finished and graduated four years later. However, those who didn't drop out evidently attended school regularly--school officials reported the daily attendance rate as a reasonably high 95%.

The Curriculum

Laurel High's curriculum in 1977-78 can only be described as limited. The basics required by state law for graduation were covered fairly well, but there was not much else. Courses were one year long, and most departments offered only three or four courses, which meant that no possibility for choice existed at all in those subject areas. The English and Math departments, however, each offered seven or eight courses, because these two departments used a tracking system--"Basic" (low ability) and "Regular" (everybody else) classes.

41

The English department also offered three electives:
Senior English, Journalism, and Yearbook.

Overall, the impression was of a fairly drab
curriculum. Each course seemed to be as much or as
little as the teacher was willing or able to make it.

Atwater

The Community

The Atwater district is part of a large city in the
Northwest. Its population in 1977 was 11,193. Atwater
is a fairly typical middle-class community, not too
affluent but not excessively poor (8% of Atwater
families were earning less than $5,000 annually, but
42% were earning over $15,000 a year at the time of the
Study).

A majority of the homes were single-family dwellings, modest tract houses for the most part.

There is quite a lot of light industry in the
Atwater district; these plants employ some residents,
and others work in the city itself. Atwater has no
downtown or central business district of its own.
Residents do their shopping in the city or at large
suburban shopping malls.

The Atwater community in 1977 was virtually all
white, though there were a few Asian-Americans (2.9%),
blacks (2.7%), Mexican-Americans (2.1%), and American
Indians (1.4%).

The Parents

158 parents with students at Atwater High responded
to the Study questionnaire. The average annual income
reported by this group was $19,000. Twelve percent of
the Atwater High parent sample told us that they
themselves had never finished high school, another 44%
said they finished high school but went no further, and
11% went to some kind of trade or business school. The
remainder—33%—had some exposure to higher education,
but only six per cent completed a four-year college

42

degree and another six per cent completed a postgraduate degree.

Atwater High parents were, by and large, long-term residents of Atwater--three out of four had lived there for nine years or longer.

Most of the Atwater High parents who participated in the Study felt that they knew a moderate amount about the school, but a relatively low percentage (16%) felt they knew a great deal about it. Parent apathy was seen as a problem by several members of the Atwater Board of Education and school district officials, and one out of every five of the responding parents admitted that they never had any contact with teachers. On the other hand, Atwater High had a higher percentage of parents participating in a Parent Advisory Board (11%) than did any other high school in the Study, and well over half of the parent sample told us that they attend special school events. Finally, larger percentages of Atwater High parents took part in meetings to discuss local political issues (30%) and other community problems (45%) than at any other high school in the Study except Dennison.

Over half of the parents said that a conflict with working hours hindered their involvement in school-related activities, and one out of four said that they felt it was the business of the principal and the teachers, not the parents, to run the school. Nevertheless, as is frequently the case in smaller schools, parent participation at Atwater High was relatively high in most categories compared to the other twelve high schools.

The School

Atwater High School had 25 teachers and 450 students in grades 10-12 at the time of the Study. Our sample consisted of all 25 of the teachers and 336 (75%) of the students. Two of the teachers were Asian Americans and the rest were white; most of the student body (96%) was also white.

The school building is a one-story structure, with wings for each department branching off the central core. Within the previous three years, Atwater High had been redecorated inside, with new lighting, new

43

ceiling tile, some new furniture, and newly painted classrooms.

The principal was in his third year at Atwater High in the Fall of 1977. He had been hired by the Board three years earlier with instructions to help the teachers to improve the school program, and since then he had been instrumental in initiating several curricular changes. The teachers, however, were none too happy about their new administration: 72% said they did not trust the principal and 80% said that conflicts between the principal and staff members were not easily resolved. We will investigate this further in Chapter 3.

The principal was the only administrator at Atwater High. He had a secretary. One full-time counselor was available for the entire student body of 450 (not an unusual load as compared to the work loads of other high school counselors in the Study). Atwater High also had one full-time Special Education teacher.

The school had one full-time librarian and one part-time library aide. The library budget of $11 per student per year was one of the highest in the Study, but the actual number of books in the library was among the lowest in the Study. The librarian's title was "Media Resources Specialist," and much of the library budget evidently went into media modes other than books.

The daily schedule consisted of six 55-minute periods. The school day began at 8:00 a.m. and ended at 2:30 p.m.

The Teachers

Teacher salaries at Atwater High were among the highest in the Study--beginning teachers started at $11,026, and the median salary during the 1977-78 academic year was $15,632. Only one other high school

--the largest in the Study, Manchester High--had a higher median teacher salary.*

Teacher turnover at Atwater High School was reported by district officials as nonexistent: in the previous year, no teachers had either left or joined the faculty. Nevertheless, it was not a particularly old faculty in 1977--over two-thirds of the teachers were under the age of 40. All but two were married, and sixteen of the twenty-five teachers were men.

Five teaching periods (or four teaching periods and one study hall duty) and one planning period constituted the daily teacher work load.

The Atwater High School faculty placed very high on a satisfaction index composed of questions about school facilities, counseling and library services, school safety, and so on. As has already been mentioned, however, they were not happy with the kind of leadership that was being provided by the principal.

The Students

The 450 students at Atwater High had a more or less average daily absentee rate of eight per cent. The dropout rate, averaged across the three grade levels (10-12) was 6.3%; about 82% of the students who entered Atwater High in 10th grade actually remained to graduate three years later.

School officials estimated that vandalism at Atwater High cost the district only about $500 a year--a very low figure compared with other high schools in the Study.

Thirty per cent of the sampled students said that they planned just to finish high school but to go no further, another thirty-three per cent planned on going to trade school or junior college. Twenty-four per cent expected to go to a four-year college and another

---

* Annual per pupil expenditure was also second highest in the Study, at $1,807 per student per year. Evidently the property taxes paid by the many light industries in the Atwater district provided the district schools with a budget that was unusually comfortable for a school of this size.

two per cent wanted to go beyond that, to post-graduate work. About ten per cent didn't know what they wanted to do in the future.

The student day included six classes, or five classes and one study hall.

The Curriculum

Atwater High School in 1977 had a standard curriculum organized by trimesters, which allowed for slightly greater diversity than would have been possible in a school that size which had a conventional semester plan. There were a few unusual courses (for example: Entomology, Self-Defense, Computer Science, Parenting, The Nature of Prejudice, and "Future Shock"), but for the most part, the small 25-person faculty just about managed to cover the standard basics expected of a high school.

There was evidence of department planning in the four major academic areas, but the other areas were either too small (such as foreign languages: one teacher) or too diverse (such as vocational subjects) for teachers to plan together on curriculum. There were no interdisciplinary or team-taught courses. All in all, the general impression was of strong teachers doing good work within a fairly traditional curricular format.

Crestview

The Community

Crestview High School is located in a rural/suburban area just outside of a medium-sized Midwestern city. The population of Crestview in 1977 was approximately 11-12,000 and the median income, according to the 1970 census, was $13,300. It is a low-to-middle-class community with extremes of income that range from below poverty level--old people living solely on Social Security, young single-parent families on welfare--to middle-class employees of local light industry or heavy industry located in the nearby city. On the whole,

46

Crestview can be fairly characterized as primarily a blue-collar community.

Most of the homes in the Crestview area were modest, single-family units with a median value of $20,200 in 1977. They varied in age between 15 and 50 years. No new homes were being built; the population was aging and the school enrollments were declining. About 15% of the housing did, however, consist of two large apartment complexes and many families with school-age children lived in these. Both apartment complexes had a high transiency rate and something of a crime problem; drugs were easily available.

The Crestview district was virtually all white, and many Crestview residents had moved to the area from the Appalachian states.

The Parents

330 Crestview High parents responded to the Study questionnaire. The median income reported by this group was $14,500 annually; one-fourth of them, however, said that they earned less than $10,000 a year.

Over one-third of the Crestview parent sample told us that they had not graduated from high school themselves and just five percent said that they had completed college (and, in a few cases, graduate school). Only Fairfield, Laurel and Rosemont parents had a similarly low educational level. Furthermore, a number of Crestview parents contacted during the course of the Study indicated that they would rather not answer the questionnaire because they could not read it.

About one-fourth of this parent sample said that politically they considered themselves to be conservative or strongly conservative. Over 60%, however, said they thought of themselves as politically moderate.

Seventy-one percent of the Crestview High parents who participated in the Study said that they had lived in the Crestview area for nine years or longer. Slightly over ten percent had moved there within the previous three years.

Parent participation in school-related activities at Crestview High was low, though one-third did say

that they attend special school events and there was
quite an active Mothers Athletic Association. When
questioned about their lack of participation in school
activities, half of the Crestview High parent sample
said it was due to conflict with their working hours,
and one-fourth said that it was their belief that it is
the job of the principal and the teachers to run the
school. A vocal minority, however, were willing to
speak up on certain school matters: 17% said that they
had objected to some curriculum materials because they
taught the theory of evolution. And a huge majority
(95.6%) said that it would be alright with them to
allow prayers in school.

The School

Crestview High had 44 teachers and 1,091 students
at the time of the Study. All 44 of the teachers and
576 (53%) of the students constituted the sample populations of these two data sources.

The school was housed in a two-story building constructed about 15 to 20 years earlier, a well-kept and
tidy example of a typical midwestern high school.
District officials estimated the annual vandalism expenditure at only about $1,000.

Crestview's principal was new at the time of the
Study, having been hired for the job the year before.
His assistant principal and the school secretary were
also new and still adjusting to new responsibilities.
There were two full-time counselors and two librarians.
Crestview did not have any special facilities, teach-
ers, or programs for children with learning problems or
special educational needs in 1977.

The daily schedule at Crestview High consisted of
seven class periods. As a rule, students took six
classes and one study hall.

The Teachers

All 44 Crestview High teachers participated in the
Study. It was a fairly young faculty; three-fourths of
the teachers were under 40 years of age. Approximately
the same proportion were married, and over half (57%)

48

were male. All but one were white; the lone exception identified himself as "other."

Starting salaries at Crestview in 1976-77 were $9,337, and the median teacher salary at that time was $14,451. Teacher turnover was a moderate eleven percent, and the average number of years most teachers had taught at Crestview was 7.7.

The work load included six class periods and one planning period, or five class periods, one planning period, and one study hall duty.

Crestview High teachers seemed quite satisfied with their work, with their new principal, and with each other. They felt some frustration at what they perceived to be lack of student interest in learning, however; 37% of the teachers identified this as the single biggest problem at Crestview High.

The Students

Student absenteeism, estimated by Crestview officials at 11 to 13%, was the second highest high school absenteeism in the Study. The average dropout rate across all four grades was 7.5% annually, and approximately 73% of the students who entered Crestview in the ninth grade actually graduated four years later.

The school district estimated that only 5% of Crestview graduates went on to four-year colleges or universities. Of the students sampled, about one-fourth said that they expected to go to college. Nearly 40%, however, said that they would finish high school but go no further.

The Curriculum

Crestview High had a standard comprehensive curriculum with a more or less equal balance between academic and vocational courses as listed on the master schedule. The four academic subject areas (English, Math, Science, and Social Studies) were ability-grouped into three levels: honors, average, and basic.

Teachers seemed to work individually on their own teaching assignments; there was no evidence of either intra- or inter-departmental cooperation in curriculum matters.

Fairfield

The Community

The Fairfield community, located near a large city in the Southwest, has a dual personality. About 85% of its total geographic area consists of sparsely-populated farm and ranch land. The remaining 15% is a densely-populated suburban area, with a large proportion of its adult population employed by two large Air Force bases nearby. There are no industries located in the school district itself.

The total population of the Fairfield district in 1977 was 15,000. Ethnically, about 48% were Hispanic, 46% were white, and the remainder were black, Asian, and American Indian.

The average family income for families who had children attending the Fairfield schools was $7,000 to $8,000. Nearly all (99%) of the dwellings in the school district were single-family homes with an average assessed value of $11,500.

The Parents

304 Fairfield High parents responded to the Study questionnaire. Their median annual income of $12,800 was the second lowest of the high schools in the Study. Compared to the ethnic distribution of the community as a whole, a disproportionate percentage of parents who responded to the Study questionnaire were white (65%); only 27% were Hispanic. This may have skewed the estimated annual income figure, giving the impression that it was higher than it actually was, since the incomes of white families in the Study tended to be higher than those of nonwhite families.

Only 8% of our Fairfield High parent sample reported that they had graduated from a four-year college or completed graduate school. Approximately 29% said that

50

they had never completed high school,* and 37% said they had graduated from high school but had gone no further. Thus, two-thirds of our Fairfield High parent sample had only a high school education or less.

Fairfield had the second-lowest percentage in the Study of parents who were long-term residents of that community (47%). This is not too surprising in an area where military bases are located. Almost one-fourth of the responding parents said that they had lived in Fairfield three years or less.

Fairfield High parents did not participate in school activities very much, with the exception of special events and PTA (41%); and one-third of them admitted that they did not feel that they knew very much about the school. One-fourth said they felt it was the job of the administration and the teachers to run the school; on the other hand, much larger percentages say that they would like to be involved in school decision-making. About half said they couldn't participate due to conflicts with their work schedules, however.

The School

Fairfield High had 57 teachers and 1,137 students at the time of the Study. Our sample consisted of 44 of the teachers and 696 (61%) of the students. The student body was 53% white and 42% Hispanic.

Fairfield High, Fairfield Junior High, and Fairfield Elementary Schools are all grouped together on a single thirty-acre site.

The high school building was a typical 1950s single-story, "finger-style" construction, with outdoor hallways. A large vocational complex was located in a separate set of buildings which resembled large tin barns.

There was one principal and one assistant principal at Fairfield High at the time of the Study. The principal was feeling frustrated by restrictions imposed by the school district and was thinking of leaving the

---

* 15% said they never completed 8th grade.

following year. There was also a very strong person in the position of Vocational Director. This person treated the vocational teachers as a separate staff, accountable only to him. The principal was forced to work around this situation.

Fairfield High had a conventional six-period day, and students could take six classes or five classes and a study hall.

There were three full-time counselors; one worked exclusively with vocational students and the other two took care of the academic students. Fairfield High had two full-time librarians in 1977.

The Teachers

Teachers' starting salaries at Fairfield in 1977 were the lowest in the Study--$8,000. The median salary at that time was also among the lowest in the Study, at $10,700. The highest-paid teacher at Fairfield High in 1977 was making just $12,780. Teachers' contracts were issued on a year-by-year basis, so Fairfield teachers had little job security.

The teacher work load was five classes and a planning period, or four classes, a study hall, and a planning period.

Fairfield High scored extremely low on the Teacher Satisfaction Index (on a scale of zero to seven, Fairfield scored a one). It's hardly surprising, then, that Fairfield school officials reported one of the highest teacher turnover rates in the Study--30% annually.

Considering that the Fairfield High student body was 42% Hispanic at the time of the Study, it's worth noting that only 10% of the faculty were Hispanic. 86% were white.

The high teacher turnover rate at Fairfield creates job space for younger teachers, and 66% of the sampled teachers were under the age of 40. About four out of every ten were male.

The Students

Student attendance at Fairfield was reported as being about 90% on a typical school day. According to demographic data provided by the district, the average dropout rate was 11%; only 63% of the students who entered 9th grade actually graduated from Fairfield High.

Fairfield High students were divided into two distinct groups, vocational and academic. Rarely, if ever, did the two groups encounter each other in the classroom, especially after ninth grade when the final decision about which curriculum to enter must be made.

Fairfield High had by far the highest vandalism estimate in the Study--$12,000 to $15,000 annually was the figure given. The next highest school estimated its annual vandalism costs at $4,000, and the others were even lower than that.

The Curriculum

Most Fairfield High teachers offered conventional programs, and seemed content to get by with relying on published materials and curriculum guides provided by the State education agency. Others, however, seemed to be struggling to offer something more--despite clear limitations of money, supplies, and equipment in most departments. Only the Vocational courses seemed to have everything they need.

Woodlake

The Community

The Woodlake School District is located in a rural/suburban area in the Pacific Northwest. The community is greatly affected by the existence of a large naval air base which is in the district. Military population figures provided to the Study of Schooling suggest that fully one-third of the 1977 population of 37,200 were either military personnel on active duty, reservists, retired, or civilians employed by the base. A large percentage of Woodlake teachers were wives of base personnel, and a large number of students in the district were likewise from military families.

Of the total Woodlake population of 37,200, all were white except for very small percentages of Hispanics, Asians and blacks.

The Parents

475 Woodlake High parents responded to the Study questionnaire. (This was 52% of the total parent population for Woodlake High, the best parent response for any high school in the Study). Of this group, one-fourth indicated that they had lived in Woodlake for three years or less. Almost half, however, said that they had lived in the area for nine years or longer.

Politically, the Woodlake parents characterized themselves as moderate to conservative. Their median income was $18,400. About 8% reported earning less than $10,000 a year but 24% said they earned over $25,000 a year; Woodlake was a fairly affluent community with little real poverty.

Only seven percent of Woodlake High parents did not finish high school themselves--this was the lowest percentage of parent high school dropouts in the Study. However, less than one-fourth reported that they had graduated from college and/or completed a postgraduate degree. The largest percentage (28%) reported that they had graduated from high school but had gone no further (into the Navy, presumably), while another 24% said that they had attended college for awhile but had dropped out before completing a degree.

Nearly one-third of the Woodlake High parents who responded to the Study questionnaire said they felt they knew very little about the school. Nonetheless, they gave it a grade of B-.

Almost one-third of the Woodlake High parent sample indicated that they attend meetings to discuss local political issues and/or other community problems. 40% said they attend special school events, but only 18% said that they participate in the PTA.

57% of the parents cited conflict with working hours as the reason for their low involvement with school-related activities, and about one-fourth said that they believe it is the job of the principal and the teachers (and not the parents) to run the school. The transiency of the population and the absence of a real sense of community were mentioned by several school board members and school district personnel as reasons for low parent involvement in school activities.

The School

Woodlake High School was a three-year school with a student body of 1,202 and a teaching staff of 57 in 1977. Our sample consisted of 53 of the teachers and 642 (53%) of the students.

The school building was brand-new, located on a spacious site which had at that time not yet been landscaped. It was designed for team teaching, with pods for each subject area and teacher work areas in the center of each pod. The school had all the latest and most modern equipment.*

The principal of Woodlake High had been in that job for twenty years, longer than any of the other high school principals in the Study.

In addition to the principal, the administrative structure at Woodlake High also included one assistant principal, three full-time counselors, and one full-time librarian. The head of the English Department also served as Dean of Students.

The Teachers

Teachers' starting salaries at Woodlake High in 1977 were neither the lowest nor the highest in the Study: $9,990. The median salary also was right in the middle--in the rank-order of eleven schools for which we were able to obtain this information, Woodlake's median teacher salary of $13,586 ranked sixth.

---

* Woodlake was the beneficiary of Federal funds available to districts in which military bases are located: PL-815 funds for buildings and PL-874 for equipment and materials.

85% of the Woodlake High teachers were married, and a higher percentage (68%) were male than at any other high school in the Study. Approximately half were under 40 years of age. Of the 53 teachers who participated in the Study, 51 were white, one was "other" and one was black. Politically, over one-third said they were conservative and nearly half said they were moderate.

On the whole, the teachers at Woodlake High seemed pretty happy with their work situation. They placed very high on two different satisfaction indices and gave the school an overall grade of B+. No doubt they were pleased with the new building, and with its excellent facilities and equipment. They also seemed to feel that they had quite a bit of influence on decision-making within the school. And finally, it is conceivable that the stability of the administration--the principal had been at Woodlake High for twenty years--was a source of reassurance for the teachers.

The teacher work load at Woodlake High was five classes and one planning period daily.

The Students

Student attendance at Woodlake was reported by district officials as being 91% on a typical day. Figures on the dropout rate were not provided. As student attitudes seemed quite positive at Woodlake, however, one might guess that the dropout rate was relatively low. Woodlake students gave their school a grade of B+ and responded with strong agreement to the statement, "This school gives students a good education." Furthermore, they did not seem to feel that their school had many major problems, and they were quite happy with the library and counseling services available to them.

40% of the Woodlake student sample said that they expected to go to college, and another 5% hoped to continue on to graduate school.

Compared to other high schools in the Study, high percentages of Woodlake High students said that they participated in special-interest clubs and school or community service activities.

The Curriculum

Woodlake High had a conventional six-period day, and students commonly took six courses; there were no study halls or free periods for students.

The Woodlake curriculum was also fairly conventional, with the usual range of courses found in most American comprehensive senior secondary schools. Several courses were, however, provided which were particularly congruent with the needs and values of the Woodlake community. Marine Biology and Oceanography, for example, were part of the Science curriculum, and Naval ROTC I, II, and III were also available.

Tracking practices were not especially strong at Woodlake, although some ability grouping existed as a result of student selection of, for instance, "Consumer Math" as opposed to the Algebra-Geometry sequence. On the whole, though, most students had the same courses--everyone took U.S. History, World Problems, and Composition Basics, for example. There were some electives, but not the great range of options found at some of the other high schools in the Study.

Bradford

The Community

Bradford is a suburban community not far from a large Midwestern city. In the high school attendance area, the 1977 population was approximately 7,598. Most households had a fairly comfortable annual income of between $15,000 and $20,000.

Bradford is a working-class community. Most jobs are associated with major industries in the greater metropolitan area and are somewhat dependent upon a growth economy nationwide. Layoffs are common during periods of national recession.

Housing is fairly homogeneous and consists primarily of single-family tract houses. In some areas the housing is federally funded, but there are no areas of extreme poverty and little evidence of extreme wealth.

Ethnically, the Bradford community is about 95% white.

The Parents

382 Bradford High parents responded to the Study questionnaire. The average annual income of this group was $19,600 in 1977. About one-fourth of these parents reported that they themselves had never completed high school, and only seven percent reported graduating from college or completing a postgraduate degree. By far the largest percentage--about 48%--reported that they went as far as graduating from high school and, since only small percentages reported going on to any form of higher education (including trade schools and junior colleges), it seems that the dominant pattern in the Bradford community has been to complete high school and then go right to work. This is made possible by the presence nearby of many large industries which require a steady supply of unskilled labor and which, since all are unionized, offer a pay scale which can seem very attractive to a young person just out of high school.

A large majority (77%) of Bradford High parents responding to our questionnaire reported that they had lived in the Bradford community for nine years or longer; only 7% said that they had moved to Bradford within the previous three years. Politically, our parent sample at Bradford High was moderate to conservative.

One third of the sampled parents felt that they knew very little about Bradford High, and the parents as a group gave Bradford High a grade of C-, which was the lowest grade given by parents to any school in the Study. Parent participation in school activities was generally quite low at Bradford. One-third of the parents sampled did say that they attended special events, and approximately one-fifth said that they attended meetings to discuss local political issues and other community problems. This is interesting, in view of the fact that according to some board of education members and school district personnel, Bradford parents only get involved in school matters when specific issues arouse their interest. There was also some feeling that parents generally don't understand the complexity of running a school system.

58

The School

Bradford High was a three-year high school (grades 10-12) with 63 teachers and 1,350 students at the time of the Study. Our sample consisted of 48 of the teachers and 741 (55%) of the students.

Bradford High's five-period day was the shortest daily schedule found at any high school in the Study: most high schools had at least six, and sometimes more, periods.

The administrative structure included one principal and two assistant principals. There were two librarians, a staff of six counselors, and eight department heads. There were two Special Education teachers.

Bradford High is located in a conventional multi-story building dating from the 1950s. Neither attractive nor unattractive, it is a typical suburban midwest school facility. School officials estimated annual vandalism costs at approximately $4,000.

The Teachers

Teachers' salaries at Bradford High started at $10,799 in 1977 and the median salary was $13,776. The teacher workload was all five class periods each day, with no planning period, and teacher turnover was a rather low 4% annually.

Of the 48 teachers who responded to the Study questionnaire, 47 were white and one was "other." A majority of Bradford High teachers were male (62.5%) and just over half were under 40 years of age. Most of the teachers did not live in the Bradford community themselves.

Bradford High teachers are represented by the local chapter of the American Federation of Teachers.

The Students

The student body at Bradford High was 90% white, 8% black and 2% "other" at the time of the Study. Student attendance was reported by school officials to be approximately 92% daily, and the dropout rate averaged about 10% over the three grade levels. Just under three-fourths of the students who entered Bradford High in the tenth grade actually graduated.

Bradford High students seemed somewhat unhappy with the quality of the educational experience they were getting. They gave the school a grade of only C and disagreed, more than students at any other high school in the Study, with the statement, "This school gives students a good education." One-fourth of the students sampled felt that poor teaching was a major problem, and there was a good deal of agreement with the statement that "Too many students are allowed to graduate from this school without learning very much."

The Curriculum

Bradford High had a five-period day during the 1977-78 school year, and all five periods were fully scheduled with classes. That is, there were neither study halls for students nor preparation periods for teachers.

Although Bradford is located in a state which emphasizes accountability, there was no evidence of competency-based curriculum development at Bradford High-- no tightly structured course guides, no behavioral objectives, and no sign of school-wide curriculum planning. The course offerings were standard for a comprehensive high school, with a wide variety overall but much more limited in terms of what any given student could actually take. As in most of our other high schools, this was due to the tracking system in operation at Bradford: once a student was assigned to a track for one subject area (usually Language Arts), this affected his or her track placement in other subjects as well.

Inasmuch as Bradford is a working-class community with a predominant pattern of going right to work after high school, it is rather striking that Bradford High had one of the most meager vocational programs of the thirteen high schools in our sample. Just 14% of the FTEs at Bradford High were in vocational subjects--only two other high schools had lower (13%) allocations of teacher time to vocational subjects.*

Palisades

The Community

Palisades High is located in an affluent white suburb of a major city in the South. The area is almost totally residential, with big houses on large wooded and beautifully-landscaped lots, some very big estates, expensive apartment buildings and condominiums, and a large, exclusive shopping center.

Palisades was the only high school in the Study where busing for the purpose of racial integration was actually happening; half of the student body came in by bus from an almost equally affluent black neighborhood across the city. Partly because both white and black students came from upper middle class families, but also because everyone involved worked very hard at it, racial tension aggravated by economic class differences has been minimal. Desegregation was accomplished smoothly in the early 70s, and in 1977 the atmosphere seemed to be one of harmony and cooperation.

The Parents

461 Palisades High parents responded to the Study questionnaire. Of this number, 56% were white, 42% were black, and 2% were "other." Both the white and the black parents of Palisades High tended to be well-educated, and to hold white-collar professional and managerial positions in the nearby city. A higher percentage of Palisades High parents graduated from college and/or completed a postgraduate degree (42%) than at any of the other high schools in our Study, and this high level of educational preparation is reflected in the figures for parent income: the median income of Palisades High parents was $20,800 in 1977 and 40% of them reported earning over $25,000 a year.

---

* For purposes of comparison, Fairfield High allocated 42% of its FTEs to vocational subjects, Euclid 41% and Dennison 35%.

Only 56% of the Palisades High parent sample said that they had lived in that area for nine years or longer; about 18% indicated that they had moved there within the past three years. Both communities are still upwardly mobile, and both neighborhoods are evidently seen as desirable places in which to live.

As a group, Palisades parents were politically moderate.

Palisades High parents had the highest percentage of parent participation in PTA in the high school sample (67.8%), but parent participation in other ways was fourth highest when compared to the other twelve high schools. Parents themselves listed "conflict with my working hours" most frequently as the reason for not being more involved. Interestingly, it was the perception of several school board members and school district administrators that Palisades parents do not get as involved as they might in school matters because of "...administrators who see parents as a threat," and who thus do not really encourage much parent participation.

The School

Palisades High had 68 teachers and 1,402 students in 1977. Our sample consisted of 59 of the teachers and 768 (55%) of the students.

Palisades High is a large brick building three stories high which dates from the 1950s. It is neither very attractive nor unattractive in itself, but it is located in a beautiful wooded area which considerably enhances its appearance.

The school day consisted of six periods of conventional length. The administrative structure included one principal, two vice-principals, and one registrar. There were also eight department chairpersons, three counselors, two librarians, and seven specialists: a nurse, a speech therapist, someone in charge of homebound students, and specialists in the areas of Learning Disabilities, Hard of Hearing, Visually Impaired, and Reading.

The Teachers

Starting salaries for teachers at Palisades High in 1977 were the highest in our sample, at $11,700. The median salary in 1977 was $14,772. The highest teacher salary in the Study was earned at Palisades High: $23,772. Teacher turnover was reported by school officials as a moderate 11% annually. Teacher work load was five classes and one planning period daily.

Of the 59 teachers who participated in the Study, about 31 were white, 24 were black, and 4 "other." Palisades High thus came closer than any other racially mixed high school in the Study to having a faculty with a racial balance approximately the same as that of the student body.

Palisades had one of the lowest percentages of male teachers in the Study--37%. Just over half of the faculty were under 40 years of age, and the average number of years taught at Palisades High was six. Most of the Palisades High teachers did not live in the Palisades area themselves--few would be able to afford it.

The Students

Palisades High's 1,402 students were, in 1977, 50% black and 50% white and, as has already been mentioned, all but a few of the black students came to school by bus from another part of the city. From middle-class, upwardly-mobile and education-oriented families, the black students at Palisades were just as interested in getting through high school and into college as were the white students--exactly the same percentage of each race, 46.7%, said that they expected to go to a four-year college or university, and about 16-17% of both groups said they would probably go beyond college and into graduate school. (Palisades school district officials estimated in 1977 that 65% of Palisades High graduates go on to four-year colleges or universities. This was the highest estimate of college-bound students in our sample of 13 high schools).

The Palisades High dropout rate, averaged across all four grade levels, was a comparatively low 4.5%, and a correspondingly high percentage of students (83%)

who enter ninth grade actually remained through the
four years and graduated from Palisades High.

On the other hand, daily attendance figures were
reported at approximately 88%, which is surprisingly
low for a school which seems to have such an education-
oriented student body.

The Curriculum

Palisades High had a conventional six-period day,
and students commonly took six courses; there were no
study halls or free periods for students.

The academic courses were organized into four
tracks, and not only did the two upper tracks have
higher status,* but they also tended to have more interesting content. As was found to be the case in all
of our racially mixed schools, there were more white
students in the highest-track courses and more black
students in the lowest-track courses, but this pattern
was far weaker at Palisades than at some of the other
high schools.

Course offerings were more or less standard for a
comprehensive high school, although the college-preparatory tracks had much more variety than did the two
lower tracks.

There was little evidence of departmental planning
and none at all of school-wide curriculum development.
Use of behavioral objectives was sporadic.

Vista

The Community

Vista High School is located in a suburban community not far from a medium-sized Midwestern city. The

---

* In at least one department there was some evidence in the
curriculum materials of a condescending attitude on the part of
teachers towards students in the Basic and Average track courses
of that department.

population of Vista in 1977 was 27,000 and the median income, according to the 1970 census, was $15,400. There was little poverty in Vista, although it could not be described as a particularly affluent community.

Vista is virtually all white, and many residents have moved there, over the years, to escape the multi-ethnicity of the nearby city. Politically, the community is moderate to conservative.

90% of the homes in the Vista district were single-family dwellings, with a median value of about $37,000 in 1977. Most people owned their own homes, and nearly two-thirds of the Vista High parents responding to our questionnaire said that they had lived in the Vista area for nine or more years. About ten percent said they had moved to Vista within the previous three years, so the community, while basically stable, was still growing.

Some light industry provides jobs, but a great many Vista residents commute to work in the nearby city.

The Parents

638 Vista High parents responded to the Study questionnaire. Just under ten percent of these said they had not finished high school themselves; about one-fourth had graduated from college and/or completed a postgraduate degree. The remainder just finished high school, and some had a few years of college but did not graduate.

Except for the band program, which drew the vigorous support of those parents whose children played in the band, parents were not very active in school-related activities. School board members and district personnel said that this was due to parent apathy and to a lack of appropriate participatory mechanisms. Half of the parents gave conflict with working hours as a reason for their non-involvement and about one-fourth said that they believe that it is the job of the principal and teachers to run the school. (This belief on the part of the parents, leading to their lack of involvement in school activities, might be viewed by school personnel as "parent apathy.")

The School

Vista High had 84 teachers and 2,312 students at the time of the Study. Our sample consisted of all 84 teachers and 834 (36%) of the students.

Vista High had a rather unusual master schedule of ten 40-minute classes per day and an unconventional mini-course curriculum which had started within the previous three years in conjunction with the opening of a new school building and the admission, for the first time, of 9th graders to Vista High.

The administrative structure at Vista included one principal, two assistant principals, two administrative assistants, and a Director of student activities. Six full-time counselors were available, each with a student load of about 400. A team of two Special Education teachers managed a multi-aged (grades 8-12) self-contained EMR classroom.

The Teachers

Teachers' salaries at Vista High started at $8,840 in 1977 and the median salary in that year was $13,019. Teachers actually taught four full hours each day--six forty-minute classes. This was the lowest actual teaching load, in terms of _time_, reported in all of our thirteen Study high schools. It was not, however, the lowest in terms of total daily pupil contacts; with an average of 24 students in each of the six classes, most Vista teachers were dealing with about 144 students every day. Too, teachers had to contend with the added pressure of encountering new groups of students every nine weeks because of the quarter-course schedule. Teacher turnover at Vista High was reported by district officials as being fairly high: 23%.

All of the teachers at Vista High in the 1976-77 school year were white. On the average, they considered themselves politically to be moderate to conservative. A fairly large percentage--about 60%--were male, and an even larger proportion, 75%, were under the age of 40.

The Students

Vista officials reported an annual vandalism expenditure of about $3,000, an average daily student attendance figure of 93%, and a fairly low dropout rate of 3.5%. About 86-87% of the students who entered 9th grade actually graduated from Vista High; this is the second highest percentage of students remaining in school through graduation in our sample of thirteen high schools. Approximately 45% of Vista graduates were reported to go on to college or universities. This estimate tallies with student data indicating future plans: about 43% of our student sample said that they would probably go to a four-year college or university and another seven percent said they expected to go beyond college to complete a postgraduate degree.

More than at any other high school in the Study, drug and alcohol use was reported by students to be a problem at Vista High at the time of the Study.

The Curriculum

The unusual mini-course schedule has already been mentioned. The Vista High course catalogue was, as a result, extremely thick and in theory, students at Vista had considerably more opportunity for choice than did students at the other twelve high schools in the Study. However, it was also true that the Vista curriculum was rigidly tracked, and this acted as an unofficial but nonetheless effective limitation on student choice.

The overall impression of the Vista High curriculum of 1976-77 was that it had been carefully structured by the teachers. Most of the courses had been so completely planned in advance that there seemed to be little room for improvisation or adjustment by individual teachers. This was true of the more unusual courses, and even more true of the standard offerings. No department stood out as being exceptional--indeed, a feeling of sameness and uniformity permeated the Vista High curriculum. It is astonishing that a program which looks so exciting on the master schedule can give such an impression of drabness when examined more closely. On the other hand, it is possible that meticulously structured course guidelines constituted a defense mechanism for the teachers, which allowed them to cope with an unusual and demanding teaching schedule. Technically, it might have been possible for a teacher at Vista High to teach as many as 24 different courses a year. In fact, almost never were teachers asked to teach six different preparations every quarter, but they might have three, or even four. Knowing that course guidelines are there thus becomes an important source of emotional reassurance for teachers. It is ironic that an innovative daily and yearly schedule can in fact lead to a less innovative curriculum.

Newport

The Community

The Newport community is part of a large city on the West coast. Its most distinctive feature is its remarkable ethnic heterogeneity: 58 nationalities and 36 different languages are found in the Newport district.*

Newport is also a very mobile community, compared to the other twelve communities in the Study. 83% of the available housing units are rented, and only 17% are owner-occupied. Apartments are far more numerous than single-family dwellings. Also, compared to our other schools, Newport High had the highest percentage of parents reporting that they had lived there for three years or less (about 30%) and the lowest percentage who reported having lived there for nine years or longer (46%). Many of the latter are elderly people who have lived in the Newport area for many years.

The 1977 population of the Newport area was 115,923 and the average family income was $12,462 annually. The economic range within the community, however, is almost as dramatic as the ethnic heterogeneity: of 24,200 families, half earned less than $10,000 a year; 38% earned from $10,000 to $25,000, seven percent earned over $25,000 and two percent earned over $50,000.

---

* (Information provided for the Study of Schooling by Newport Junior High, based on school demographics collected in the Fall of 1976.)

As in any big city, all sorts of employment opportunities are available to Newport residents. A smaller than average percentage, however, work with their hands; most employed people in the Newport area occupy clerical, professional, or management positions.

The Newport community has its full share of urban problems, including crowded living conditions, poor housing, traffic congestion, poor facilities for public recreation, drug abuse, and crime. Education, however, is not considered a problem, and the Newport community is proud of its schools, which rate as equal to or above other city schools on student achievement tests.

The Parents

358 Newport High parents responded to the Study questionnaire. The average annual income of this sample was $14,200--about $1,700 higher than the average family income in the Newport community as a whole. (In general, parents who responded to the Study questionnaire in all thirteen communities tended to have incomes slightly higher than the overall average for their community.)

The Newport High parent sample had a fairly high educational level--only about 17% reported that they did not finish high school themselves, while fully one-third graduated from a four-year college or university and/or completed postgraduate work. Newport parents tended to be slightly more liberal in their political beliefs than parents at most other schools in the Study.

Parent participation in school activities was rather low, which is not unusual at the high school level. 63% of the parent sample said this was because of conflicts with their working hours, 10% said they had trouble getting babysitters, and 18% said that they had transportation problems. Interestingly, 17% mentioned that the language difference was a deterrent to participation for them; at only one other high school (Rosemont, with a 100% Hispanic population) did a higher percentage of parents give this as the reason for not participating in school-related activities.

The School

Newport High had 85 teachers and 2,508 students at the time of the Study. Our sample consisted of 78 teachers and 841 (34%) of the students. The school occupies a city block; surrounding blocks are crowded with small businesses of every imaginable kind. The school buildings are old but fairly well maintained and while the interiors are ordinary, the exteriors of the original buildings are architecturally distinctive. Some "portable" units, now a permanent fixture, were in use.

The administrative structure at Newport High consisted of one principal, two assistant principals, an administrative dean, two deans of students, a career advisor and a full-time nurse. Newport High had a full-time school psychologist and eight full-time counselors (but only three of them could speak a language other than English). Two librarians managed a medium-sized library of about 13,400 books; they estimated a rather low number of books (50) circulating in a single day (five high schools had a higher daily circulation).

As one might expect, Newport High had quite a large program in English as a Second Language. Both the principal and a good many of the teachers, however, felt that an even larger ESL program was needed.

Newport High also had one teacher for students designated as EH (Emotionally Handicapped), and was just beginning to develop a new program for students specially designated as gifted.

An Alternative School existed within Newport High in 1977. It served about 150 students who had a wide variety of educational needs, from remedial work to accelerated classes. Students who applied for this program had to be self-reliant, however, in order to be accepted.

The Teachers

Newport teachers as a group had a high level of educational attainment: 45% had Masters' degrees and 10% had Doctors' degrees. 80% of the sampled teachers were white, and the remaining 20% consisted of approximately equal numbers of blacks, Asians, and others.

Over half of the teachers were men, and about the same percentage were older than 40 years of age. The average teacher had been at Newport High for 8.5 years. The teacher work load was five class periods and one planning period daily.

Newport High teachers indicated that a low level of staff cohesiveness and cooperation existed at Newport, and in general the teachers there seemed to prefer working autonomously. Group consensus would be difficult to achieve even within departments, and nearly impossible at the all-faculty level.

Newport teachers were represented by a local organization which was an amalgamation of the AFT and the NEA.

The Students

The student body of Newport High reflected the heterogeneity of the Newport community, with substantial proportions of Asian students (Koreans, Vietnamese, Chinese, and Japanese), Mexican-Americans, blacks, and white students of different ethnic backgrounds-- German, Italian, and Armenian, for example.

Student attendance at Newport High was reported by school officials to be approximately 88%. No data on dropout rate were provided, but the highly mobile nature of the community suggests that there is likely to be a good deal of coming and going by students, and a relatively low percentage of students who enter Newport in the 9th grade complete all four years there, compared to the other schools in the Study.

The Curriculum

Newport High had a standard six-period day, with no study halls. The overall impression of the Newport curriculum is one of great diversity in most subjects and even between different sections of the same course. This was due to the high level of individual autonomy enjoyed by the Newport teachers, and to the absence of standardized syllabi or course content specifications (if such curriculum guides existed, they were not being used).

Newport High's curricular emphasis on academic preparation rather than on vocational training can be seen in its allocation of 62% of its FTEs to academic courses and just 13% of its FTEs to vocational courses. This seems fairly well-matched with the needs of the student body, fully half of whom say they expect to go to college and/or on to graduate school (another 22% say they will probably go to junior college).

Rosemont

The Community

Rosemont High School is an urban school in a large Southwestern city. The population of the Rosemont district in 1977 was 43,530 and the high school population was virtually 100% Mexican-American.

The average family income in the Rosemont district was about $4,382.50 annually, the lowest in our sample. Twenty percent of Rosemont families lived below the poverty level at that time.

The Rosemont community is primarily a residential area, although there is some industry, a stockyard, and a small college within the district. About half of the homes are owner-occupied, with median values ranging from approximately $6,800 to $9,600 in 1977. Forty-seven percent of the homes are rental units; many of these are in government low-income housing projects.

One out of every twenty housing units was vacant in 1977, and the population of 43,530 was 15% lower than the official 1970 census figure, suggesting that the Rosemont district was experiencing a period of decline at the time of the Study. Only 7% of Rosemont High parents responding to our questionnaire said that they had moved into the area recently (within the previous three years), but 75% said that they had lived in the area for nine years or longer. Unlike some Mexican-American communities in the Southwest, the Rosemont district did not seem to be experiencing growth caused by the arrival of new immigrants from Mexico.

The Parents

447 Rosemont High parents responded to the Study questionnaire. Their average annual income of $5,200 was the lowest in the Study--and about half of the respondents reported earning _less_ than $5,000 a year.

The median education level of Rosemont parents was 6th grade, and nearly four-fifths of our parent sample reported that they had not graduated from high school themselves. Less than 1% had graduated from a four-year college or university, and/or completed a post-graduate degree. This level of educational attainment of parents was much lower than at any of the other twelve high schools in the Study. It is interesting, therefore, that parent participation in school activities and parent involvement in school decision-making are both quite high at Rosemont High compared to the other schools. One might expect that parents who did not finish high school themselves would feel somewhat uncomfortable in school settings, particularly in cases such as Rosemont, where school business is transacted in a language which is not the native tongue of many parents. And in fact, 21% of the Rosemont High parent sample did identify the language difference as a reason for their non-involvement in school activities.

The School

Rosemont High had 121 teachers and 2,702 students at the time of the Study. Our sample consisted of 113 teachers and 763 (28%) of the students.

The school was housed in a beautiful new building, opened in 1974 and well taken care of by the students, who seemed quite proud of it. The cost estimate for vandalism was only $1,520 for the year just prior to the Study.

In 1977, Rosemont High had an eight-period day, with 50-minute periods; the day began at 8:00 a.m. and ended at 3:15.

Rosemont's administrative structure was typical of a school this size: one principal, two assistant principals, and two deans. Five full-time counselors had a student load of about 500 each. Three full-time librarians managed a library of 25,000 books, the largest in the Study; however, annual library costs per student at Rosemont High were the <u>lowest</u> in the Study, at $1.75. There were two Special Education teachers, one for EMR and one for LLD.

The Teachers

Teachers' salaries at Rosemont High started at $8,900 and the median salary in 1977 was $11,000. The teacher work load was five class periods, two planning periods, and a lunch period each day. Teacher turnover was a moderate 12% annually.

Although the student body of Rosemont High School was virtually 100% Mexican-American, only slightly over one-fourth of the teachers were Mexican-American. 63% were white and 8% were black. Just over two-thirds of the Rosemont High faculty were under 40 years of age, and about 40% were male. Most Rosemont High teachers characterized themselves as politically moderate.

The Students

Student attendance at Rosemont was reported as being about 90% on a typical school day. According to demographic data provided by the district, the average dropout rate was 4.8%, and about 82% of the students who entered 9th grade actually graduated from Rosemont High. As of September 1, 1977, 36.5% of all Rosemont area students--over one-third--were over-age for their grade; more students at Rosemont than at our other schools had been held back one or more grades during the course of their years in school.

Despite these figures for dropouts and over-age students, many of the students sampled at Rosemont High indicated that they expected to go on to some form of higher education--14% to junior college, 29% to a four-year college or university, and 5% beyond college, to graduate school. Just over 30% said they would just finish high school; and 11% admitted that they didn't really know what they would do.

When asked to identify the one biggest problem at Rosemont High, by far the largest percentage of the student sample (37%) said the biggest problem was how the school is organized (class schedules, not enough time for lunch, passing periods, etc.). 17% said the biggest problem was drug and alcohol use, and 16% felt it was student misbehavior.

On the whole, though, Rosemont High students seemed fairly proud of their school, and gave it a grade of B (at no high school in the Study did students, as a group, give a grade higher than B+).

The Curriculum

Rosemont High had a curriculum which was distinctly academic in its orientation. Although it also provided a good selection of vocational courses, including work-study programs, the emphasis was on college preparation. Rosemont, for example, offered one of the most impressive foreign language programs in our sample, including Russian, Latin, and German as well as French and Spanish. Two-thirds of the FTEs were allocated to academic subjects, and only 21% to vocational subjects.

The curricular offerings as presented in the master schedule are quite impressive in their scope and variety, but in practice once students have chosen certain options, they get locked into a more more narrowly-defined program for the duration of their high school experience. The work-study programs, for example, are three years long and once a student has begun one of these, the pressure to stay put is quite strong. Tracking practices operate in much the same way, limiting student choice and stratifying the student body.

Finally, it is interesting to note that despite the strong academic orientation of the curriculum at Rosemont High, only 29% of our student sample said that they expected to go to college. Nearly the same number--31.4%--said they expected simply to finish high school and go no further.

Manchester

The Community

The Manchester community is located within a large Midwestern city. Its population of 65,236 in 1977 was

75

about 36% white and 64% black. The student body of Manchester High, however, was 99% black.

Three of every ten Manchester families earned less than $10,000 a year at the time of the Study; about sixty percent earned from $10,000 to $25,000, and twelve percent earned over $25,000.

Manchester is basically a residential community. There are some stores and restaurants in the area, but no major industry. Most people who live in Manchester commute to work in other parts of the city.

Homes range in value and appearance from very modest to very expensive, but in general Manchester can be described as an economically middle-class community.

The Parents

482 Manchester High School parents participated in the Study. The average annual income reported by this sample was about $16,200 but this figure is somewhat deceptive, since the distribution of parent income was more heterogeneous in Manchester than in any other community except Newport. In fact, about one-fourth of the responding parents reported earning less than $10,000 a year, while at the other extreme, about one-fifth reported earning over $25,000 a year.

The majority of Manchester High parents finished high school, and quite a few went on to have some higher education. 21% of our sample did say, however, that they had not finished high school.

Manchester High parents tended to be slightly more liberal politically than parents in any of the other high schools in the Study.

The stability of the Manchester community is indicated by the fact that almost two-thirds of the parents said that they had lived in Manchester for nine years or longer; only 12% said that they had moved in within the previous three years.

37% of the Manchester parent sample admitted that they felt they knew "very little" about the school. Parent participation in a variety of school events at Manchester High was quite low; "conflict with working

76

hours" was the reason most often given. A certain amount of generally negative feeling toward the school also seemed to exist; Manchester High parents gave the school a grade of only C-, the lowest grade given to any school in the Study by any group of parents. Only one other school was graded that low by its parent sample.

One of the school district's assistant superintendents described Manchester High's problems of parent participation as being

> "...unemployment, crime, poverty, and social alienation. Parents who feel hostile and alienated have difficulty relating positively to the school. School staff feel threatened when parent hostility so manifestly outweighs parent warmth and support."

The School

Manchester High had 114 teachers and 3,006 students at the time of the Study. Our sample consisted of 66 teachers and 937 (31%) of the students.

Manchester High is an unattractive old building several stories high. From the outside, the effect is rather gloomy as the building looks more like a factory than a school. Vandalism, according to school officials, costs the school district about $3,000 a year.

The administrative structure was conventional: one principal, two vice principals, and one person in charge of student activities. In addition, there were two librarians, nine department heads, and an extraordinarily large staff of eleven counselors.

Manchester High's daily schedule was somewhat unusual. The total day, from 7:30 a.m. to 4:30 p.m., was the longest in the Study. However, neither teachers nor students put in the full nine hours. Teachers worked either from 7:30 to 3:30 or from 8:30 to 4:30, and student schedules varied from a full day for freshmen to just a few periods for seniors who had completed most of their graduation requirements.

The Teachers

Teachers' salaries at Manchester High started at $11,360 and the median salary in 1977 was the highest in the Study, $21,277. However, the teacher work load was also higher than at any other school in the Study: six 55-minute classes, for a total of 5½ hours of actual teaching time every day, plus one study hall duty and one planning period. Annual teacher turnover was estimated by district officials as a moderate 11%.

The Manchester faculty was 53% white and 44% black. Just over half of the teachers were over 40 years of age, and about half were male, half female. The average length of time that most Manchester teachers had taught at the school was 7.7 years, and most of the teachers did not live in the Manchester area themselves.

The AFT has been the sole bargaining agent for Manchester teachers for many years. This is not surprising, since the city as a whole is very much a union city and always has been. For this reason, the community understands and supports the right of teachers to bargain collectively. Everything the district does must be negotiated with the union. The sponsors of the Study of Schooling received permission to collect data at Manchester schools from the union officials as well as from the school district authorities.

The Students

Student attendance figures reported by district officials were lower than at any of the other high schools in the Study, at 84%. The dropout rate averaged 10% across all four grades, and only 66% of the students who entered 9th grade actually graduated from Manchester High.

Over half of the Manchester students sampled told us that they expected to go on to some form of higher education--39% to four-year colleges, 9.5% to junior college, and 6.6% to both college and graduate school. About one-fourth of the students sampled said they just planned to finish high school but go no further.

Student misbehavior, defined as "fighting, stealing, gangs, truancy, etc." was identified by many

78

students (42%) as the one biggest problem at Manchester High. This was a far larger percentage than that for any other problem area. For example, only 10% said that drug and alcohol use was the biggest problem, and 9% said that the way the school was organized (class schedules, not enough time for lunch, passing periods, etc.) was the biggest problem.

A possible indicator of student dissatisfaction at Manchester High is the fact that, in response to the question "What is the one best thing about this school?" nearly 20% said "Nothing." At no other high school in the Study did that high a percentage of the student sample select that response. Further, when asked to grade their school (A-B-C-D-F), the mean grade of C- given by the Manchester High student sample was the lowest in the Study.

The Curriculum

Manchester High is located in a state which emphasizes competency-based education, accountability, and curriculum development which is very prescriptive and specific. It is therefore not surprising that the Manchester High curriculum provides a syllabus for almost every course, containing stated behavioral objectives as well as suggested activities and methods of evaluation. It is a highly structured curriculum, with little room for teacher initiative or creativity.

*   *   *

These, then, were our thirteen high schools, similar in some ways but very different in others. Even a quick reading of these profiles reveals some of the themes which we will explore more fully in Chapters 3 through 6: What characteristics of a school seem to generate higher teacher and student satisfaction? What kinds of demands does a high school teaching career place on teachers? What are the effects of tracking on students? To what extent are parents and communities involved in the life of their high schools? Are high schools at all responsive to the communities they serve? Are big schools preferable to small ones? And are most schools similar in the ways in which they structure time and utilize space?

Other themes, as well, will emerge from the data and will be presented in the next four chapters. Our findings about what goes on in most high school class-rooms, for example, form the substance of Chapters 5 and 6.

As the reader proceeds through the rest of the book, data about the schools as a group and about each of the schools individually will accumulate, so that by the final chapter a much "thicker" description of each school can be presented. We will do a "reprise," to borrow a term from music, on school profiles in Chapter 7, focusing on what we have learned about each school's unique personality and its capacity for change.

CHAPTER II, NOTES AND REFERENCES

1. B.J. Benham, Analysis of Curriculum Materials Submitted by 599 High School Teachers (Unpublished Technical Report, 1978).

2. Jeannie Oakes, A Question of Access: Tracking and Curriculum Differentiation in a National Sample of English and Mathematics Classes (Technical Report No. 24, 1981).

CHAPTER III

BEING A TEACHER

Twenty-five years later, what comes back? No more nor less than we knew then: there was tiny Mrs. Bass, increasingly pregnant, ruling a class of rowdy boys with such skill that, eventually, any one of them would gladly have jumped through hoops for her. Mr. Taylor, who terrified his General Science classes with (as I have since learned) erroneous descriptions of various diseases. Tall Mrs. Vollmer, the typing teacher, who never smiled. The coaches, who lived in their own little world somewhere out beyond the wood shop and the cafeteria. Dr. Fletcher, head of the social studies department, who taught us that just about everything worth doing involved politics somehow or another. Miss McCarthy, who gave an F for the day to anyone who didn't wear green in her Home Ec. classes on St. Patrick's Day.

We didn't know much about our teachers. And beyond a little fairly mild teen-age curiosity we didn't really care. With few exceptions they were, for us, one-dimensional figures in a landscape that only constituted one part of our lives; actually, we were much more interested in each other than in the adults around us. That our teachers had private lives, personal fears, hopes, dreams, and worries, not to mention physical aches and pains--all seemed more or less unreal to us. It would never have occurred to us to ask why a teacher had chosen to become a teacher, or what he or she liked or disliked about the work. True, some of what our teachers valued was clear to us in what they chose to teach us, and the way they taught it. That was important for us to figure out--and act upon, as necessary. But anything more personal was simply none of our concern--our teachers might have been turned off, folded up and stored in a closet overnight and on weekends, for all we knew or cared.

Things haven't changed that much. Except in very small towns like Dennison, students don't generally encounter their teachers in out-of-school settings, and so by and large the same is as true now as it was then: to students, teachers aren't quite "real people."

And all of us were students once. Some people still seem to think of teachers that way--as one-dimensional. Those of us who chose education as a career, however, learned the truth firsthand: teachers are real people--neither victims nor villains, but ordinary people who chose to devote their work lives to passing knowledge, skills, and understanding along to others. It's not an easy job--done well, it consumes much more than just eight hours a day. The needs and problems of students can't simply be turned off at 3:00, and summer vacations no longer mean a chance to rest and regain needed resilience, but extra college courses, inservice workshops, and preparation for next year's teaching. Among teachers, "burn-out" has become a familiar phrase --but there are still many people who think of teaching as an easy job and of teachers as not quite real.

What is life in schools like for teachers? Information collected from the 664 high school teachers who participated in the Study of Schooling can begin to give us a glimpse of the many different aspects of their lives: their values and attitudes, their beliefs about education, their relationships with their colleagues, with their superiors, and with parents; their views of students, their satisfaction with their work environment and their own job performance, staff meetings, in-service training, and professional activities; their educational background; what they do in the classroom, and more.

This chapter will put together a picture of teachers--who they are, what they do, and how they feel about what they do--using A Study of Schooling data. Inevitably, the picture will not be complete: it wasn't possible to ask every question that might have been asked. And in any case, there will always be individual differences--664 teachers can certainly be understood to have 664 different experiences of their work situations. Nevertheless, there are commonalities of values, perceptions, and experience which can be reported. To the extent that the teachers sampled tend to share similar views, they will be reported as a total group. In cases where the responses of a subset of teachers differ from the responses of the rest, these differences will be noted and, when appropriate,

84

hypotheses about the causes and/or the meanings of the differences will be proposed.

The chapter is divided into six parts. Part One provides a description of the job of teaching and the physical setting of the classroom. It also reveals how teachers feel about their work, what functions of schooling they value, and what duties they prefer.

Part Two explores teachers' contact with parents in some detail, and Part Three covers teachers' percep- tions of staff relationships at their schools. In Part Four, we learn what kind of leadership teachers said they want from their principals. Part Five addresses several isues, focusing on teachers' perceptions of students. Finally, in Part Six, we examine the educa- tional beliefs and value systems of the teachers in our sample. Some demographic data also are included in Part Six.

I.

Day in, day out

The work day of a teacher starts early. At most of the high schools in the Study, teachers were expected to be in the school building by 7:30 or 8:00 each morning, or half an hour before the first class began. At Vista and Manchester, the first class actually began at 7:30. At Euclid, by contrast, the first class began at 8:45.

As a rule, teachers' daily work schedules called for five or six class periods and one planning period (called conference periods or preparation periods at some schools). Some teachers at some schools had four class periods, one planning period, and one period of study hall duty or other monitoring responsibilities around the school building or grounds.

Because the length of class periods varied (from a minimum of 40 to a maximum of 55 minutes), the amount of time spent actually teaching classes varied consid- erably, from a low of four hours per day at Vista to a high of five and one-half hours at Manchester. Teach- ing, of course, goes on at other times as well: ex- plaining something to a student who stays for a moment

85

after class to ask a question is teaching. Spending
the planning period or part of lunchtime giving extra
help to a student who needs it is teaching. Evaluating
student work--grading papers, giving feedback--is part
of teaching, and preparing material for use the next
day (or next week) is also part of teaching. In fact,
there isn't enough time in the course of a school day
to do all that needs to be done. Many teachers take
work home with them and put in extra hours every
evening.

We asked the teachers in our sample to tell us how
much time they spent each week preparing for the class
which we observed. Nearly three-fourths told us that
they spent anywhere from two to six hours a week for
that class alone. Since most of them taught five
classes each day, that would suggest that many of our
teachers put in from ten to thirty hours of work each
week above and beyond their eight hours a day in the
school building. Then, too, there are periodic department meetings and staff meetings which add extra hours
to a teacher's day. Finally, many teachers in our
sample indicated that they take additional college
courses in order to keep abreast of their subject
specialization, to improve in their mastery of teaching
methods, or to advance on the salary ladder.

These four walls

Many studies have explored the phenomenon of
teacher isolation. We, too, found isolation to be a
reality in the school lives of the high school teachers
who participated in A Study of Schooling. 83% of our
sample said that they teach by themselves, in self-contained classrooms. Another six per cent told us that
they teach alone in self-contained classrooms, with
occasional help, on an informal basis, from one or more
other teachers. Taken together, then, 90% of our
sample taught alone in self-contained classrooms. Of
the remainder, a few (5%) were members of teaching
teams, and fewer yet (4%), taught with the help of one
or more aides.

Most schools allowed only three to five minutes
between classes--barely enough time for a teacher to
exchange a few quick words with the teacher in the next
classroom. Nearly two-thirds of our teachers told us
that they never have an opportunity to observe

instruction in other classrooms,* and the rest said that they are able to do this only once or twice a year. It is hardly surprising, then, that most of the teachers in our Study didn't know very much about each other's educational beliefs, job competence, or behavior with students. On the average, our teachers told us that they know such things about less than one-third of their colleagues.

As a rule, then, teachers are on their own with their students for the greater part of each day. In all but the smaller schools, teachers were responsible for about 150 students a day. At the high school level, of course, "'twas ever thus."

And what do these self-contained classrooms, in which most teachers spend their working days, look like? According to our observation data, the average high school classroom looks much as most of us would remember it: a room large enough to accommodate 20-30 people adequately, with desks or tables (usually movable rather than fixed to the floor) arranged in rows.** The floors are bare wood or tile, and there are chalk boards and bulletin boards on three of the four walls (the fourth wall is generally a bank of windows). The material displayed on the bulletin board is usually commercially prepared or else made by the teacher; rarely, at the high school level, did we find student-made displays on the bulletin boards. Learning centers in corners of the classroom were observed in only five percent of the cases. On the whole, we found that teachers control decisions about the use of classroom space, and most teachers use their classrooms more or less as they find them, making few, if any, alterations. While it is true that many teachers manage to create a very pleasant classroom environment through the use of visual materials taped to the walls, interesting bulletin board displays, easy access to learning materials in the room, and an occasional potted plant or two, fundamentally the high school

---

* The percentage was even higher for beginning teachers, who presumably would benefit from chances to observe and learn from the more experienced faculty members.

** In Chapter 7, we will explore some of the ways in which the physical characteristics of the classroom determine what can (and cannot) take place there.

classroom is a small, bare box with one view of the outdoors, student desks facing forward, and one teacher's desk either in the front, facing the students, or in the back, so the teacher can keep an eye on the students from behind. The "control orientation" of schools will be one of the major themes of this book.

These arrangements are conventional and familiar. In some schools, they are also more or less enforced by the expectations of the principal--who may want a quiet, tidy classroom--or by subtle but persistent pressure from the custodial staff, who do not appreciate the extra work involved in cleaning rooms which have been altered to create less orthodox learning environments. On the whole, teachers told us that they have a lot of control over use of their classroom space, and that they are generally satisfied with the way they use the space to which they are assigned. Within the physical constraints of the typical classroom, however, as a rule teachers' decisions about use of space are limited to decisions about whether to put the desks in rows, in a V-shape, a U-shape, or a circle. Once in a great while they might be put in small groups, but this configuration is only temporary; sooner or later they end up back in the usual rows.

As far as the school as a whole is concerned, the majority of teachers told us that their "school buildings, grounds, and facilities" met their work needs. However, at four schools--Bradford, Newport, Fairfield, and Manchester--half or more of the teachers felt that the school buildings, grounds, and facilities were not adequate for their work needs. At these four schools, teachers also identified "inadequate resources" as a school problem.

*   *   *

Being responsible for the satisfactory educational progress of so many students, being mostly isolated from other adults, perceived pressures from the administration, parents, and the community, and having to adjust many personal needs and concerns to the demands of the job--all of these factors, taken together, make secondary school teaching an unbelievably exhausting career--why, then, do people choose it?

We asked the teachers in our Study to tell us their primary reason for entering the teaching profession.

Nine possible responses included (1) working condi-
tions--hours, holidays, job security, summer vacation;
(2) interest in subject, always wanted to be a teacher;
(3) recommended or influenced by others; (4) work is
rewarding, satisfying, enjoyable; (5) scholarship to
study to become a teacher; (6) like children/adults/
young people; (7) to help others, to be of service, to
teach others; (8) economic considerations; and (9)
other.

The reason most often given was "interest in
subject, always wanted to be a teacher," (22%). "Work
is rewarding, satisfying, enjoyable" was the reason
given by 19% of the teachers, and 17% of them said they
chose to enter the teaching profession because they
wanted "to help others, to be of service, to teach
others." It is interesting to note that the reasons
chosen least often were "working conditions" (8%) and
"economic considerations" (4%). The teachers in our
sample, then, seem to have entered the teaching profession because they were interested in ideas and in
working with people, not because they expected an easy
life.

And what do they believe to be the central purposes
(or educative functions) of schooling?

When asked whether social, intellectual, personal,
or vocational development was the most important
function for their school to emphasize, the intellectual function was the one chosen by the largest percentage of our teachers (46%). In other words, less than
half of our teachers selected the intellectual function
as the one that should be emphasized. Given the
hullabaloo over "basics" in recent years, this is
perhaps a surprisingly low percentage.

The personal function was the one chosen by the
next largest group (30%)--in fact, at three schools
(Dennison, Fairfield, and Vista), more teachers chose
the personal than chose the intellectual function.
Since the personal function is defined as "instruction
which builds self-confidence, creativity, ability to
think independently, and self-discipline," qualities
which I believe many teachers feel make students easier
and more fun to teach, these responses are not surprising. It is encouraging that many teachers recognize
the broader goals of independent thinking and self-

discipline as essential, if not absolutely central, aims of the educative process.

The vocational function was chosen by 15% of the teachers as the most important function of schooling, and the social function was chosen by the remaining 10%. Vocational development was defined as "instruction which prepares students for employment, development of skills necessary for getting a job, development of awareness about career choices and alternatives," and social development was defined as "instruction which helps students learn to get along with other students and with adults, prepares students for social and civic responsibility, develops students' awareness and appreciation of our own and other cultures."

It is necessary to point out, I think, that these low percentages for the social and vocational functions were, to some extent, the result of the forced-choice format of the question itself, which specifically asked teachers to choose the one most important function. When given a chance to evaluate the importance of each of the four functions separately, on the other hand, our high school teachers indicated that they believed all four are very important for the development of well-rounded students.

Although high school teachers are expected to perform many other kinds of duties, teaching is what they like best. We asked our teachers to indicate which of eleven inevitable or necessary job activities they liked best and least. Teaching (actual instruction) was chosen by 77% of those responding, and working with individual students--another form of teaching--was chosen by 38%.*

When asked to estimate how much class time they actually spent on instructional activities, whether with classes, small groups, or individual students, our teachers said that instructional activity accounted for 73% of their class time. 14% was spent on routines, such as taking attendance, making announcements, passing out materials, and so forth. 9% of the total

---

* Despite instructions, some teachers selected more than one response in each category. This is why totals add up to over 100%.

time, they estimated, was spent on getting students to behave.

Required non-instructional duties (such as meetings, clerical tasks, inventory, and study hall, lunchroom, or hall patrol duty) were liked least by 43% of those responding, and external classroom disruptions (P.A. announcements, students being pulled out of class, and the like) were liked least by 40% of the teachers. This is hardly surprising. Teaching, after all, is what teachers want to be doing. What many people outside education do not realize is that the teaching career does involve many non-instructional duties in addition to actual teaching.

II.

It comes with the territory

Teaching involves a certain amount of interaction with parents, although at the high school level such interaction occurs less often than at the elementary and junior high levels. Only about six percent of our high school teachers indicated that interaction with parents was one of the activities they liked least, although this figure might have been higher if teachers had been expected to devote more time out of an already-overloaded schedule to this activity.

As it was, our teachers indicated that they sometimes have contact with parents through parent-teacher conferences and planned after-school activities (such as the annual open house, the Christmas concert, and athletic events). At none of the thirteen schools did there seem to be a policy of regularly-scheduled parent-teacher conferences and, on the average, our teachers said that they "mildly agree" with the statement that "The only time most parents visit schools is when their children are in trouble." (At Fairfield and Laurel, teachers strongly agreed that this was the case). Parent conferences, then, which teachers say they have only sometimes, are likely to occur when there are problems and not as a regularly-scheduled mechanism by which teachers can report pupil progress. We must bear in mind, of course, that high school teachers may be responsible for up to 150 students a day. To have even one parent conference a year for every student would involve one conference every day for 150 of the 180-185 days of the school year. Frequent parent-teacher conferences for the purpose of reporting pupil progress seem, therefore, largely unmanageable at the high school level.*

In addition to parent conferences and planned after-school activities, there are other ways in which teachers might come in contact with parents: at Board of Education meetings, at PTA meetings, in church or other community organizations and events, through social gatherings, or through parent visits to the classroom. Also, parents might serve as aides or volunteers in the school. However, our teachers said that they seldom encounter parents in these ways.

Of course, 68% of our teachers told us that they do not live in the community where they teach. For these teachers, out-of-school contact with parents would be even less likely and it's not surprising, then, that over half of our teacher sample told us that they have no personal friends among the parents of their students, or else that they have just one or two.

How, then, do most high school teachers generally communicate with parents? The old standby, of course, is the report card. Virtually all of the teachers in our sample (99.5%) reported using this method of communicating with parents. A large percentage (96%) also reported having parent-teacher conferences, but as we have already seen, these tend to be situational and are most often held when problems arise. 91% reported using written progress reports--generally, though not always, incorporated as part of the report card--as a way of communicating with parents.

Other methods of communicating with parents are informal and infrequent. 84% of the teachers reported that they sometimes see parents outside the context of a planned conference. They also reported meeting parents at annual open houses or back-to-school nights. Neither method, however, reaches all parents; the

---

* A workable exception to this is the teacher-advisor system, in which every teacher has an advisory group of up to 20 students and, whether the teacher has each of her advisees in class or not, is responsible for reporting their progress to their parents several times a year.

report card remains the single most commonly used way for teachers to communicate with parents.

And what do they communicate? Student grades, first and foremost. Next comes attendance, followed by behavior and work habits.

Oddly enough, overall, more teachers said they report students' health problems to parents than said that they report students' interests. However, reporting of students' interests did vary enormously from school to school.

We asked teachers how quickly, in their experience, parents respond when contacted regarding their child. A slim majority of 56% told us that, in their experience, parents usually respond quickly; 26% said that parents usually respond with some delay; 10% said parents do not respond at all, and the remaining 8% said that they had not contacted any parents and therefore could not answer the question.

Interestingly, many high school parents (59%) said that the school responds quickly when they contact it regarding their children. 15% said that the school responds with some delay. Only 2% of the high school parent sample complained that the school did not respond at all. The remaining 24% said that they had not had any need to contact their child's school.

Both teachers and parents, then, generally see each other as responding quickly or with some delay when contacted. This is not surprising, however, when one recalls that most such contacts, apart from reporting of pupil progress, concern problems of student behavior or underachievement.

Yet another reason why parents might make an effort to get in touch with teachers would be in order to voice objections to curriculum materials. Very few of our teachers had had this type of contact with parents in the year preceding the Study, although at a few schools, small percentages of teachers had experienced some parent objections to curriculum materials. These instances were evidently few and far between, however, for even the parents themselves did not perceive that they had had much reason to object to the curriculum materials which their children were using.

*   *   *

Overall, only eight percent of our teacher sample said they felt that lack of parent interest was the biggest problem at their school. Interestingly, of 3,675 high school <u>parents</u> sampled, approximately the same percentage also said that lack of parent interest was the one biggest problem at their child's school. Put another way, 92% of the teachers and about 91% of the parents felt that other school problems were far more critical than lack of parent interest.

Interest, however, is one thing; participation is another. While parents on the whole feel that they are interested in their child's schooling and experiences in school, this interest remains fairly passive. Only small percentages of parents become involved in school-related activities.

We asked parents and teachers about parent participation in a variety of school related activities. We asked whether parents worked as classroom aides, served as PTA Board members, attended adult education classes, served on the Parent Advisory Council, attended PTA meetings, helped at special events, or came to school as guest speakers. Although both parents and teachers felt that such activities were "somewhat" important, teachers told us rather emphatically that, in their view, parents did not participate in them as much as would be desirable. And the parents themselves admitted that they did not, in fact, participate much.

The two activities in which the largest percentage of parents took part (and which, interestingly enough, were the only two that the teachers considered "very" important) were PTA (32% of the parent sample said that they did attend PTA meetings) and helping at special events (38% said they did this).

Next, we asked teachers <u>why</u> parent participation was so low. Many teachers felt that the primary reason was that, often, school-related activities conflict with parents' working hours. A large percentage of teachers also felt that many parents do not participate in school activities because they feel that it is the responsibility of the principal and the teachers to run the school. (Reading between the lines, here, we might also venture to hypothesize that many parents are, simply, uncomfortable in school settings.) The

94

difficulty of finding babysitters and transportation were also mentioned by teachers as possible reasons for low parent participation in school activities. And one-fifth of the teacher sample said they felt that one reason parents didn't participate more was because of "principal's and teacher's attitudes," which attitudes, presumably, had the effect of discouraging parents from participating.

In general, then, the parents in our sample didn't participate much in school-related activities. Nor did they appear to have much influence on decisions made for the school. The teachers in our sample seemed to feel that parents should have slightly more influence in school decision-making than they do; they do not, however, seem to feel that parents should have a lot of influence. The teachers only mildly agreed with the statement, "Parents should have a say in what is taught at this school." And when asked about specific areas of decision-making such as what and how subjects are taught, hiring and firing of teachers and administrators, setting teacher salaries, and so forth, the teachers in our sample were much less willing to grant parents additional decision-making power or influence than they were in areas such as setting standards for student behavior, and how the school budget is spent, and ways the school and community work together. In these areas, more remote from the classroom itself, teachers were more willing to allow parents greater influence.

On the whole, teachers don't seem too anxious to have parents participating in areas which the teachers consider part of their professional territory. Our teachers felt that they had a lot of control over their work. Most (75%) felt that the amount of control they had was the right amount; however, the remaining one-fourth told us that it was less than they would like. Clearly, our teachers would not readily give up some of their control to parents, and if parent groups began to organize with the intention of taking a much more active role in school decision-making, some real battles could develop over who decides what.

This is unlikely to happen, however. Our data suggest that, as a rule, parents are interested in their child's school and more precisely they are interested in their child. They are far less interested in school policies and practices in general, or in helping to formulate these for the school as a whole. We have seen that parents participate very little in the activities and organizations which could have decision-making influence: PTA, School Board, Parent Advisory Council. In fact, from the teachers' point of view, Parent Advisory Councils are seen as mostly ineffectual. Teachers felt that the PAC, if one existed at all, did not make important decisions for the school, nor did it represent the views of most parents. In effect, the teachers were suggesting that Parent Advisory Councils are just so much public-relations window-dressing; and, on the whole, parents themselves seemed to concur with this view.

Another indicator of parent willingness to leave most decisions in the hands of the school people is their perhaps surprising degree of agreement (63% overall) with the statement, "Teachers' unions should be able to bargain about things like class size, curriculum, and teaching methods." And finally, as we have already seen, as many as one in four of our parents told us that a reason that they did not participate in school activities was "my belief that it is the job of the principal and teachers to run the school."

In summary, then, it seems likely that teachers will continue to control what happens in the classroom and that, as in the past, they will continue to have little contact with parents beyond traditional reporting of progress and occasional conferences related to student behavior problems. Parents are unlikely to gain any significant degree of control over school decision-making. Nor do most of them really desire such control except, perhaps, occasionally in relation to specific issues which flare up for awhile in the community, and then die out.

III.

All in it together

Teachers, on the whole, support each other, and nine out of ten in our Study believed that their colleagues were doing a good job. How they arrived at this judgment is somewhat unclear, since—particularly at the larger schools—they admitted to knowing little

96

about the other teachers' behavior with students, their job competence, or their educational beliefs.

Furthermore, most teachers virtually never observed their colleagues teaching, and although many told us that they would like to have opportunities for such peer observation, it remains doubtful whether, if given the chance, they would actually do so: it is my observation that most teachers are uncomfortable about being watched while they work. Feeling this way themselves, they are unlikely to observe others--according their colleagues the same privacy they prefer for themselves.

Interestingly, the teachers in our sample agreed overwhelmingly (94%) that it is important for all members of the staff to know quite a bit about what is actually being taught. Knowing what is being taught, however, is not quite the same as knowing how it is being taught or why it is being taught.

We asked our teachers to evaluate 19 different possible problem areas and then to tell us which they thought, of the 19, was the one biggest problem at their school. It is interesting to see that those problems which the majority of teachers at each school regarded as major tended to be those which make it harder for them to do what they want to be doing: teaching. Lack of student interest, student misbehavior, lack of parent interest, (which may mean, to teachers, lack of home support for school work), drug and alcohol use, size of classes, and inadequate resources are the work problems as perceived by teachers overall.[1]

Those problems for which teachers may be considered directly responsible--inadequate discipline of students, poor teaching, and poor curriculum--were rated by the teachers themselves as less critical, in some cases much less so.

This pattern was even more noticeable when the teachers were asked to identify the one biggest problem, as Table 3.1 shows.[2]

The first nine problems--all of them having to do with students, parents, or the school administration-- were chosen by 504 of the 603 teachers who responded to this item. Poor teaching, inadequate discipline of students, and poor curriculum, on the other hand, were

97

identified as the one biggest problem by only 46 (7.6%) of the 603 teachers, and ranked 10th, 13th, and 15th respectively.

Table 3.1

603 high school teachers select the one biggest problem at their school	Teachers selecting each problem:	
	%	N
1. Lack of student interest	23.9	144
2. School too large/classes overcrowded	10.3	62
3. Student misbehavior	9.3	56
4. The administration at this school	9.0	54
5. Inadequate/inappropriate resources	8.5	51
6. Lack of parent interest	8.0	48
7. Student language problems	6.3	38*
8. Standards for graduation/academic requirements	4.5	27
9. Drug/alcohol use	4.0	24
10. Poor teachers or teaching	3.3	20
11. Federal, state, or local policies & regulations that interfere with education	2.7	16
12. How the school is organized	2.5	15
13. Teachers don't discipline students	2.5	15
14. Staff relations	2.3	14
15. Poor curriculum	1.8	11
16. Lack of staff interest in good school-community relations	1.0	6
17. Busing for integration	.2	1
18. Prejudice/racial conflict	.2	1
19. Desegregation	0	0
		603

That there might be a connection between poor teaching, poor curriculum, and the lack of student interest which teachers find so frustrating, is a possibility that does not seem to have occurred to the teachers in our sample. As we have already seen, 89% felt that "most of the teachers at this school are doing a good job." Furthermore, the majority disagreed

---

* Nearly all of these 38 teachers were at Rosemont and Newport high schools.

that "teachers don't care about students," and that "average students don't get enough attention at this school." Teachers of all subject areas told us they felt that what their students were learning in their classes was useful--in some cases, <u>very</u> useful--both now and later in life.

Teachers didn't let themselves completely off the hook, however. Although only 27 out of 603 selected "standards for graduation/academic requirements" as the one biggest problem at their school, the majority of teachers at all but two schools agreed that "students are graded too easy at this school" and that "too many students are allowed to graduate without learning very much." And at six of the thirteen schools, the average teacher response to "students at this school receive a lot of individual attention from their teachers" was mild <u>disagreement</u>.

Indeed, school by school, there were quite a lot of differences in the problems perceived by teachers. But even so, at <u>no</u> school did the teachers identify as major any problem which was clearly the teachers' responsibility.

Bette Overman, in her report on perceived problems, developed a composite problem score for each school based on the variety and intensity of problems as perceived by teachers, students, and parents. The table below shows each school's composite problem score (as derived from the teacher data), those problems areas which were seen as <u>major</u> by the majority of teachers at each school, and the size of the school (Table 3.2).

We will return to these data shortly, in connection with teacher job satisfaction, and again in later chapters, as we compare teacher perceptions of school problems with those of students, parents, and administrators. What we can see at this point is that, on the whole, teachers do not see themselves as responsible for any of the most critical problems at their school.

And this may very well be a fair judgment on the part of the teachers. As Goodlad points out in his book on A Study of Schooling,[3] some of the problems identified by teachers are school or school district-based, but are beyond the power of teachers to solve without the active cooperation of school boards, school district staff at all levels, and parents. Others, such as drug and alcohol use and student misbehavior, are social problems and cannot be solved by schools alone. "It is interesting and simultaneously discouraging," Goodlad notes, "that the election campaigns of school board members tend so frequently to focus on these highly visible youth problems and to obscure board responsibility for the circumstances of teaching."

Table 3.2

School composite problem scores and major problems perceived by teachers at each school; size of school

School	Score	Size*	Major problems
Newport	2.09	L	st. language, school size, student interest
Bradford	1.95	M	student interest, parent interest
Manchester	1.94	L	st. misbehavior, student interest, school size, parent interest, inad. resources
Rosemont	1.90	L	student language, parent interest
Fairfield	1.88	M	student misbehavior
Laurel	1.83	S	student interest, parent interest
Vista	1.75	L	student misbehavior, school size
Crestview	1.75	M	student interest, parent interest
Palisades	1.71	M	no problems
Atwater	1.69	S	seen as
Woodlake	1.62	M	"major" by
Euclid	1.51	S	teachers at these
Dennison	1.24	S	five schools

We asked the teachers to tell us what percentage of the staff at their schools were spending "a lot of time and effort" on the major problems of the school, and to estimate the chances of success in solving those problems. It is perhaps a measure of teachers' feelings of impotence and frustration that, at Bradford, Fairfield, Newport, Manchester and Rosemont, the

---

* School size correlates with composite problem score: .70, sig. = .01.

teachers said there was very little chance of success in solving the school's major problems. And at the other eight schools, teachers estimated the chances for such success at only about 50-50.

*   *   *

A finding of considerable importance, and one which adds considerably to our growing impression of the climate and personality of each individual school, is that teacher job satisfaction is quite clearly related to the number and intensity of problems which teachers perceive to exist at their schools.

The teacher satisfaction score for each school was a complex composite based on data derived from 120 questions dealing with various aspects of the teachers' work and the school itself. Six high schools emerged from this analysis as "less satisfying" and three as "more satisfying" in the eyes of teachers (the remaining four were in between). The six less satisfying schools were also the first six in rank order on the composite problems scale, and the three more satisfying schools were those with the lowest composite problems core (see Table 3.2).

Less Satisfying	Moderately Satisfying	More Satisfying
Newport	Vista	Woodlake
Bradford	Crestview	Euclid
Manchester	Palisades	Dennison
Rosemont	Atwater	
Fairfield		
Laurel		

These three sets, based on the composite teacher satisfaction scores, recur in other ways and forms elsewhere in the data. We shall have several occasions to notice that other aspects of school life fall into much the same school-by-school pattern.

One of the factors which makes the work environment either more or less satisfying for teachers is the quality of staff relations--how positive the teachers feel about each other at each school.

Included in the Teacher Survey were 100 items about the school work environment. Analysis of the responses to these items yielded eleven item clusters, which were then treated as scales, each scale having one score--a composite of all the items in the scale. The scales which related most directly to the quality of staff relations were:

1. Staff Task Orientation -- four items about the degree to which teachers perceive that they and their colleagues solve problems and get things done;

2. Staff Affection -- twelve items about whether staff members help, support, and trust each other;

3. Staff Self-Renewal -- five items about the degree to which teachers perceive themselves and their colleagues as being open to change and professional growth; and

4. Staff Openness -- seven items about the quality of communication between staff members.

At all of the high schools in the Study except for two, teacher responses to the items in these four scales revealed positive feelings about the quality of staff relations. Generally, then, our teachers felt good about their colleagues.

At Dennison Secondary School, the feelings were even more positive. In fact, Dennison teachers were highly positive on all eleven of the work environment scales, as well as on the composite satisfaction index already mentioned. Since Dennison was such a small school (10 teachers, a teaching principal, and 61 students), and so isolated geographically, it is a happy circumstance for everyone there that the teachers felt so positive about their work environment.

The two schools at which teacher responses about staff relations were more negative were Newport and Rosemont High Schools. At Newport, in particular, there seemed to be a good deal of staff friction. The impression conveyed in other areas of the data--for example, from the curriculum materials submitted by teachers--was one of a rather independent and individualistic group of teachers, each most interested in doing his (or her) own thing and not very interested in cooperative efforts. Staff relations were seen as a problem at Newport, and the responses to the staff cohesiveness items on the work environment instrument--particularly the items about staff respect and affection--certainly support this view.

Both Newport and Rosemont were large, urban schools, with many problems. Both were also rated "less satisfying" places to work by the teachers working there. Supportive and harmonious staff interaction is more difficult to achieve in very large schools, especially if other aspects of the working environment are also seen by teachers as less than satisfactory. Too, even in smaller schools, teachers spend little time together other than informally at lunchtime and preparation period, and formally at staff meetings and occasional in-service meetings. There is not much occasion for real closeness to develop. Nor, in fact, do the prevailing norms really encourage such closeness.

And yet, teachers at almost all schools told us that they had a good many close personal friends among their colleagues.* Informal conversation in the teachers' lounge undoubtedly leads to some personal friendships, but the existence of these doesn't necessarily ensure a friendly in-school working environment. And, as we have already seen, teachers say they do not know much about most of their colleagues' educational beliefs, classroom behavior, or job competence; thus, it seems to be a fair speculation that, aside from discussion of "problem kids," teachers' lounge conversations tend to be more about personal than professional matters. It is ironic, to say the least, that the demands of teaching prevent teachers from maintaining professional relationships with each other.

IV.

The Head Honcho

Other studies have found that, more than any other person in the school, the principal sets the tone and is instrumental in creating the working environment within which the teachers must function from day to day.

---

* This was not true at Laurel, which is interesting in itself.

We asked the teachers in our Study many questions about their principal, their relation with him and their perceptions of his effectiveness in various aspects of his role. The responses we received varied so greatly that it is difficult to summarize them across schools. For example, the range of responses to the statement, "The staff members trust the principal," varied by 62 points, from a low of 28% agreement at Atwater to a high of 90% agreement at Dennison. Instead, what seems to emerge is a continuum, from negative to positive relative to principal leadership. The thirteen schools fall into clusters on this continuum, as follows:

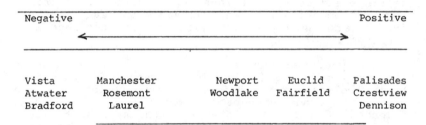

How teachers at thirteen high schools felt about their principal. Based on the composite Principal Leadership scores for each school staff.

What sort of leadership earns a positive response from teachers? The principal who was perceived by the teachers in our Study as providing good leadership allowed his* staff considerable freedom of action, and was open to new ideas. He was supportive and encouraging, and the teachers felt that he trusted them and respected their judgment. Basically democratic in his leadership style, he often sought out the teachers' ideas, and consulted with them before making any decision that would affect them. The teachers felt included in the school's decision-making process, and agreed that "The administrators and teachers collaborate in making the school run effectively." Staff meetings were not seen as a waste of time, but when

---

* As it happens, all of the principals at the thirteen high schools in the Study of Schooling were male.

they were called, were viewed by the teachers as being about moderately important matters.

On the whole, teachers at all of our schools felt that they had <u>some</u> influence in making school deci-sions, but that they should have <u>more</u> influence.[4]

Areas of decision-making for the school as a whole over which teachers perceived that they <u>do</u> have some influence were curriculum and instruction, pupil behavior, communication with parents, extracurricular and community related issues and activities, and dress codes for both students and teachers.

Areas of decision-making in which teachers per-ceived themselves to have no influence included teacher and student class assignments, procedure and content of staff meetings, fiscal management, and the selection and evaluation of both teaching assistants and of professional staff.

Since, as we have seen, teachers feel more job satisfaction and are more positive towards their principal at schools where they feel included in the decision-making process, an administrator interested in improving the work environment of his or her school would be likely to search for new areas and ways in which to involve teachers in making decisions. This involves recognition, by the principal, of an important discrepancy: we found quite clearly that principals thought the teachers had more influence in school decisions than the teachers themselves thought they had. Involving teachers in more areas of decision-making, then, also involves making an effort to see things from the teachers' point of view. This may be difficult for some principals, whose daily experience is so very different from that of the classroom teach-er.

There are, however, several areas in which teachers now perceive they have no influence but in which they <u>could</u> have some influence, if the principal were able and willing to involve them. Surely teachers could be involved to some extent in negotiating their own class assignments, planning and running staff meetings, and the selection and evaluation of teaching assistants. Too, some form of peer observation could be used that would involve teachers in evaluation of professional staff.

Fiscal management and the initial selection of professional staff are more clearly the principal's responsibility--in some cases, these actually are taken care of primarily at the district level. On the whole, these are areas in which teachers would probably not even want to be involved.

But that they do want to be more involved in some way is clear: while 72% of them said that they have some influence, and only 18% said they had "a lot" of influence in "making decisions for this school," 70% said that they should have a lot of influence.

It is interesting to note that the principals at Dennison, Crestview, Palisades and Fairfield were all new to their positions at the time of the Study--that is, in their first or second year at the school. A "honeymoon effect" may have been operating in one or two cases, but being relatively new to the job doesn't guarantee success as a principal in the eyes of the teachers: at Atwater High, where the principal was only in his third year, the teachers were consistently negative in their views of the leadership he was providing. Nor does mere longevity necessarily produce poorer leadership, in the eyes of teachers: at Euclid and Woodlake, where the teachers were quite happy with their principals, the men had been on the job for ten and twenty years respectively.

We asked teachers to tell us why they do the things the principal suggests or wants them to do, by rank-ordering the following five possible responses:

1. I admire the principal for personal qualities, and I want to act in a way that merits the principal's respect and admiration.

2. I respect the principal's competence and good judgment about things with which he/she is more experienced than I.

3. The principal can give special help and benefits to those who cooperate.

4. The principal can apply pressure or penalize those who do not cooperate.

5. The principal has a <u>legitimate right</u>, in that position, to expect that the suggestion he/she gives will be carried out.

At Atwater and Bradford, two schools at which teachers were very negative about their principals, the majority of teachers ranked "legitimate right" first, followed by "punishment" and "reward" at Atwater and "reward" and "competence" at Bradford.

At Fairfield, Dennison, and Euclid, three schools at which teachers were positive about their principals, most teachers ranked "competence" first, followed by "personal qualities" "legitimate right" or "reward".

At most of the schools, however, the teachers gave "legitimate right" followed by "competence" and "personal qualities" as the reasons for doing as the principal requested.

Case Study: Atwater

At Atwater High School, there was quite a bit of tension between the teachers and the principal at the time of the Study. The principal was in his third year then. When he first arrived, he had made an effort to get the teachers' support for a trimester plan to replace the semester schedule then in use. Additionally, there was a general belief among the teachers that he had been hired by the Board with a mandate to "shape up" the staff. Whether this was true or not, it was hardly an auspicious way to begin.

As we have seen, teachers respond more positively when they are treated with trust and respect, and when they feel included in the school's decision-making process. Unfortunately, at Atwater, the staff perceived that the new principal was determined to institute the trimester system despite their objections and that he put considerable pressure on them to cooperate.

And they <u>did</u> cooperate, to some extent, because on the whole they believed that "the principal has a legitimate right, in that position, to expect that the suggestions he/she gives will be carried out." They also believed that the principal might penalize those who did not cooperate, and reward those who did. Admiration for the principal's personal qualities and respect for his professional competence were ranked low by the majority of Atwater teachers.

And so the teachers voted to try the new plan, and during the second year of the new principal's tenure, a trimester system of sorts was instituted at Atwater High. Lacking the wholehearted support of the teachers, however, it failed; and by the third year--the year of the Study--all of the program areas except fine arts and the vocational subjects had modified their schedules, and some had even gone back to the old semester schedule.

Although the teachers were very much involved in the decision to modify the trimester plan, the whole experience evidently left a residue of bad feeling towards the principal which, in that third year, he was trying to overcome. Among other things, he had formed a faculty advisory council to help him with school decision-making but, as one teacher told us somewhat skeptically, "it hasn't had a chance to prove itself yet."

Breaking the sound barrier

Actually, with the exception of tiny Dennison, on a day-to-day basis the teachers in our Study didn't have much contact with their principals. This was especially true at the larger schools.

We asked the teachers how often they talked with their principal about staff relations, pupil discipline, parents, curriculum and instruction, or their own job performance. On all these issues, most teachers indicated that they talked with the principal about once a month; many, however, told us that they never talk with the principal about some of these matters.

Furthermore, the teachers told us that they--rather than the principal--usually initiate the discussions of curriculum, parents, pupils, and staff relations. When it comes to their own job performance, however, at all but three schools most of the teachers say the initiative comes from the principal. The exceptions were Dennison, Laurel, and Newport. Dennison and Laurel were both very small schools, at which communication between teachers and principal would be fairly easy. At Dennison, where the teachers felt strongly positive about their principal, one can envision the staff members feeling fairly comfortable in raising the issue of their own job performance, with the expectation of receiving real help.

At Laurel, as we have noted several times before, the teachers felt rather negative about the principal. Substantial percentages of the teachers at Laurel told us that their conversations with the principal--particularly about parents, curriculum, and staff relations--were not at all helpful; the remainder said that these conversations were only somewhat helpful.

Finally, when we asked the teachers whether they would like to have such discussions with the principal more often, less often, or about the same, most of the teachers at Laurel said about the same. A picture of a rather laissez-faire principal leadership style begins to form when we examine all the data from Laurel--a situation which the teachers, feeling generally negative anyway, weren't really interested in changing. We already know that many Laurel teachers commuted from long distances; we know the salaries were lower there than at any other high school in the Study, and we know that teacher turnover at Laurel was very high.* These factors and others combine to make Laurel a less than ideal place to work, in the eyes of the teachers who were working there.

The teachers at Newport High were similar to those at Laurel in perceiving that they had to (and did) initiate whatever communications they had with their principal. At Newport, as at Laurel, substantial percentages of teachers felt that such communication--when it did occur, which wasn't often--was not at all helpful, or only somewhat helpful.

But whereas the Laurel teachers didn't seem to want to change the situation, at Newport many teachers told us that they would like to have more opportunities to talk with the principal about pupils, parents, curriculum, staff relations, and even their own job performance. Newport was, of course, a very large and heterogeneous school--we have already seen that the teachers there viewed the size of the place as one of its major problems (Table 3.2), and as a final note, it

---

* Chapter 2 profile of Laurel.

is interesting to see that at all of the large high schools in the Study, sizeable percentages of teachers said that they would like opportunities to talk with their principal more often.* An emerging hypothesis might be that teachers find the work environment to be, in many ways, less supportive and satisfying at very large schools. We will come back to this theme period- ically, as we dig deeper into the data.

*   *   *

Evaluation vs. Supervision

We asked teachers to tell us how satisfied they were with the teacher evaluation system in use at their schools. Table 3.3 shows the percentage at each school who were somewhat dissatisfied, and Table 3.4 shows the changes that teachers, across all thirteen schools, would like to see made in the teacher evaluation system.

Each school had a slightly different profile of desired changes. For example at Vista, where many teachers expressed a wish to talk to their principal more often about their own job performance, only one teacher out of 81 said he or she wanted less frequent evaluations. But about half said they would also like to have different people do the evaluations and/or have different criteria used.

Despite the fact that they did not feel very positive about their principal, the teachers at Vista still wanted more frequent help in evaluating (and presumably in improving) their own teaching. This was also true at Atwater High where, despite very negative feelings about the principal, 64% of the teachers wanted more frequent evaluations of their teaching. One begins to suspect that increased supervisory activity on the part of these principals might raise their standing in the eyes of their staff. At any rate, this would be an hypothesis worth testing.

---

* Manchester, Rosemont, Newport, and Vista. Many teachers at medium-sized Crestview and Bradford also wanted to talk to their principal more often.

Table 3.3

Percentage of Teachers Not Satisfied with the
Teacher Evaluation System Used at Their School

Dennison	0.0
Euclid	21.7
Crestview	22.7
Atwater	32.0
Woodlake	32.7
Palisades	35.1
Manchester	35.4
Vista	38.5
Laurel	41.2
Rosemont	42.2
Fairfield	45.4
Newport	59.8
Bradford	61.7
overall:	40.4

Table 3.4

Changes in Teacher Evaluation System
Desired by Teachers

(N=625)

20.6%	Less frequent evaluations
42.0	More frequent evaluations
46.0	Have different people do the evaluations
49.8	Different ways of communicating results
58.8	Use of different criteria

111

V.

At the center of it all

Students are the single most crucial fact of life for teachers, and their contact with students takes place primarily--though of course not exclusively--in the classroom setting. Chapters 5 and 6 examine the classroom encounter in detail.

Only a few questions about students in the Teacher Survey were not specific to the classroom. Taken together, they form a mixed bag: some of the questions are about school problems caused by students; others relate in a general way to programs offered to students; while yet others are about matters of school policy concerning students or about the teachers' beliefs about what is good for students.

It is impossible to synthesize these questions into a single conceptual whole. Furthermore, whether considered singly, together, or in clusters, teacher responses to these questions fail to give us an affective impression of how teachers _feel_ about students, in general.

Nevertheless, this seems an appropriate point at which to present these teacher responses to "school-general" items about students. It will lead us into an extended discussion of teachers' educational beliefs and values, and beyond that into an exploratory description of what our teachers were actually like, as people.

Drug or alcohol use

Although only 24 teachers out of 603 selected "drug and alcohol use by students" as the one biggest problem at their school, teachers at most of our schools did consider it to be somewhat of a problem.

Interestingly, the schools at which drug and alcohol use was not seen by teachers as a problem were: Dennison and Euclid, the two small, isolated, rural schools; Laurel and Palisades, the two schools located in the deep South; and Woodlake, the school at which

112

many students were members of military families stationed at the nearby naval air base.

Perceived prejudice

At Laurel and Palisades (each with about a 50-50 balance of white and black students), at Newport, with its large and ethnically heterogeneous student body; at Bradford, a white midwestern school with only a few black students; and at Crestview (which served an all-white, working-class community), teachers saw student prejudice and racial conflict as something of a problem.* This phenomenon--of student prejudice, as seen by teachers--was found primarily at the schools serving mixed white/black student populations. Though present, it was not as strong at the school which served a mixed white/Hispanic student body (i.e., Fairfield). Nor was it found at Manchester and Rosemont, the two schools at which the student populations were, respectively, 100% black and 100% Hispanic.

Students who don't speak English

Teachers at Newport and at Rosemont High Schools were frustrated by student language problems. At Rosemont, serving a low-income Mexican-American community, the mother tongue of most students was Spanish. At Newport, sizeable percentages of students were dominant in languages other than English--Korean, Vietnamese, Chinese, Japanese, Spanish, Armenian, German, and Italian, for example. Newport High had quite an extensive program of English as a Second Language; however, many teachers felt than an even stronger ESL program was needed if students were to become competent in English.

Overall, 80% of the teachers sampled felt that students should have some influence in school decision-making; two out of three, however, felt that students already did have some influence. School by school,

---

* Interestingly, at these schools from 1/3 to 1/2 of the teachers also agreed that "Many teachers at this school are prejudiced." --"Responses of Students, Teachers, and Parents to 4 Questions About Racial/Ethnic Prejudice in Their Schools," Benham, 1979 Study of Schooling Technical Report.

there were large differences. At Manchester, for example, only about 17% of the teachers felt that the students were <u>entirely</u> left out of the decision-making process--that they had <u>no</u> influence--and Manchester was the largest school in <u>the</u> Study, with 3,006 students. Some mechanism for the involvement of students was evidently in use at Manchester.

At Laurel, by contrast, 71% of the teachers felt that the students had no influence at all; and Laurel was a very small school (271 students), at which one might have thought it would have been relatively easy to involve students in school decision-making. Evidently, whether or not students are involved is not a function of school size. Perhaps it is more closely related to factors such as the leadership style of the principal and existing traditions of student participation.

Vandalism

Vandalism by students was seen as a problem by large percentages of teachers (70-77%) at Newport, Vista, and Manchester, and by approximately one-half of the teachers at Fairfield, Rosemont, and Bradford. At the other seven schools, vandalism was seen as a problem by less than half of the teachers.

Only at Manchester did over half the teachers (53%) feel that student violence was a problem at their school. Interestingly, however, only 18% of the Manchester faculty agreed that "physical punishment for discipline purposes should be allowed at this school," while very large percentages of teachers at some schools with little or no student violence agreed with this statement. The belief of teachers in our sample in the value of corporal punishment, it seems, was unrelated to their perceptions of actual violence existing at the school where they worked. Such belief, I suspect, is much more likely to be a function of more fundamental aspects of the individual teacher's value system, which he takes with him wherever he teaches, regardless of the conditions at any particular school.

114

Job experience for students

Three out of four teachers sampled agreed that high school students should have job experience as part of their school program. This suggests that most teachers would be in favor of an increase in work-study programs and other forms of out-of-school learning. However only one out of three also agreed that "there are other places in this community where students could be taught, but this school doesn't make use of them."

There were big differences between the schools, of course. Not surprisingly, teachers at rural Euclid, Dennison, and Laurel didn't feel that there were many "other places in the community where students could be taught." What is surprising is that less than half of the teachers in all but one of the high schools located in or near cities agreed with this statement. Only at Manchester High did over half the teachers--actually, just 58%--agree that "there are other places in this community where students could be taught, but this school does not make use of them." One can only hypothesize that, while teachers agree with "job experience" in theory, they are opposed to it in practice. It would be interesting to test this in a study specifically designed for the purpose. Perhaps the teachers fear that a large-scale work-study emphasis would detract from the academic mission of the school. Some teachers may feel, not without some justification, that school resources are already spread too thin. Some may feel that the school cannot handle the complexity (and extra expense) of adding coordinated work-study for all students to the curriculum. Or perhaps, after all, it's simply a question of the latent but strong societal belief that students, especially teenagers, should be retained on the school grounds during the school day, where they can be more easily watched and controlled.

In fact, most teachers are generally in favor of keeping students in school not only throughout the school day, but throughout the conventional three or four years of secondary schooling--only about one-third of them agreed that "students should be able to leave school as early as age 14 if they can pass a standard examination." An even larger percentage strongly disagreed with this proposition. All in all, two out of every three teachers felt that early leaving--no

115

matter how bright or well-qualified the student--was
not a good idea.

Teachers do, however, like the idea of all students
having to pass a standard examination in order to
graduate with a high school diploma. Overall, eight
out of ten agreed with this suggestion; at no school
did less than 60% of the teachers agree with the
concept of an "exit exam" for students. The accountability movement thus manages, in practice, to hold the
student--rather than the teachers, administrators, and
school boards--responsible for reaching certain learning goals (defined at the state or even at the national
level), irrespective of the quality of the programs and
of the teaching which the student experienced during
his or her years of high school.

                *   *   *

In the classroom, teachers seem to regard students
with mixed feelings. While in general teachers believe
that it is important that they maintain order and
control in the classroom, they also seem to feel that
student participation in classroom decision-making is
important.[5] Our observation data, however, showed that
teachers did not, in actual practice, allow much
student decision-making in the classroom.

Showing an interest in the problems and concerns of
students is regarded by teachers as contributing to a
good learning atmosphere in the classroom, but this
evidently is not expected to take up too much time, for
mastery of basic skills was seen by teachers as the
single most important substantive task to be accomplished by students while in class. Indeed, conversations between teacher and students on matters of
concern to the students are often cut short by the
pressure felt by the teachers to "cover the text"
within a prescribed amount of time, regardless of other
educational considerations. It is not too unusual to
find high school teachers who refuse to allow their
students to attend assembly programs, no matter how
worthwhile, for example, for fear that it would put the
class "behind schedule".

Most of their time each day is spent with students;
their relationships with them, control over them, and
feeling about them are of utmost importance to teachers. We will explore the teacher-student relationship

116

in more detail in Chapter 6. Some of these issues will also come up again in Chapter 4, as we look at many aspects of schooling from the <u>student</u> perspective.

VI.

The teachers themselves

So far, we have looked at data about the teachers' work load, the rooms in which they spend most of their working time, their reasons for going into teaching and their beliefs about what schooling is for, contact with parents, relationships with other teachers, the extent to which teachers are--or are not--involved in school decision-making, feelings about the principal, and a variety of issues concerning students.

We turn now to the teachers themselves. What kind of people are they? 664 individuals, of course. But a respectable body of research (including the work of Holland and others investigating psychological relationships between career choice and personality type) exists which suggests that people with certain clusters of traits may be more inclined to select one career area rather than another. Furthermore, as people with similar traits gravitate to certain career areas, they create a characteristic environment which, in circular fashion, then attracts more of the same kinds of people. This is the foundation of those stereotypes which have, over time, become associated with certain types of work. Needless to say, like all stereotypes these are simplistic and fail to include the many atypical people one may find in any line of endeavor, including high school teaching. And yet we may also see that teaching, with its peculiar blend of challenge and security, its isolation and autonomy, power and powerlessness, and the physical and psychological exhaustion which are an inescapable part of it--teaching too, perhaps, attracts people with various combinations of identifiable characteristics.

It would take a different type of study to establish this definitively, of course. And yet perhaps, to a limited extent, our Study data can shed some light in this area. We have already seen how isolated teachers are within their classrooms. Most of them do not often actively seek help from each other, observe each other

117

teaching, or interact with each other about their own professional growth and improvement. In some ways, they know surprisingly little about each other--as professionals.

Teachers do not feel that they or their colleagues are to blame for any of their school's most serious problems; and--as common sense would suggest--those who teach at schools where relatively few problems exist express more satisfaction with their jobs than those who teach at schools where there are many problems.

By and large, principals leave their teachers alone and rarely intervene in matters which are clearly part of the teacher's classroom domain. On the whole, teachers respect and appreciate this.

Teachers have virtually complete control over all aspects of life in their classrooms, and they like it that way. They are willing to work extremely hard--and they do--in return for few tangible rewards, but that autonomy and power in the classroom is one of the aspects of the teaching career that high school teachers cherish most and which they'd be reluctant to give up. This is one reason, I believe, why team teaching never really caught on at the high school level.

In preparing a technical report on resistance to change in schools, Ken Tye reviewed other Study data which further strengthens this picture of teachers as isolated but powerful within their own limited "territory,"[6] and content with that state of affairs. He found little sharing or cooperation between departments, and no instances of interdisciplinary team planning or teaching whatsoever. Tye also found little school-wide in-service education at the high school level. We will return to these findings again in Chapter 7.

Frances Klein's analysis of the data on sources of[7] influence on the curriculum decisions made by teachers revealed that teachers rely primarily on their own background, interests, and abilities, and on their own judgment of the needs and interests of the students, in deciding what to teach and how to teach it. They told us that they do not make use of district consultants, and that state and district curriculum guides, textbooks, commercially prepared materials, and other

118

teachers had only a small to moderate influence on their decisions about what to teach.

High school teachers in the Study sample said that district or regional resource people were available to them, but that they didn't make use of them. And though many teachers belonged to several professional organizations and read a certain amount of professional literature annually, they told us that they felt that such organizations and such readings were only "somewhat" helpful.

What it boils down to is that teachers are nearly absolute rulers in their own classrooms, do not seek much outside contact, and rely primarily on their own training (good or poor as that may have been), experience, and judgment in planning and carrying out their jobs. They want to teach, and tend to be frustrated most by students' lack of interest in learning.

*   *   *

What else were we able to learn about the teachers in our sample? Some schools had markedly older and more experienced faculties than others. At Manchester, for example, more than half of the teachers were over 40 years of age and they had an average of almost 16 years of teaching experience. By contrast, nine out of the ten teachers at Dennison were under 40 years old and the average number of years of teaching experience was only four and one-half. Laurel and Euclid, the two other relatively isolated, small, rural schools, also had comparatively young and inexperienced faculties. Schools located in or near major cities tended to have older and more experienced teaching staffs.

On the average, there were slightly more male than female teachers in our sample. The male/female ratio varied, of course, from school to school, with Laurel having the lowest (35%) and Woodlake having the highest percentage (68%) of male teachers.

Despite the fact that over half of the teachers in our sample were male, our data suggest that men may not be entering high school teaching as much as they used to do. Of 340 male teachers, one-third were "oldtimers," with 16 or more years of experience; half had over 11 years of experience, and only 8% were beginners. Of 309 female teachers, on the other hand, only one-fourth were old-timers; 39% had eleven or more years of experience, and 14% were beginners. Furthermore, while almost one-fourth of the male teachers said they'd been at that school for eleven years or more, only 15% of the women had been there that long. Conversely, while almost half of the female teachers (48%) said they had been at that school for three years or less, only 36% of the male teachers had come that recently.

Table 3.5

Some Teacher Demographics

school	mean years of experience	% under 40 years	% male	% white
Dennison	4.5	90.0	50.0	100.0
Laurel	5.6	82.4	35.3	76.5
Euclid	6.7	86.9	65.2	100.0
Fairfield	8.7	65.9	43.2	90.9
Vista	8.8	75.0	59.5	100.0
Crestview	10.4	76.7	56.8	97.7
Rosemont	10.7	68.2	39.8	63.3
Atwater	11.4	68.0	64.0	92.0
Woodlake	11.5	49.1	67.9	96.2
Bradford	12.2	54.3	62.5	97.9
Palisades	13.9	53.4	37.3	52.5
Newport	15.3	44.8	55.1	80.8
Manchester	15.7	44.3	48.5	53.0

Finally, a higher percentage of male than female teachers told us that if they had it to do over, they would not choose to go into teaching--35% of the men said they wouldn't do it again, as opposed to 28% of the women.

Overall, eight out of ten teachers in our total sample were white. Even at the schools where the student body was entirely nonwhite (Manchester, Rosemont) the majority of teachers were white. High school teaching has long been known as a white, middle-class profession; attempts made during the 1960's and 70's to redress the balance had evidently not made much of a dent at the schools we studied in 1977. And recent

120

cutbacks in student loan programs, coupled with shrink-
ing numbers of students going into teacher training
programs suggest that the teaching profession will
continue to be white and middle class--as well as
increasingly elderly--for the foreseeable future.

Table 3.6

Some Teacher Family Income Data

school	% under $15,000	% over $20,000	median annual teacher salaries*
Dennison	70.0%	0.0%	(NA)**
Euclid	52.2	13.0	$11,841
Rosemont	42.2	40.4	11,000
Vista	45.2	41.6	13,019
Fairfield	47.7	43.2	10,700
Laurel	35.3	29.4	9,590
Palisades	31.6	50.9	14,772
Newport	20.8	49.4	(NA)
Crestview	18.6	51.2	14,451
Atwater	16.0	68.0	15,632
Woodlake	15.1	60.4	13,586
Bradford	10.9	80.4	13,776
Manchester	4.9	83.6	21,277

*   As reported by the districts
** Data not available

Table 3.6 shows the percentage of teachers who
reported an annual family income of under $15,000 and
those who reported an annual income of $20,000 or more,
and the median annual salary paid at each school. At
the schools where the larger percentages of teachers
reported yearly family incomes of $20,000 or more, it
is likely that larger percentages of the teachers were
members of two-income families, as the median salary
figures at all but one school were well under $20,000 a
year. These days, a teacher's salary is scarcely
adequate to support a family unless the spouse also
works (80% of the teachers we sampled agreed that
"teachers are not paid enough at this school"). Over
half of our male teachers told us that they hold other
paying jobs for all or part of the year. Considering

the physical and emotional demands of the teaching profession, it is remarkable that so many male high school teachers can find enough energy to hold another job as well. It is hardly surprising that one out of every four male teachers in the Study listed "more money" as the single most compelling reason that would cause them to leave their present positions. Too, as we have already noted, higher percentages of male teachers than female told us that they would not choose teaching again.

Female teachers married to working husbands are much less likely to need to take a second paying job in addition to their teaching. 83% of the female teachers we surveyed told us that they did not hold a second paying job. Most of them do, of course, perform another job--only they don't get paid for it.

Table 3.7

Family Income During Childhood Compared With Present Income

	Low	Medium	High
During Childhood	27.6%	69.6%	2.7%
	Under $10,000	$10,000 to $25,000	Over $25,000
At Time of Study	7.2%	62.9%	29.9%

Table 3.7 suggests that teaching is still a profession which can provide upward mobility to some extent, despite the low salaries earned by teachers when compared to salaries earned by people in other trades and professions. About one of every five teachers we sampled came from a home in which the family income was in the low range, but had evidently shifted into the middle-income range themselves. A comparable percentage of teachers whose parents were middle-class seem to have moved into an upper-class income range themselves.

*   *   *

122

Half of the high school teachers in the Study sample characterized themselves as political moderates. One-fourth told us they were liberal, and the remaining one-fourth said they considered themselves to be politically conservative. There were some differences among schools, although at every school but one the moderates were in the majority. The lone exception was Manchester, where a higher percentage characterized themselves as liberal than moderate.

One of the questions that was asked during the teacher interview was, "Do you think schools should or should not be used to solve problems in our society?" Of 311 high school teachers who were interviewed, 219 (or 70%) said yes, they did believe that schools should be used to solve certain social problems. The other 30%--presumably including most of those who described themselves as politically conservative--disagreed that schools should be used for this purpose. I suspect the percentage who disagreed would have been much higher if the question, as asked, had stipulated that such problems be "solved" through the curriculum itself. Instead, however, the question referred to extra-curricular programs such as health care, busing for desegregation, and free lunch programs for poor children. As a rule, programs such as these--outside the classroom--are expected to bear the burden of providing solutions to the larger problems of society. Even in Social Studies classes, as we saw in the analysis of curriculum materials included as part of the Study[8], social problems are generally approached rather abstractly, and we never encountered an instance of a high school Social Studies class going out into the community, making use of community resources, or making the actual problems of the community itself a focus for study.

So, although 70% of the teachers who responded to this question said yes, schools "should be used to solve problems in our society," my hunch is that they would balk if asked to find ways to do this through their actual teaching. It would certainly require extensive alteration of the curriculum in most subjects. This, then, may be an example of teachers agreeing to something as a matter of principle, but not being in a position to act upon the principle on an everyday basis; certainly a familiar dilemma for most of us at one time or another.

Widening horizons

Teachers, it seems, do not travel abroad any more than most people. About two-thirds of our sample told us that they had been to other English-speaking countries, slightly over one-third had been to Western Europe, and 40% had been to "other regions of the world." In most cases, they went for vacation and stayed less than six months; although some of those who went to Western Europe and "other regions" were there on military duty, and it is probably those individuals whose stay was from one to three years. In all fairness, it must be noted that teachers' salaries, as well as rising inflation and cost of living, do not permit a great deal of overseas travel.

The high school teachers who participated in the Study of Schooling agreed overwhelmingly (97%) that "It is important that every child have the opportunity to study and learn about the political and economic systems of other countries." However, at no school did teachers seem to feel that their school was doing a particularly good job in this area. This finding is especially pertinent in the cases of Fairfield, Rosemont, and Newport, which had fairly high percentages of students from other countries--or whose parents had immigrated from other countries. Perhaps the pressure for assimilation was even stronger at these schools than at schools with few immigrant families. It would be interesting to study the schooling experiences of foreign-born students in American schools at this point in our history, though we might not like what we learn about ourselves; in this regard, we might start by noting that 60% of the teachers at Newport and 70% of those at Fairfield and Rosemont agreed that "the immigration of foreigners to this country should be kept down so that we can provide for Americans first." (At all of the thirteen schools, half or more of the teachers agreed with this statement.)

In fact, our teacher sample was surprisingly nationalistic, even isolationist, when asked certain pointed questions about the role of the United States in the world today. One-third agreed that "Our country should not cooperate in any international trade agreements which attempt to better world economic conditions at our expense," and nearly half agreed that "A populous country should not receive food or aid from the United States until it can prove that it is working

124

toward the control of its birthrate." On the other hand, only 29% agreed that "If necessary, we ought to be willing to lower our standard of living to cooperate with other countries in getting an equal standard of living for every person in the world." Two-thirds agreed that "Schools are not placing enough emphasis on patriotism and respect for the flag."

On the average, male teachers, teachers with higher family incomes, teachers with 16 or more years of teaching experience, and teachers who were politically moderate-to-conservative tended to be more nationalistic.

Conclusion: ordinary people

In the final analysis, it seems fair to say that the teachers in our sample were fairly typical, average American workers and citizens. Simultaneously happy and frustrated with their jobs, they were pleased with their classroom power and yet disconcerted by students' lack of interest in learning.

On the whole, these teachers were rather limited in their horizons--again, not unlike many Americans. Most had not travelled widely, nor did they seek new knowledge in areas not specifically applicable to the teaching of their subject speciality. They did, however, feel competent and well-prepared in their subject fields.[9]

By and large, these teachers were isolated from sources of professional stimulation and growth, and tended to rely on their own background and experience in making decisions about what and how to teach.

Our teachers indicated higher job satisfaction in schools which had fewer problems, and these tended to be the smaller schools (Laurel, where teacher satisfaction was very low, was the exception). The issue of the optimum workable size for a high school has been a matter of debate for many years; our data suggest that medium-sized and smaller schools, while they sometimes have more limited curriculum and resources, are perceived by teachers as more manageable, more livable, and more satisfying places to work than very large schools. To the extent that teacher satisfaction leads to student satisfaction and enjoyment of school (and our data suggest that this connection does exist) we may question the wisdom of the consolidation of small and medium-sized high schools which has, in the name of efficiency, dominated school planning for the past 35 years.

In general, teachers receive pro forma support from their principal, who tends to be an administrator-manager rather than an instructional leader. They do not, in fact, see much of their principal and at some schools teachers clearly wished for more contact than they were getting. Often, it was a matter of wishing that sometimes the principal would approach <u>them</u> instead of waiting for teachers to approach him first. Furthermore, teachers in less satisfying schools did not view their principals as supportive.

One-third of the teachers told us that "personal frustration or lack of satisfaction with my own job performance" would be the main reason they would consider leaving their present teaching positions. It would be interesting to know more precisely what teachers had in mind when they selected "personal frustration" or "lack of satisfaction with my own job performance" as a likely reason for leaving their jobs. The item as written and the strong response of teachers--one out of every three--suggest a level of self-awareness and self-criticism not found elsewhere in our data.

Another 39% admitted that they might be lured away by a better-paying or higher-status job. It is certainly true that teaching lags far behind the other professions in terms of both status and money. The teaching profession has a difficult time attracting excellent trainees for this very reason, and society more or less expects any college student with clearly above-average potential to choose law, medicine, or business rather than teaching.

Nevertheless, and seemingly against all odds, many good people do go into education, and some stay. They find rewards there that might be incomprehensible to those who leave school at the age of 18 and never look back. To their credit, very few teachers said they'd leave their present positions because of problems with students, the administration, or their colleagues. Similarly, few felt that inadequate resources and

126

materials (though many saw this as a big problem in their schools) would cause them to leave. On the whole, they stay--and they persevere, confronting their 150 students a day and working to impart as much as they can to them of the knowledge and skills which constitute their chosen field.

*   *   *

Dr. Fletcher died a few years ago. Mrs. Bass left teaching to raise her family. Mrs. Vollmer is nearing retirment age. Many of the rest are still there--each yearbook picture shows them a little grayer than the year before. Some would like to retire early, but will probably hold onto their jobs a few years more because of the uncertain economic situation.

Those who are gone have been replaced by others, many with attitudes, opinions, and feelings not unlike those of the teachers who participated in A Study of Schooling. Neither teachers nor teaching, it seems, have changed very much in the past quarter-century.

CHAPTER III, NOTES AND REFERENCES

1. Bette C. Overman, Variety and Intensity of School-Related Problems as Perceived by Teachers, Parents, and Students, (Technical Report No. 17, 1980).

2. B.J. Benham, The One Biggest Problem at This School, as Perceived by Teachers, Parents, and Students, (Unpublished Technical Report, March 1979).

3. A Place Called School by J.I. Goodlad, (New York: McGraw-Hill, 1984) Chapter Six, "Teachers and the Circumstances of Teaching."

4. David Wright, Teachers' Perceptions of Their Own Influence Over School Policies and Decisions, (Technical Report No. 16, 1980).

5. David Wright, Teachers' Educational Beliefs, (Technical Report No. 14, 1980).

6. Kenneth Tye, Changing Our Schools: The Realities, (Technical Report No. 30, 1981).

7. Frances Klein, Teacher Perceived Sources of Influence on What is Taught in Subject Areas, (Technical Report No. 15, 1980).

8. B.J. Benham, An Analysis of Curriculum Materials Submitted by Teachers Who Took Part in the Study of Schooling, (Unpublished Technical Report, 1978).

9. Kenneth Tye, op. cit. p. 45: "Only about 3.6% of the teachers at the secondary level reported that they did not feel adequately prepared to teach the subjects they were teaching."

CHAPTER IV

STUDENT PERCEPTIONS

Seven thousand, six hundred and seventy-seven high school students took part in A Study of Schooling, each a unique being with dreams, worries, frustrations, plans and fears. Ego-involved as all human beings are; with self-concepts that may be resilient and fragile by turns or simultaneously. In short, just like you and me, regardless of our ages, and not greatly unlike other American high school students.

These students had different experiences at school to some extent, depending on the characteristics of the school they happened to attend. One such characteristic would be the size of the school. Attending Dennison Secondary School with sixty other young people, most of whom one has known since first grade and many of whom are siblings or cousins, would feel very different than would being one of 3,006 students at Manchester High.

Another factor would be where the school was located. The life of a student in an isolated farm setting such as Euclid and that of a student who lives in a cosmopolitan urban setting such as Newport are vastly different. Not only are different types of experiences available to each, but the culture of the surrounding community, its values and its assumptions, differ as well. To some extent, these differences are also reflected in the school curriculum. The rural schools we studied provided agricultural courses, those located near the ocean provided Marine Biology, and those located near large military bases provided ROTC programs, for example.

Ethnicity, too, causes schools to differ. The atmosphere of a school is created through the interactions of the people who spend their days there. Cultural factors affect how people relate to each other, what they value, and implicit as well as explicit norms governing behavior. Rosemont High, where all the students were Mexican-American, was a very different place from all-black Manchester and all-white Crestview.

The experiences of students at ethnically heterogeneous schools would be different in yet other ways. Our data suggest that a black student at 90%-white Bradford High, for example, would have a more difficult school life than would a black students at racially balanced Palisades. We shall explore this more fully later in this chapter. A white student at Fairfield, with its evenly-balanced population of Mexican-American and Anglo (white) students, would experience school differently than he or she would at predominantly white Vista or Atwater.

The socio-economic status of the community and that of the student's family also can affect the type of experience a young person has in high school. The problems and concerns of a very poor student who attends school in an affluent suburb will differ from those of a wealthy student at the same school. The kinds of programs available at Woodlake, with its wealth of federal impact aid, open doors for Woodlake students that the students at nearby Atwater can only dream about.

School size, location, ethnicity, and SES are all characteristics of the community in which the school exists. All have an impact on the students' experiences in the school, but they are not peculiar to the school alone; they are external. We will see numerous examples of such impact in this chapter.

Of the many internal characteristics of the high school which shape a student's life there, we found none so powerful as the system of tracking or curricular placement which separates students and assigns them to one of several possible schooling experiences. This phenomenon existed in varying degrees at all of the thirteen high schools we studied.[1] At some of the schools students in the vocational curriculum and those in the academic curriculum seemed to be, literally, worlds apart. At others, the experiences of students in a low-achieving 10th grade English class differed not only in content but also in teaching practices, grouping patterns, and many other ways from the experiences of students in a high-achieving 10th grade English class in the same school. The findings of the

130

Study which pertain to classroom differences by track level will be discussed in chapter 6.

Despite all these sources of difference in the kinds of experiences that young people have in their high schools, we also found enormous <u>similarities</u> across schools, as well as similarity of <u>outlook</u> among students across the whole sample. Having said that each of our 7,677 high school students was different from all the others, I now must acknowledge that in many respects they were also very much alike. This is the paradox that recurs time and again in this Study: our subjects are different, yet they are the same. It is true of the thirteen high schools, true of the 664 teachers, and it is true of the 7,677 students.

This chapter is divided into four parts. Part One presents the student sample in more detail. Part Two presents students' views of school as a work place, and Part Three presents their views of school as a social place.

Part Four will examine some of the responses of a subset of the sample: the 568 disenchanted young people who, when asked "What is the one best thing about this school?" chose, from a list of twelve possible responses, to say "Nothing."

I.

The Students in Our Sample

a. Gender

The 7,677 high school students in the Study were about evenly divided by sex. On the whole, gender does seem to make a difference: girls evidently have a more enjoyable time in school than do boys. Girls responded more positively to the statements, "I like school," and "It is worth going to school because it will help me in the future." Boys, on the other hand, tended to agree more than girls that "Average students don't get enough attention at this school," and "Many teachers at this school don't care about students."[2] With the exception of sports, higher percentages of girls than of boys indicated that they are involved in a variety of extracurricular activities: clubs, student government,

music and drama, honor society, and service activities.
Finally, as we shall see in chapter 6, girls reported
having more positive classroom experiences than did
boys.

b. Ethnicity

About 60% of the students we sampled were white,
21% were black, 16% were Mexican-American, and 4%
"other" (Asian-American, Puerto Rican, and Native
American). The thirteen high schools differed greatly
in their ethnic composition. Vista, Crestview, Atwater, Bradford, Woodlake, Euclid, and Dennison were
predominantly white. Rosemont was 100% Mexican-American, and Manchester was 100% black. Laurel and Palisades were 50-50 black/white, and Fairfield was about
50-50 Mexican-American/white. Newport was, ethnically,
extremely heterogeneous: 47% white, 18% Mexican-American, 17% Asian-American, 9% black, and 9% "other."

In general, the high school students in our Study
sample believed that schools should be desegregated,
but they were less enthusiastic about achieving this
social goal through the use of busing. Mexican-American students were the least negative about being
personally involved in a busing program, followed by
black students and then by white students attending
ethnically mixed schools. White students attending
all-white schools were the most negative about being
personally involved in busing, though they were just as
supportive of the idea of desegregated schools as were
all the other kinds of students. Even they, however,
were not as negative about busing as were the teachers
and parents who responded to the same set of questions.

c. Ethnocentrism and knowledge about the world

One small sub-study which was built into the larger
Study of Schooling was the Global Education Substudy.
It consisted of two sets of questions, intended to
measure both attitudes toward and knowledge about world
interdependence.

There were ten questions in the Ethnocentrism
Scale. The responses to these questions, examined one
by one, are interesting. They reveal that the high
school students we sampled were, as a group, proud of

their country but generous in their attitude of responsibility towards other countries and peoples. For
example, while 60% agreed that "the American people are
the best in the world," only one-third felt that
"schools should teach students that our country is the
best in the world." Nearly three-fourths disagreed
with the suggestion that "A country where people have
too many children should not get food or aid from the
U.S." and that "People from foreign countries should be
prevented from living in the U.S." Nearly two-thirds
agreed that "The United States should share its food
with other countries," and over half agreed that
"Helping other countries is a good way to use our
money." Approximately eight out of every ten students
sampled disagreed that "Schools should not waste time
teaching about other countries."

On the whole, we found the tendency toward ethnocentrism declined a little in the higher grades of high
school, and global knowledge, as might be expected,
increased. The boys in our sample had higher global
knowledge scores, on the average, than did the girls,
but they also had more of a tendency to ethnocentrism.
Students who did not plan on going on to higher education had lower global knowledge scores and higher
ethnocentrism scores. They also tended to value the
Vocational function of schooling more highly than any
other. Those students who planned to go on to some
form of higher education, by contrast, valued the
Personal function highest, had more knowledge of the
world, and had less tendency to ethnocentrism. These
findings suggest that global education curriculum
projects, frequently aimed at the higher-achieving,
college-bound pupils, should be also directed toward
those who do not plan on college attendance but who
need expanded horizons just as much.

d. Self-Concept

The Study also contained a small subsection on
student self-concept. Making use of work done by
Coopersmith,[3] the staff developed three self-concept
scales: General Self-Concept, (containing items such as
"There are a lot of things about myself I'd change if I
could," and "I'm pretty sure of myself"); Self-Concept
in relation to Peers (I'm popular with kids my own
age," "Kids usually follow my ideas," etc.); and
Academic Self-Concept (I'm proud of my schoolwork," and

"I am able to do school work at least as well as most other students," etc.).

There are many problems involved in the measurement of self-concept. For this reason, these data were examined very conservatively. Only those relationships which were beyond doubt are being reported in the Study of Schooling publications, and I leave speculation about their significance to the reader--and to further research.

As the table below shows, all three kinds of self-concept tended to rise in the upper grade levels. Overall, the General Self-Concept received the lowest mean scores, followed by the Academic Self-Concept. The Self-Concept in Relation to Peers received the highest mean scores at each grade level.

Table 4.1

Three Kinds of Student Self Concept,
by Grade Level

grade level	General S-C $\overline{X}$	Academic S-C $\overline{X}$	S-C Peers $\overline{X}$
9	2.6	2.8	3.0
10	2.7	2.8	3.0
11	2.7	2.8	3.1
12	2.8	2.8	3.1

As a group, girls tended to have higher mean scores than boys did on the Academic Self-Concept scale. On the other hand, boys' mean scores were higher than those of girls on the General Self-Concept scale. There was no statistically significant difference between the means of the two sexes on the Self-Concept in Relation to Peers scale.

e. Future Plans

The student survey also contained several questions about the students' future plans. We wanted to know what the students themselves wanted to do, what they thought their parents would like them to do, and what they felt they probably would do, after leaving high school. As it turned out, there wasn't much difference between the three. The students we sampled seemed to feel that what their parents wanted them to do, and what they themselves wanted to do, was what they probably would do.

Seven possible answers to these these questions were listed; students were asked to select only one of the seven. Table 4.2 shows the percentage of students who chose each possible answer:

Table 4.2

High School Students' Responses to Three
Questions About Their Future Plans

	A-12 "I would like to--"	A-13 "My parents would like me to--"	A-14 "Actually, I will probably--"
QUIT	3.4%	.5%	1.7%
FINISH HIGH	26.3%	24.0%	25.6%
TRADE/TECH	12.2%	8.3%	11.8%
JR. COLL.	6.5%	6.6%	11.5%
4-YEAR COLL.	34.0%	47.2%	34.4%*
GRAD SCHOOL	8.1%	9.1%	7.0%
DON'T KNOW	9.5%	4.5%	8.0%
	N=7051	N=7012	N=7014

* These figures are similar to those received by the researchers in the NCES Studies (National Longitudinal Study and High School and Beyond Study)--34% of the NLS 1972 seniors and 38% of the HS&B 1980 seniors expected to attend a 4-year college or university.

The largest percentage, about one-third, expected to go to a four-year college or university after finishing high school. The next largest percentage, just over one-fourth, told us that they just wanted to finish high school. The way the question was structured made these questions mutually exclusive; the students who chose "finish high school," therefore, were telling us that they either did not want to, or did not think that they would go to a four-year college. Nor did they evidently plan on going to a trade school or a junior college. Presumably, then, they intended to enter the work force right after high school.

There were enormous differences between the schools in the percentages of students who expected to go to college, from only 18% at Laurel--less than two out of every ten students--to a high 63% at Palisades--over six out of every ten.[4] The responses for "Finish high school" at these two schools were just the reverse: from only 12% at Palisades, to 42% at Laurel. All the other eleven schools fell somewhere between these two on the question of students' future plans.

When responses to the questions about future plans are correlated with self-concept scores, we can see the beginnings of a pattern which suggests that students who plan on some form of higher education have higher self-concepts, of all three types, than those who plan to quit school, who just want to finish high school, or who don't know what they'll do.

Furthermore, students whose future plans do not include some form of higher education are more likely to agree that "if you don't want to go to college, this school doesn't think you're very important."

These two patterns, taken together, raise some interesting questions about how school feels to those students who evidently--for whatever reasons--haven't had enough success in school to want to continue their education beyond high school. I found that the responses of these students to many other questions on our survey differed from the other students in our sample. These patterns will be discussed in detail in Part Four of this chapter.

f. Job Preparation

Overall, nine out of ten students agreed that high school students should have job experience as part of the school program. In fact, over half of the students who responded to this item indicated that they strongly agreed with it. What's more, students who were planning on going to college wanted job experience in high school, too. The intensity of the response from the students who were not going on to college was slightly greater--as the percentages of the "strongly agree" column below show--but when it comes to overall agreement, the responses from the two groups are nearly identical:

Table 4.3

Regardless of their future plans, most students agree that high school students should have job experience as part of their school program

	Mildly Agree	Strongly Agree	Total Agree	N
Students whose future plans include junior college, 4-year college, or grad school	39.1%	49.7%	88.8%	3701
Students who just plan to finish high school, or go to a trade or technical school	31.7%	59.5%	91.2%	2616

Summary: The Students in Our Sample

To summarize, then. Our student sample consisted of approximately equal numbers of boys and girls. In general, girls reported feeling more positive about school experiences than did boys, and their academic self-concepts, as a group, were higher than those of boys. Boys, however, had higher general self-concepts.

Over half of our sample planned on going to college, either at a junior college, a four-year college, or a university plus graduate school. One-fourth planned to finish high school and go to work, and 12% told us they wanted to go to a trade or technical school. 8% said they didn't know what they would do, and 2% indicated that they would probably drop out before graduating.

Some schools were definitely predominantly "college-prep," others clearly were not geared to sending students on to college. Since we found that students planning on going to college tended to have higher self-concepts, we are faced with the possibility that large percentages of students at vocationally-oriented schools may have lower self-concepts, while similarly large percentages at predominantly college-prep high schools have higher self-concepts. These patterns could contribute to the overall atmosphere and morale of the school, and might be reflected in student satisfaction measures. Some of our data suggest that this is indeed the case, as we shall see in Part Two of this chapter.

On the whole, our students were proud of their country but generous and responsible in their attitudes towards other countries, especially the poorer nations. Younger students, boys, and students who were not planning on higher education were slightly less so, though the difference was not extreme.

Our students were firm in their support of desegregated schools, whether or not they attended desegregated schools themselves, but negative in their attitudes towards busing. Parents and teachers, however, were even more negative than students.

Our students were very positive in feeling that high schools should provide all students with job experience as part of the high school program.

Clearly, these young people are oriented toward the market value of school attendance: nine out of every ten of them agreed that "it is worth going to school because it will help me in the future," and 74% or more of the students sampled at every one of the thirteen high schools agreed that "what I'm learning in school will be useful to me later in life."

II.

Students View the School as a Work Place

Although our students seemed well-oriented towards the prevailing notion that school is primarily a place where one prepares for the world of work, many of them valued other functions of schooling besides the vocational one, as Table 4.4 shows:

Table 4.4

6,670 high school students told us which function of schooling is most important to them.

If you had to choose only the ONE most important thing for you, which would it be?

SOCIAL (to work well with other people)	15.9%
INTELLECTUAL (to learn basic skills in reading, writing, arithmetic, and other subjects)	27.3%
PERSONAL (to become a better person)	25.6%
VOCATIONAL (to get a better job)	31.1%

These data on which function of schooling students value most highly for themselves become even more interesting when examined school by school (Table 4.5). Now, we can see that at four schools--Manchester, Laurel, Rosemont, and Palisades--the intellectual function was the one selected by the largest percentage of students. It is probably not a coincidence that

139

these four schools had the highest percentage of academic FTE's[5] in the Study--from 65-69% of their faculties taught academic subjects. The curriculums of Palisades and Rosemont, in particular, were academically-oriented.[6]

It seems to me to be very important that we take note of the fact that Palisades and Laurel were ethnically mixed schools (half black, half white), Manchester was an all-black school, and the student body of Rosemont was entirely Mexican-American. I would venture the hypothesis that ethnic minority students still value the traditional function of schooling; noticeably more than white students do. Certainly, many students at these schools--particularly Rosemont, Manchester, and Palisades--had high hopes for going to college: 48%, 55%, and 70%, respectively, told us they probably would go to either a junior college, a four-year college, or to university and graduate school.

The figure of 48% at Rosemont is especially significant when one recalls that both parent income and parent educational level at Rosemont were the lowest in the Study.[7] Nevertheless, there is evidence that Rosemont parents and students still view schooling as the way to enter the American mainstream, and they were happy with the academic emphasis being provided at their high school. Although nearly two-thirds of the students said they felt pressure to perform well academically, almost all of the Rosemont students (87%) agreed that their teachers were doing a good job and that "this school gives students a good education." Eighty-four percent of the Rosemont students told us, "I like school." At no other high school in the Study was the student response to that item more positive.

The vocational function drew the highest percentage of responses at Fairfield, Vista, Crestview, Bradford, and Atwater. It can hardly be a coincidence that these five schools were located in working-class communities. With the exception of Fairfield, these schools had standard comprehensive curriculums.

Fairfield High stands alone among the thirteen high schools we studied in being the one with an extremely vocationally-oriented curriculum. Less than half of its faculty taught academic courses;[8] at Fairfield, there is nearly one vocational or arts teacher for every academic teacher in the school. As one might

140

expect, the curriculum reflects this vocational emphasis, offering a wide range of work-study options and three-year technical training sequences in a variety of occupations.

TABLE 4.5

The function chosen as "most important to ME" by the largest percentage of students at each school.

Intellectual		Personal		Vocational	
Manchester	43.5	Euclid	36.3	Fairfield	36.9
Laurel	37.9	Newport	33.1	Vista	35.3
Rosemont	36.1	Dennison	32.7	Crestview	34.6
Palisades	31.4	Woodlake	30.4	Bradford	34.6
				Atwater	32.3

This vocational emphasis was evidently acceptable to many of the students, since over one-third of them (37%) chose the Vocational function as the most important to them. The Personal function was next, with 23% and the Social and Intellectual functions each drew a response of around 20%. To put it another way, only two out of every ten students at Fairfield High School thought that the Intellectual function of schooling was the most important.

Student Satisfaction

As we looked at student responses to questions about their school as a work place, over and over again we saw the same five schools emerging as relatively satisfying places in which to work. These were Dennison, Euclid, Woodlake, Rosemont, and Palisades. Likewise, five schools consistently appeared to be relatively unsatisfying places insofar as their students were concerned. These were Bradford, Manchester, Fairfield, Laurel, and Newport.

Let's take a look at some of the variables on which these groupings appeared consistently at the high and low ends of the rankings. First of all, we asked the students who participated in the Study of Schooling to

give their school a "grade," A-B-C-D-F, as they themselves would be graded in their own schoolwork. On the
average, students in cluster 1 schools gave their
schools a grade of "B," while students in cluster 2
schools gave their schools a grade of "C." These were
the highest and lowest grades given; that is, no school
got an "A" or a "D" or "F" as an average grade, from
its students.

Cluster 1: High Student Satisfaction	Cluster 2: Low Student Satisfaction
Dennison	Bradford
Euclid	Manchester
Woodlake	Fairfield
Rosemont	Laurel
Palisades	Newport

At cluster 1 schools, 84% or more of the sampled
students agreed that "this schools gives students a
good education." At cluster 2 schools, on the other
hand, from over one-fourth to almost one-half of the
students disagreed with that statement.

At cluster 1 schools, less than half of the students felt that "average students don't get enough
attention at this school," whereas more than half
agreed with that statement at cluster 2 schools.

At Bradford, Newport, Manchester, and Fairfield,
students generally agreed that "too many students are
allowed to graduate from this school without learning
very much," while students at Palisades, Rosemont,
Woodlake, Euclid, and Dennison disagreed with that
statement.

Very few students at Dennison, Euclid, and Woodlake
agreed that "many teachers at this school don't care
about students," while about 90% told us that "most of
the teachers are doing a good job." It is interesting
to notice that teacher satisfaction was also high at
these three schools (see Chapter 3). Evidently there
is some truth in the commonsense assumption that happy
students are found in schools where the teachers are
happy.

Conversely, teacher satisfaction was low at Newport, Bradford, Manchester, Laurel, and Fairfield, and

at these schools almost half of the sampled students agreed that "many teachers at this school don't care about students," and told us that "if I had my choice, I'd go to a different school." Relatively lower percentages of the students at Bradford, Manchester, Fairfield, and Newport felt that most of the teachers at their schools were doing a good job.

To their credit, students at Bradford, Newport, Laurel, and Fairfield don't put all the blame on teachers. Many students at these schools agreed that "many students at this school don't care about learning (72.8%)."

We have already seen that Rosemont and Palisades had very academically-oriented curriculums, so it comes as no surprise that over 60% of the sampled students at these schools agreed that "in this school, we feel we have to get good grades all the time." At Fairfield and Bradford, by contrast, less than half of the sampled students felt such a pressure to perform well academically. Clearly, schools differ greatly in this aspect of their "personalities."

Case Study: Bradford

One of the biggest problems identified by the teachers at Bradford High School was "standards for graduation and academic requirements," and more than at any other high school in the Study, Bradford High teachers felt that "students are graded too easy at this school." Furthermore, Bradford was the only high school in our sample where the largest percentage of teachers said that the social function of schooling gets more emphasis than the intellectual function.[9]

One gets the impression that the teachers at Bradford High are aware that the academic standards at their school are low, but that they do not see themselves as being to blame for the situation: the other three problems they identified as the "biggest problem" were "lack of student interest" and "inadequate resources," and "the administration."[10]

By contrast, many students and parents at Bradford High indicated that they thought that poor teaching was definitely a problem at their school.

143

Finding this pattern interesting, I decided to explore a little further. Elsewhere in the data there are four questions relating to the issue of academic quality. These were asked of both students and parents. Examination of school by school crosstabulations of these four variables revealed a striking pattern of student and parent dissatifaction with the academic situation at Bradford High School. For example, more than at any other school in the sample, students and parents at Bradford disagreed that "most of the teachers at this school are doing a good job," and agreed that "too many students at this school are allowed to graduate without learning very much." Bradford students ranked lowest of all the thirteen high schools in agreement with "this school gives students a good education," and highest on "many students at this school don't care about learning." Bradford High parents ranked higher than the parents at any other high school in agreeing that students ought to pass a standard exam in order to graduate from high school.

As we saw in chapter 3, Bradford High was one of the "less satisfying" schools in the Study, as far as teachers were concerned. It also had the second-highest composite problems score in the Study, which tells us that it is a place where many problems exist to distract teachers and students from the business of teaching and learning.

Over 40% of the Bradford High students we sampled told us that they would go to a different school if they could.

In searching for a possible reason for such pervasive dissatisfaction among Bradford students, teachers, and parents, one cannot avoid the hypothesis that some of the difficulty lies in the type of leadership that was being provided by the principal at Bradford at the time of the Study.

Other data from the Study make this hypothesis seem even more plausible. For example, most of the teachers at Bradford felt that the school's administration was a problem. In fact, 30% were of the opinion that it was a major problem. Forty per cent disagreed with the statement, "the staff members trust the principal." As a group, the Bradford faculty had the lowest mean score in the Study on the Principal Leadership Scale. This means that, on the whole, they tended to feel that adequate leadership was not being provided: they rated their principal lower on leadership behavior than did the teachers at any of the other twelve high schools.

Half of the Bradford faculty disagreed that their "principal often seeks out the ideas of his staff members," and that "the principal is continually learning, seeking new ideas." These teacher responses are corroborated by the qualitative impressions formed by Study of Schooling staff who spent time at Bradford both during and after the Fall 1977 data collection. Such impressions yielded a picture of a principal who was neither good nor bad, but simply ineffectual and perhaps somewhat timid. Yet, he was a survivor--the 1977-78 school year was his 14th as principal of Bradford High.

Laissez-faire leadership does not, however, seem to have been quite what was needed at Bradford. When nearly half the faculty feels that morale is low, when students, teachers, and parents agree that academic quality is poor and when a school clearly has many complex problems which get in the way of constructive teaching and learning, one might expect that a more vigorous leadership style would be appropriate--and appreciated.

Yet, this principal didn't even seem to be aware of his staff's unhappiness. Asked in an interview to rate the "general adult working climate" of his school from one (low) to ten (high), this principal gave it a 9. His teaching staff, as a group, gave it only a 6.6. The numbers themselves are of less importance than the discrepancy, which indicates that the Bradford High principal really was out of touch with his staff.

It might seem that I have strayed far, in this case, from my central theme of student satisfaction with school as a work place. But the Bradford situation shows us how organic an entity a school really is, and how an unsatisfactory condition can be felt throughout the whole system. For we began by noticing signs of strong and pervasive student dissatisfaction, then found similar parent and teacher unhappiness. In exploring the teacher responses, we discovered that one of the many problems at Bradford was laissez-faire leadership on the part of the principal. Allowing for the all-too-human tendency to "pass the buck" (in this case, students and parents blamed the teachers, and the teachers blamed the principal), it is still fair to conclude that Bradford High School, caught in a downward spiral of complex problems, negative attitudes, and weak leadership, was a very unhappy place. In compiling this picture of Bradford, we have barely scratched the surface of the available data. In the course of this chapter and the next, we shall have opportunities to see how other data tend to support this depressing picture.

Schoolwork and Student Attitudes

On the whole, our students seemed quite positive about schoolwork. Almost three-fourths of them told us that they liked school (although only 57% felt satisfied with their own school performance). As Table 4.6 shows, for each of the eight areas, our student sample indicated that they like all subjects, especially the more active, less "academic" subjects.[11] Yet even these--science, math, and social studies--are enjoyed by nearly two-thirds of our students.

Table 4.6

Comparison of high school student responses
to two questions about which subjects they like
and which they consider to be important.

In general, how do you like the following subjects?		In general, how important are the following subjects?	
Subject Area	% who said they like it	Subject Area	% who think it is important
Arts	82.6%	Math	94.3%
Voc. Ed.	80.8	English	93.6
Phys. Ed.	79.8	Voc. Ed.	85.9
English	72.1	Science	79.2
Math	65.1	Social Studies	77.8
Social Studies	65.0	Phys. Ed.	67.4
Science	64.1	Arts	65.3
Foreign Language	52.8	Foreign Language	65.1

When students were asked how important the various subjects are, however, a different pattern emerges. Almost everyone agrees that Math and English are important, though not everyone likes them. And those subjects which were among the most popular--Arts and Physical Education--were not considered to be important by as many students. Only Vocational Education is able to win a large percentage in both categories--the subjects included under this rubric are both liked and considered important. Again, we see the emphasis which high school students place on getting ready for the world of work.

On the whole, students who participated in A Study of Schooling seemed fairly content with the curriculum available at their schools. They seemed to regard other problems as more pressing, although at six of the thirteen schools (Fairfield, Bradford, Newport, Manchester, Atwater, and Laurel), poor curriculum ("poor courses or not enough different subjects offered") was considered a minor problem. Of these six schools, all but Atwater were in "cluster 2"--schools at which general student satisfaction was low. Perceived inadequacy of the curriculum, therefore, seems to be another contributor to student dissatisfaction with school as a work place, in some schools.

If students overall were more or less content with what was being taught at their school (across the whole sample, only 4% told us that poor curriculum was the one biggest problem), they were less pleased about what they perceived to be lacking; that is, with what wasn't being taught. Fully two-thirds of the students we asked told us that "There are things I want to learn about that this school doesn't teach." As Table 4.7 shows, agreement ranged from about 50% to nearly 80%. And, once again, we see several of our "cluster 1" (high student satisfaction) schools at one end of the ranking, and several of our "cluster 2" (low student satisfaction) schools at the other end.

Analyses of curriculum materials submitted by teachers,[12] master schedules, and other curriculum data from teacher and student surveys and teacher interviews made it possible to develop a set of descriptive categories for the curriculum of the schools we studied.[13] Table 4.8 presents each school in one of the categories, together with some descriptive demographic information about the community in which the school was located, and the size of the school.

Table 4.7

Percentage of high school students who agreed that "There are things I want to learn about that this school doesn't teach"

School	% agree
Rosemont	49
Dennison	55
Palisades	62
Bradford	62
Vista	66
Newport	66
Crestview	70
Woodlake	71
Euclid	71
Atwater	73
Manchester	74
Fairfield	77
Laurel	79

Several things stand out. First of all, it is interesting that the five schools with the most standard (i.e., similar, familiar, comprehensive) curriculums are all mid and lo-mid class, white, and suburban. The two with a standard, but more limited, curriculum are both small and rural. The two with a standard curriculum which is somewhat more diverse are both large, urban, and middle class. Evidently, demographic factors have a substantial impact on a school's curriculum. It would be interesting to study this further.

*   *   *

Another aspect of student satisfaction with the school as a work place is the degree to which students perceive that they have some control over their own school programs. We asked students to respond to two statements relating to student choice and student influence on curriculum decision-making. Almost 40% said they did not have enough freedom in choosing their

148

classes and 82% agreed that "students should have a say in what is taught at this school."

Table 4.8

The curriculum of each school falls into one of six different descriptive categories. Some data about the school community is also included.

School	SES	Location	Ethnicity	School Size	
STANDARD CURRICULUM					
Vista	Mid	Sub	W	2312	large
Crestview	Lo/Mid	Sub	W	1091	medium
Woodlake	Mid	Sub	W	1202	medium
Atwater	Mid	Sub	W	450	small
Bradford	Lo/Mid	Sub	W	1350	medium
STANDARD/LIMITED					
Laurel	Lo	Rural	W/B	271	small
Euclid	Mid	Rural	W	262	small
STANDARD/DIVERSE					
Newport	Mid	Urban	Mixed	2508	large
Manchester	Mid	Urban	B	3006	large
VOCATIONALLY-ORIENTED					
Fairfield	Lo/Mid	Rural	W/Hisp	1137	medium
ACADEMICALLY-ORIENTED					
Rosemont	Lo	Urban	Hisp	2702	large
Palisades	Hi/Mid	Urban	W/B	1402	medium
INNOVATIVE					
Dennison	Mid	Rural	W	61	small

Teachers seemed to agree that students should have more influence in school decision-making than they now do. Whether the teachers would really want students to

149

be involved in having, as the students put it, "a say in what is taught," we cannot be sure.

Library and Counseling Services

Most high schools offer two kinds of support services to students as part of their learning program. These are library and counseling services.

We asked the students in our sample to respond to two statements about library services at their school. Overall, about eight out of every ten agreed that "it is easy to get books from the school library." The school by school responses differed greatly, however, ranging from a low of 52% agreement at Fairfield to a high of 93% at Dennison.

Just over two-thirds of the students agreed that "things in the school library are useful to me." The range of school by school responses wasn't as extreme in this case--from 57% agreement at Bradford, to 82% at Dennison.

Table 4.9

Student views of library services at 13 schools

	It is easy to get books from the school library percent agree	Things in the school library are useful to me percent agree
Fairfield	52%	64%
Vista	68	60
Rosemont	73	80
Manchester	80	69
Palisades	83	71
Crestview	84	61
Bradford	86	57
Newport	87	71
Atwater	88	63
Laurel	88	78
Euclid	91	77
Woodlake	92	78
Dennison	93	82
overall	79%	68%

One can't help being curious about why so few students at Fairfield found it easy to get books from their library. The reason, however, was not hard to find: at Fairfield, the library was open to students only before and after school, and during lunch. During the school day, it has to be used for classes because of crowded school conditions. No wonder so many Fairfield students considered it difficult to get books from the library! At the other twelve high schools in the Study, the library was open to students all day, in most cases from around 7:30-8:00 a.m. to 3:00 or 4:00 p.m. Fairfield was the only exception.

One is tempted to consider the possibility that this situation at Fairfield had something to do with the school's overwhelmingly vocational orientation. Granted that when a school is very crowded, additional class space must be found and libraries are often used in this way--as are cafeterias and auditoriums. Yet, closing off the library to students during the school day might be an administrative decision which, perhaps unconsciously, reflects the comparatively low emphasis on academics at Fairfield.

As a matter of fact, by several other indicators Fairfield wasn't even the most crowded school in the Study. Woodlake, Newport, Palisades, and Manchester had higher average student/teacher ratios. The principals at Vista, Newport, and Manchester indicated excessive school size and/or crowded conditions as the one biggest problem at their school. Teachers, parents, and students at each of these schools agreed with the principals that school size and crowded classes were a problem. These data, by raising questions about the use of library space for classes as a school response to crowded conditions, suggest that we might legitimately hypothesize that student access to (and perhaps, attitudes toward) library facilities and services may be related to a school's predominantly academic or vocational orientation. This is an example of the sort of research questions raised by the Study of Schooling which might make workable dissertation topics. All of A Study of Schooling books and reports are full of such ideas for further research; this was one of the primary purposes of the Study.

151

Counseling and Guidance

We asked our students to respond to three statements about the counseling services available to them in their schools:

1. If I have a personal problem, it would be easy for me to get help from a counselor. (56% agree)

2. It is easy for me to get help from a counselor when planning my school program. (66% agree)

3. If I need help planning for a career, it would be easy for me to get help from a counselor.
(69% agree)

If the overall responses shown above are considered a measure of relative satisfaction with counseling services, one must conclude that only a slim majority felt generally satisfied with such services. Almost half indicated that they felt that their school's guidance department didn't do a very good job of helping them with personal problems. One-third were less than satisfied with the help they could receive in planning their school program, and over 30% told us that it would not be easy for them to get help with career planning. These are fairly sizable percentages. The obvious question to ask is whether most of the negative students attended certain schools, or whether the dissatisfaction was more or evenly distributed among the thirteen schools.

Turning to the school by school responses to these three questions, we find (and by this time, are we surprised?) Fairfield High School students were the most unhappy with their school's guidance services, especially the program-planning and personal problems aspects of guidance department responsibilities. The fact that fewer Fairfield students were unhappy with the career planning aspect of guidance services suggests that it was into this area that the Fairfield guidance counselors put most of their effort--again, hardly surprising in view of Fairfield's extraordinarily strong vocational emphasis.

The guidance function most likely to be neglected--or poorly performed, in the opinion of students--was the provision of help with personal problems. Many students at Manchester, Vista, Euclid, and Newport, as well as those at Fairfield, felt that they couldn't get adequate help with personal problems from their guidance counselors. Vista, Manchester, and Newport were large schools, with correspondingly complex coordination and scheduling problems and comparatively impersonal school environments. At all three of these schools, as well as at Bradford, students were assigned to counselors alphabetically, further de-personalizing the process and making it even less likely that students would feel comfortable taking a personal problem to their counselor, since students assigned to one counselor would be discouraged from consulting a different one of their own choosing.

It is interesting to contrast student attitudes at Rosemont High with those at Vista, Manchester, Newport, and Fairfield. At Rosemont, which was also a very large school (in fact, second largest high school in the Study), about two-thirds of the students said it would be easy for them to get help with a personal problem. Why should Rosemont students, on the whole, feel so positive compared to the students at the other large high schools in the Study? Data provided by the counselors themselves offer several clues.

Of the five counselors at Rosemont, two were Mexican-American, two were white, and one was black. At the other twelve high schools in the Study, including Manchester, Fairfield, Palisades, and Laurel, all the counselors were white. One suspects that having some non-white counselors might have made it easier for the 100% Mexican-American student population at Rosemont to feel more positive about and comfortable with their guidance staff. On the other hand, it is incredible that all ten of the guidance counselors at 100% black Manchester, and all eight counselors at ethnically diverse Newport, were white.

Also, of the five counselors at Rosemont, three could speak a second language—presumably Spanish. This surely must have helped Rosemont students to feel more comfortable in seeking help from their guidance staff.

Three of the eight counselors at ethnically and linguistically diverse Newport could also speak a second language. All three of the counselors at Fairfield could speak at least one language other than English; as at Rosemont, we can probably assume that it

153

was Spanish, since half the student body of Fairfield was Mexican-American. It would certainly make sense to hire support staff who could converse with students in their mother tongue.

Quite a different situation was found at Euclid, where only one counselor was available to serve all 262 students. Most of the students at Euclid (about 70-75%) were content with the help they were able to get with program and career planning. But only about half felt that it would be easy to get help with a personal problem from this counselor. Evidently something about this person prevented students from feeling entirely comfortable with him.

Actually, it has long been my view that most students will be more likely to take a personal problem to a _teacher_ they know and trust than to a counselor. Herein lies one of the many strengths, in my opinion, of the teacher-advisor system.

When the teacher-advisor system is properly used, students select an advisor when they enter 9th or 10th grade and remain with that advisor throughout their high school years. Every teacher, administrator, coach and librarian in the school had an advisee group of approximately 15-20 students. Each group is heterogeneous in terms of age, sex, ethnicity, and academic ability. Every June, when the seniors graduate, four to six places open up in each advisee group, and four to six freshmen fill these places the following fall. Teacher-advisors are responsible for all the program planning, paperwork, record-keeping and parent reporting for their advisees, and are also the ones to whom those 15 to 20 students are most likely to take their personal problems.

High schools that use a teacher-advisor system find it works best when advisee groups meet at least three times a week for 30-45 minutes each time, since not much can be done in less time. To keep the advisory periods from becoming just another version of home room, they cannot be interrupted by PA announcements or filled with administrative routines. Teachers are expected to use the time with their advisees for program planning, group discussions of student problems and concerns, self-awareness building activities, career-awareness experiences (such as guest speakers from different careers), and helping individual students with particular needs and problems.

Teachers and other adults who become part of a teacher-advisor system often feel that they need help in developing their own counseling skills, and in developing relevant and student-focused curriculum plans for their advisory periods. The guidance counselors are freed, by the teacher-advisor system, from most of the traditional "guidance" paperwork, and thus can serve as teachers for the teacher-advisors, designing and conducting inservice programs to help the teaching staff to acquire basic counseling skills. Guidance personnel in a teacher-advisor system also find that they have more time to work with special student problems which are beyond the abilities of the teacher-advisors, and to do more group counseling of students with particular problems. In data obtained from the counselors at our thirteen high schools, over and over again they identified "too much paperwork--too little time to really work with students" as the biggest frustrations of their job.

Crestview, at the time of the Study, was the only high school of our thirteen in which a true teacher-advisor system was being tried. There, every teacher and every administrator had a group of 15 advisees and met with them every day. The students had chosen their advisors and, barring unforeseen conflicts, would remain with that advisor for four years. There were also two full-time guidance counselors at Crestview, and because of the way the three items about guidance services were worded in our student questionnaire, the Crestview students responded in terms of these counselors rather than in terms of their own teacher-advisor. Unfortunately, therefore, we can't really assess how the students at Crestview felt about their "TAG" program.

We do know, from interviews with Crestview teachers and the principal, that it was a new program, partly funded by a government grant, and that it had been started by a committee of teachers with administrative support. Some teachers were very positive about the TAG program, others less so, but none were actually negative. It was as if they sensed the program's potential, or perhaps they were simply reserving judgment until the program had been given a fair trial.

155

As we have seen, then, all of the thirteen high schools offered guidance services for students, and students were happier with these at some schools than at others. In general, students at the larger schools were less satisfied and those at small schools were more satisfied with counseling services, although, as we have seen, Rosemont and Euclid were exceptions to this rule. One is left with the impression, from the student data, that guidance services could be much improved. The data from counselors tends to support this impression as well: time and again counselors indicated that their work load is too large, they do not get enough clerical help with record-keeping, their budgets and their work spaces are inadequate, they are bogged down with red tape and paperwork and do not really have the time to provide the kind of help that students need and should be getting.

Summary: students view the school as a work place

Although the Vocational function of schooling ("to get a good job") was selected as the most important by the largest percentage of our student sample, the Personal ("to become a better person") and Intellectual ("to learn basic skills") functions weren't far behind. An interesting finding was that the Intellectual function was selected as the most important by the largest percentages of students at only four schools-- and that these were four of the five schools with the largest populations of nonwhite students. Black and Hispanic students, clearly, are well aware of the importance of developing intellectual competence. For the most part, it was the students at predominantly white, middle-class schools who tended to feel that the reason for going to school was primarily vocational--to get a good job.

At four schools, the largest percentage of students selected the Personal function as the most important. One question that emerges from these school to school differences in student perception about the functions of schools is this: does the general "ambience" of a school have anything to do with the function of school- ing seen as most important by a majority of its stu- dents? We found considerable evidence that it does. For example, an analysis of the congruence between what students felt was important and what they perceived their school emphasized revealed that where such congruence existed, the students were happier with their school as a work place.[14]

In the view of our students, some schools were more satisfactory work places than others. The more satisfactory--and satisfying--schools were characterized by students' feeling that their school give a good education; that their school gives all students enough attention, including the average students; that the teachers at their school care about students and about teaching, and do a good job of teaching; that students at their school care about learning; and that there is some pressure to perform well academically. Schools at which most students share these kinds of positive opinions, we found, get a high "grade" from their students.

On the whole, we found students to be quite positive about their schoolwork, although many didn't feel that they were doing as well as they should be academically. About three-fourths told us that they like school, and most seemed to like all the subjects. There was a tendency, though, for smaller percentages of students to like the subjects which the students themselves rated "more important"--Math and English in particular. Conversely, larger percentages of students like the "less important" subjects: Physical Education and Fine Arts.

The students in our sample schools seemed generally satisfied with the curriculum that was available to them, but many (at least two-thirds, 67%) wished for an even broader selection of learning experiences. Too, many students told us they wished they could have more of a voice in school-wide curriculum decision-making.

Student satisfaction with library services varied from school to school, but on the whole, most found things in the library useful and easy to get. The same cannot be said of the counseling services available to students. Disappointingly large minorities--from 31% to 44%--told us that it was not easy for them to get help with career planning, program planning, or personal problems. Of the three, students felt they were least able to get help with personal problems. Counselors themselves confirmed this, by telling us that they are really too bogged down with record-keeping to give the students personalized help. One school, Crestview, had just begun using a teacher-advisor system, but it was too early to judge its effectiveness as compared to the more traditional guidance department structures in use at the other twelve Study high schools.

The School as Workplace: Other Considerations

High school students come to school around 8:00 a.m. They arrive on foot, by bus, or in cars and spend up to half an hour with their friends before going to their first class. Once the first class bell rings and the day has officially begun, a student is kept running from class to class with only a few minutes between classes and a short break for lunch.

Most high school campuses are "closed"--that is, students may not leave the school grounds before the official end of the day unless they have special permission. This makes it easier to control the young people, but communicates a negative message: we (adults) don't think you (young people) can be trusted to act responsibly. This may, in fact, turn out to be a self-fulfilling prophecy. It certainly deprives teen-ages of the opportunity to learn to take responsibility for their own behavior, and it can lead to an "us versus them" school climate that would be very destructive. At Newport, where the campus had just recently been closed, several teachers reported increases in hostile student behavior and a noticeable decline in overall student morale.

Many junior and senior students are granted official permission to leave school during the day as part of a supervised vocational training program, and some are excused early because they hold paying jobs.

A fairly recent pressure to finish up and get away from school as soon as possible has led administrators in many schools to drop the Study Hall option from the daily schedule. This may have the effect of forcing students to be more thoughtful in their choice of courses; as one teacher at Woodlake observed, "We have done away with Study Hall, and discipline has improved tremendously. There is no place for them to go if they drop out of a class, so they are more careful in their selection of electives."

158

The effects of abandoning Study Hall need to be studied. No doubt there are both advantages and disadvantages. For some students, because of home situations or part-time work commitments, there is no better time in which to do homework. Somehow, time for homework must be found, for according to our data, most teachers of academic subjects want their students to do about half an hour of homework a night. A student whose daily schedule includes English, History, Algebra, Biology, and Spanish, therefore, can expect at least two and a half hours of assigned homework a night for at least four nights a week.*

We did not ask students to tell us how much time they spend on homework, but I would hypothesize that relatively few spend as much as two and a half hours each night. It would be interesting to investigate whether students who had a Study Hall period in their schedules actually spent more time, or less time, on homework than do students in schools without Study Hall periods. There might be a tendency to do what one can in Study Hall and let the rest slide. When we recall that the teachers in our sample reported being most frustrated by lack of student interest in learning, we might further hypothesize that non-completion of homework assignments by students is one of the symptoms by which teachers gauge "lack of student interest."

III.

Students View the School as a Social Place

Despite the fact that school is a place where students go to work each week day and do, in fact, maintain a tightly structured work schedule while they are there, we found, as have other researchers before us, that it is the social rather than the educative

---

* In the High School and Beyond 1980 baseline data, 28,240 high school seniors--over 65% of the sample--reported spending less than 5 hours per week on homework. A Study of Schooling did not ask students how much time they spent on homework, but if this HS&B finding is any indication, students are spending far less time on homework than teachers would like and feel is necessary. When students get home, are they required by parents to spend sufficient time on their homework?

role of school which is of the most importance to young people. School is a gathering-place; whether or not you see your friends at other times or in other places, you can be sure of seeing them at school. Give high school students a choice of getting an education at home using TV, home computers, and correspondence courses, and I am quite sure most would reject your offer. Students generally would choose to go to school, even if they didn't have to. Life would just be too solitary otherwise--the fun of being in school is the social contact with peers.

We asked students to tell us what they considered to be the one best thing about their school. Table 4.10 shows the percentage who selected each of the 12 possible responses:

Table 4.10

6,828 students told us what they considered to be the "one best thing" about their school.

My friends	33.5%
Good student attitudes	12.4
Sports activities	12.2
Nothing	8.3
The variety of class offerings	7.8
The classes I'm taking	7.0
Little or no prejudice	5.9
Fair rules and regulations	4.0
Teachers	3.4
Extracurricular activites other than sports	2.6
The campus, buildings, and other equipment	1.6
The principal and other people in the office who run the school	1.4

By far the largest percentage of students, overall, selected "My friends" as the one best thing. At every school, "My friends" was the largest response. It is interesting to note, however, that there was a good deal of difference between schools in the size of the percentage who chose "My friends."

160

There is quite a difference between 21% at Rosemont and 51% at Crestview. Oddly enough, the four schools at the high end--Crestview, Bradford, Vista, and Fairfield--were all schools at which the Vocational function of schooling was selected as the most important by the largest percentage of students. Could there be a relationship here? Is it possible that at these schools, "my friends" takes on added importance in part because the educative/intellectual function of schooling is considered less important? Further study would be needed to answer this question.

Table 4.11

Percentage of students at each school who chose "My friends" as the one best thing about this school.

Crestview	51.0%
Bradford	45.7
Vista	44.3
Fairfield	41.5
Laurel	33.5
Atwater	32.6
Newport	30.6
Euclid	30.6
Palisades	28.7
Dennison	25.5
Woodlake	23.6
Manchester	21.1
Rosemont	20.8
overall	33.5%

---

*   *   *

As far as popularity is concerned, athletes were No. 1 at all schools except Laurel, where "good-looking students" received a higher percentage and athletes came in second. Good-looking students were rated No. 2 at all schools except Manchester, where "Gang members" were popular, as we have already noted.

"Smart students," on the whole, were low on the totem pole; in general, we would have to say that smart students wouldn't be considered popular in most of the schools we studied, unless they were also[15] either athletic or good-looking--and preferably both.

Students who are active in student government are also rarely seen as the most popular; not surprisingly, perhaps, in view of the fact that almost one-third of our student sample agreed that "Student government is a waste of time."

Table 4.12

Overall responses to a question about who were considered the most popular students in the school.

N=6931

Athletes	55.0%
Good-looking	23.6
Gang members	7.0
Smart	7.0
Student gov't	4.6
Wealthy	2.8

Most students felt that it was easy to make friends at their school. This feeling was not necessarily stronger at the smaller schools, however, or weaker at the larger schools: as many as 27% of the students at Laurel (population 271) didn't feel it was easy to make friends there, while only 15% at Rosemont (population 2702) felt that it wasn't easy to make friends there. Social customs and cultural norms play a role in an area such as this, of course. It is possible that the ethnic homogeneity of Rosemont (100% Mexican-American) caused the students to feel included and accepted by their peers more or less automatically. At Laurel, on the other hand, there was still a good deal of uneasiness between the recently desegregated white and black students, nurtured by the skepticism or outright negativism of their parents and the community.

It is also true that most of the students in the schools we studied didn't feel in any danger from other students. We asked that they respond to the statement, "There are places in this school where I don't go because I'm afraid of other students." Only 17%, overall, admitted to feeling that way. The percentages were highest at Fairfield (22%) and Newport (23%), and lowest at Dennison (2%).

While most students didn't feel unsafe while in school, larger percentages were uneasy about walking home from school, particularly if their school was large and located in an urban area. Over 30% of the students at Newport, Rosemont, Fairfield, and Manchester agreed that "It's not safe to walk to and from school alone." At Dennison, Euclid, Woodlake, and Atwater less than 10% felt that way.

Drug and alcohol use--the biggest problem?

From a list of thirteen possible problem areas, students were asked to rate each as either a major problem, a minor problem, or not a problem at their school; and then, from the thirteen, select the one they considered to be the biggest problem at their school.

The thirteen problem areas, and the percentages of students who chose each as the "one biggest" are shown in Table 4.13. The problem area selected by the largest percentage of students overall was "drug/alcohol use." This figure, however, masks the fact that at some schools drug and/or alcohol use was really quite a serious problem, while at other schools it wasn't a problem at all. It would certainly be a mistake to use these overall data to assert that "U.S. high school students say drug and alcohol use is the biggest problem in their school," as the mass media are wont to do.

School by School

Drug/alcohol use was the problem area which the largest percentage of students at Vista, Bradford, Euclid, Atwater, and Crestview considered to be the "biggest" problem at their school. It got the second-largest percentage at Woodlake, Newport, Manchester, and Fairfield. From about 30-45 percent of the students at Vista, Bradford, Newport, Manchester, Crestview and Fairfield rated it a major problem.

163

We also asked questions about drug use and alcohol use separately. Alcohol use is a problem here, said 38% of the students at Bradford and Euclid, 52% at Vista, and 33% at Newport and Crestview. Drug use is a problem here, said 54% of the students at Newport, 60% at Bradford, 55% at Fairfield, and 71% at Vista.

When all of these variables are combined, we can see that basically the same schools turn up again and again: Vista, above all; then Bradford, Crestview, Newport, and Fairfield. By the same token, drug and alcohol use seemed not to be a problem at Laurel and Dennison. At the remaining schools, it was rated as a minor problem, but even here there were important differences: mean scores at Euclid, Atwater, and Woodlake indicate that the drug/alcohol situation there wasn't considered as much of a problem as it was at Palisades, Rosemont, and Manchester.

Table 4.14 shows a continuum of drug/alcohol use "problem seriousness" at our thirteen schools, from the students' viewpoint.

Do students actually come to class drunk, or high? Not very often, if the responses of teachers are any indication--in fact, in the large majority of classes such incidents are probably extremely rare. When asked to rate drug/alcohol use as a problem, the teachers at most schools rated it a minor problem. However, when asked to select the one biggest problem at their school, very few teachers selected drug/alcohol use. At only one school--Crestview--did drug/alcohol use fall into the "top three" of teacher responses; and even then, only four teachers out of 42 selected it as the biggest problem. Other Crestview teachers were much more concerned, as were teachers at the other schools, with problems such as lack of student and parent interest.

There may be several explanations for this seeming lack of concern on the part of the teachers in our sample. Perhaps, although teachers are aware of some drug and alcohol use by some students, this behavior rarely intrudes upon their own classrooms and is therefore of less concern to most teachers than are other problem areas.

The same cannot be said of parents. While teach-ers, on the whole, didn't seem terribly worried about

164

drug and/or alcohol use by students, parents <u>were</u>. At nine of our thirteen high schools, drug/alcohol use was the problem area selected as the "one biggest" by the largest percentage of parents; at a tenth school it came in second.[16]

Table 4.13

6613 students at 13 high schools selected the "one biggest problem" at their schools.

18.4%	Drug/alcohol use
17.9	Student misbehavior (fighting, stealing, gangs, truancy, etc.)
14.3	How the school is organized (class schedules, not enought time for passing periods, lunch, etc.)
9.5	Poor student attitudes (poor school spirit, don't want to learn)
7.8	Poor or not enough buildings, equipment, materials
6.5	Poor teachers or teaching
5.5	School too large/classes overcrowded
5.0	Too many rules and regulations
5.0	The principal and other people in the office who run the school
4.4	Poor courses or not enough different subjects offered
2.5	Teachers don't discipline students
2.0	Prejudice/racial conflict
1.2	Busing for integration

Table 4.14

Drug/Alcohol Use: More of a Problem
at Some Schools Than at Others

		$\overline{X}$
Serious problem	Vista	2.24
	Bradford	2.18
High moderate	Newport	2.08
	Crestview	2.04
	Fairfield	2.00
	Manchester	1.98
Low moderate	Rosemont	1.89
	Atwater	1.89
	Euclid	1.86
	Palisades	1.84
	Woodlake	1.75
	Laurel	1.70
Not a problem	Dennison	1.07

As one might expect, parents were more worried about drugs than they were about alcohol. Whereas just under half of the parents, overall, agreed that alcohol use was a problem at their child's school, just over two-thirds of these parents agreed that drug use was a problem. Parental concern about drug use by students ran very high (55-88%) at all but two schools--Laurel and Dennison. In fact, even at those schools where many students agreed that drug use was a problem, parent percentages of agreement were even higher than those of the students, despite the fact that most parents hardly ever come to school and must depend, for their impressions, upon what they hear from their children or other sources. One can hardly avoid the suspicion that perfectly legitimate fears about drugs make parents vulnerable to local rumor and media misrepresentation about how serious a problem it really is in most high schools.

Alcohol, of course, is a more familiar danger, within the personal experience of most parents in a way that drugs are not. Even so, parent concern about alcohol use by students was quite high (38-64%) at all but three schools--Laurel, Dennison, and Palisades.

Perhaps it would be wise to take all of these data with, as the saying goes, a grain of salt. It may be true that parent impressions of the seriousness of the drug and alcohol problem are exaggerated. It may be equally true that student responses, too, are inflated. One can easily imagine a student exaggerating about the extent of a problem as a way of seeming knowledgeable and "with it." One can also envision a situation in which a student, seeing one or two drunk or stoned students (or even just hearing a rumor about such an incident) would come to the conclusion that drugs, or drinking, were indeed a "problem" at that school.

This is a good example of a variable for which the "Rashomon effect" can be clearly seen: the story you hear depends on who is telling the tale. The truth probably lies somewhere in between the various perceptions; we shall see this again and again in this book.

The same may be true of violence in schools. We have all heard or read about incidents of violence--muggings, stealing, attacks on teachers, and so forth. Such things do happen in high schools, but they certainly weren't common in the schools we studied. We hear about them because "headlines sell newspapers." What goes on in the vast majority of high schools day after day isn't considered newsworthy: a lot of teaching and learning, some headaches and confusion, and relatively little violence.

Although "student misbehavior" came in a close second to drug/alcohol use as the "one biggest problem" across all of our schools, it was actually selected as the biggest problem by less than two out of every ten students in the sample. At only one of the thirteen schools--Manchester High--did students themselves rate "student misbehavior" as a major problem--in fact, at Manchester, 42% of the sampled students said that it was the school's biggest problem. About two out of every ten students sampled at Manchester considered gang members to be the most popular students in the school. Evidently there was some gang activity at Manchester, but it was not readily visible to Study staff members who spent time visiting there: students seemed well-dressed and well-behaved; as much so as at other high schools in the Study.

Manchester High is located in an upwardly-mobile, urban middle class black community. As we have already seen, many Manchester students valued the Intellectual function of schooling, and 55% of them planned to go to college. Virtually none (less than 1%) expected to drop out of high school before graduating. All in all, it may have been that when Manchester students identified "student misbehavior" as a major problem, they were not merely identifying a problem but were, in effect, expressing dissatisfaction with what they perceived to be an undesirable situation.

Further exploration would be needed at Manchester in order to establish the truth of this, or to discover other reasons and meanings behind the students' perceptions. My purpose in describing the Manchester situation in some detail is to once again underline the complexity of schools, and the impossibility of making quick "capsule descriptions" that will fit the common stereotypes. Manchester was an inner city high school, depressing to look at. It had many problems. But it also had many strengths, and these must be noted as well.

At most of our schools, teachers were more concerned about lack of student interest in learning than they were about actual bad behavior. Our observation data shows that very little class time was spent by teachers in dealing with student misbehavior. High schools--at least those we studied, and they were pretty typical-- are simply not the dangerous, chaotic places we sometimes hear about.

Nor do teachers fail in their duty to discipline students when misbehavior does occur, as we are led to believe every September when the Gallup Poll is released. At only one school--Fairfield--did students identify "teachers don't discipline students" as a problem, and even at Fairfield, the students said it was only a minor problem. Teachers and parents, on the whole, felt that lack of discipline was only a minor problem--at no school in the Study did teachers or parents, as a group, say that lack of teacher discipline was a major problem.

Student Perceptions of Student and Teacher Prejudice

A very important factor in the social climate of some of our schools was the relative presence or absence of prejudice that was perceived to exist between teachers and students of differing racial or ethnic backgrounds. Racial or ethnic prejudice can poison the atmosphere of a school for white and non-white students alike, as well as for the teachers and other adults who work there.

The table below shows percentages of student agreement with two statements: "Lots of students in this school don't like other students because of their race or color," and "Many teachers at this school don't like some students because of their race or color." It also shows the percentage of nonwhite students enrolled at each school at the time of the Study.

Table 4.15

Student perceptions of student and teacher prejudice at their schools, total school population and percent of nonwhite students enrolled in 1977.

| | Students perceive: | | | |
	student prejudice	teacher prejudice	total students in the school	% of nonwhite students
Euclid	12.9%	9.2%	262	0%
Dennison	15.8	5.3	61	3%
Woodlake	18.8	12.9	1202	20%
Atwater	20.3	12.3	450	4%
Rosemont	24.8	22.1	2702	100%
Manchester	25.0	27.1	3006	99%
Vista	31.5	14.5	2312	2%
Fairfield	43.9	34.2	1137	47%
Palisades	45.8	38.2	1402	50%
Crestview	46.3	24.0	1091	1%
Newport	46.8	39.1	2508	53%
Bradford	70.5	32.7	1350	10%
Laurel	70.5	49.8	271	48%

A number of interesting questions are raised by the data in Table 4.15. For example, Fairfield and Palisades both had student populations that were about 50-50 white-nonwhite. At these two schools, around 45% of the students agreed that "Lots of students at this school don't like other students because of their race or color." While one might expect that this response

169

came primarily from nonwhite students, such was not the case. 40% of the white students at Fairfield and 47% of the white students at Palisades also agreed that student prejudice existed at their schools.[17]

The responses from Bradford and Laurel catch the eye, too. At Laurel, we aren't really surprised to find that 70% of the students say that yes, students at this school are prejudiced. We already know that Laurel, a small rural Southern school, had been desegregated just a few years before the Study and that the entire community was still very nervous about it. The responses from Bradford are more surprising--and more disappointing.

Of the total student body of 1,350 at Bradford, 10%--or135--were nonwhite. Of these, 108 (8%) were black and 27 (2%) identified themselves as "other." A student body that is 90% white could, one would think, assimilate a small percentage of nonwhite students with generosity and compassion. Certainly, 10% is not a threatening proportion, on the face of it.

The fact is, however, that Bradford was a lower middle-class blue collar community, located not far from a big city which has a large black population. In the mid-1970's, as the Supreme Court was preparing to rule on the constitutionality of metropolitan busing, Bradford residents were especially uptight about a possible influx of nonwhite students into their schools.[18]

70% of the students sampled at Bradford agreed that "Lots of students at this school don't like some students because of their race or color." Given the strength of this response (and even after assuming that some of this agreement came from nonwhite students--but they weren't numerous enough to be responsible for much of it), I would hypothesize that the nonwhite students at Bradford High, especially the 108 black students, have a pretty tough time at that school. I picture them sticking pretty close together in the halls and cafeteria, and maintaining a fairly low profile in class. Outnumbered as they are, in an environment where they are not made to feel welcome, basic safety would suggest being very careful not to attract attention or cause trouble. They'd be wanted on the basketball team, but that's about all.

170

Teacher prejudice is another sort of problem. On the average, about 23% of the white high school students in our sample agreed that the teachers at their schools "don't like some students because of their race or color." 25% of the Mexican-American students, 30% of the Asian-American students, and 33% of the black students also agreed that some teachers at their schools were prejudiced.

As Table 4.15 shows, the schools with mixed populations--Fairfield, Palisades, Newport, and Laurel--were the schools where higher percentages of students felt that some teachers were prejudiced. Again, one might assume that such responses came primarily from nonwhite students, but this was not the case. At Laurel, for example, 48% of the white students also agreed that many teachers there didn't "like some students because of their race or color." If teachers show prejudice, any student can recognize it, white or nonwhite. The same is true of student prejudice, as we have already noted.

On the whole, most students agreed that "Students of all races get an equally good education at this school." At ethnically mixed Laurel and Fairfield, the nonwhite students didn't agree quite as much as the white students did, but the difference isn't very great: about 73% of the nonwhite and 80% of the white students agreed that students of all races got an equally good education at these three schools. At none of the high schools did students, as a group, identify racial prejudice as a major problem, although it was rated as a minor problem at Fairfield, Crestview, Palisades, Newport, Laurel, and Bradford. Furthermore, the majority of students in our sample (77%) agreed that schools should be desegregated--specifically, that "Students of different races or colors should go to school together."[19]

*   *   *

Extracurricular Activities

It sometimes seems, on the surface of it, that the life of a school revolves around its extracurricular program--especially its sports activities. For many students, it is true, participation in extracurricular activities is a tremendously important part of school. Such activities generally have a number of characteristics which distinguish them from the regular school program: they are usually self-selected, and are not mandatory; though they may be competitive in other ways, they don't involve pressure for good grades; and they provide opportunities for the development of skill mastery in areas the students themselves consider important. For reasons such as these, students who participate in extracurricular activities generally find them enjoyable and satisfying (we also found that students who are involved in extracurricular activities had higher self-concepts than those who did not).

It would follow, then, that the more students in a school who are involved (by their own choice) in some form of extracurricular activity, the more positive and enthusiastic a place that school might be. A corollary of this would be that the greater variety of extracurricular activities offered by a school, the more students would be likely to become involved in one or more of them. I am actually suggesting, as an hypothesis, that a school where many students were active in a wide range of extracurricular activities would be a happier, healthier school than one at which varsity sports dominated while other activities were either nonexistent or, at best, weak. Let's see if our data have anything to tell us about this aspect of students' lives.

We asked the students to tell us whether or not they participated in six categories of extracurricular activities: sports teams; special interest clubs; student government; music, drama, or acting groups; honor society, and school or community service activities.

First of all, as Table 4.16 shows, surprisingly few students told us that they participated in NO extracurricular activities--less than one-third, even at the larger schools. To put it another way: overall, better than seven out of every ten students sampled told us that they participated in at least one kind of extracurricular activity (column A, Table 4.16).

Next, we found that at those schools where a larger percentage of students were involved in extracurricular activities, they also tended to be involved in a greater variety of activities. Not only that, but each student was active in several ways (Table 4.16, column B).

172

Third, there was a clear relationship between school size and student participation in extracurricular activities: in the larger schools, a smaller percentage of students were involved in such activities. In the smaller schools, not only were higher percentages of students involved but they were involved in a greater number of activities.[20]

Fourth, at the larger schools, smaller percentages of students were involved in extracurricular activities other than sports (column C).

Finally, those schools where more students were involved in a wider array of activities were schools which were given a better overall "grade" by students (column D). These also were the schools at which students seemed more satisfied with their work environment ("cluster 1" schools).

*   *   *

Much of our student data now seems to be falling into a pattern which is fairly consistent: the small and medium-sized schools are more satisfying places for students in lots of different ways; the large schools are less so.[21]

Dennison and Euclid, our two smallest schools, more or less serve as community centers: there simply isn't much social life for students if the school doesn't provide extracurricular activities. So these schools do provide such activities, and just about everyone is involved--92% at Euclid and 98% at Dennison. Furthermore, each student who is involved participates, on the average, in three different kinds of activities. Sports, service activities, special interest clubs such as the 4-H Club, and music or drama groups are the ones in which most Euclid and Dennison students told us they were involved.

Woodlake is another school at which many students are active in extracurricular activities (83%), and those students participate, on the average, in two or three different kinds of activities. Woodlake, like Euclid and Dennison, got a high "grade" from its students, and has emerged in many parts of our data as a very satisfying place from the students' point of view.

Table 4.16

High School student participation --or nonparticipation--in extracurricular activities

	A	B	C	D
Dennison	2%	3.3	48.1	B+
Euclid	8	2.9	41.1	B
Palisades	16	2.2	28.8	B-
Woodlake	17	2.5	31.6	B
Atwater	18	2.2	25.9	C+
Rosemont	20	2.2	28.4	B
Laurel	21	2.4	28.1	C+
Newport	24	2.2	24.3	C+
Fairfield	24	2.1	24.4	C
Vista	26	1.8	18.3	C+
Crestview	28	2.1	21.7	C+
Manchester	30	2.0	22.6	C-
Bradford	31	1.9	18.4	C

Column A: Percentage of students who told us they were involved in NO extracurricular activities

Column B: Of those who said they were involved in extracurricular activities, the average number of activities each participated in.

Column C: Average percentage of students participating in all activities other than sports.

Column D: "Grade" given to each school by the students attending it.

Bradford, on the other hand, had the highest percentage of non-participating students, and those students who were involved in extracurricular activities at Bradford were, on the average, involved in only one or two. 39% of the Bradford students who responded to this question told us they were involved in sports teams. None of the other five types of activities had such a high percentage of student involvement, and the average percentage of students participating was lower at Bradford than at any other school except Vista.

"My friends" and "sports," combined, accounted at Bradford for a whopping 59% of the responses to the question, "What is the one best thing about this school?" Drug/alcohol use was seen as a serious problem by students at Bradford--in fact, Bradford had quite a lot of problems. This school was given a low "grade" by its students, and was judged by them to be an unsatisfactory place to work, as we saw earlier. Added to these negative images of Bradford, then, we now have an impression of a weak extracurricular program about which no one seemed especially excited, except for the sports activities.

Significant Others

Inasmuch as the principal sets the tone for the whole school, he is inevitably involved in creating the school's social atmosphere at well as its intellectual climate. The principal can grant or withhold privileges which affect the social life of the students--whether or not dances and parties are held, for example, or whether rock music can be played in the cafeteria at lunchtime. Such things may seem small matters to adults, but they are important to teen-agers.

Yet in most schools, only a few students deal directly with the principal on matters such as these. For most students, the principal remains a remote figure, and this is especially true in the large high schools. Although most students told us that they do know their principal by sight, and many said they think their principal is friendly and helpful, at some schools--specifically Vista, Newport, Woodlake, Manchester, and Bradford--large percentages told us that they just didn't know if their principal was friendly or helpful. This isn't surprising in the case of Newport, where the principal was only in his second year at the time of the Study and was still an unknown quantity to many students. But at Manchester, Vista, Bradford and Woodlake the principals had been on the job for anywhere from eleven to twenty years. That large percentages of students still felt they didn't know whether their principal was friendly or helpful may be partly explained by school size but is also, I suspect, partly due to the leadership styles of these principals. Relating to students is not what some principals consider to be part of their proper role; this, or some similar attitude, may have been the case in these four schools.

*   *   *

A finding which is somewhat discouraging is that at nine of our thirteen high schools, from one-third to three-quarters of the students disagreed with the statement, "In general, the people at this school can be trusted." The percentages of disagreement for each school are shown in Table 4.17, along with the percentages of agreement that "Many teachers at this school don't care about students," and the "grade" students at each school gave their school.

Confronting these figures isn't easy; something is terribly wrong when, at most of the schools we studied, one student out of every three feels that teachers don't care about students and that people at the school can't be trusted.

It's no wonder, then, that many students choose "my friends" as the one best thing about school. Friends can be counted on to be supportive, even if teachers and others at the school cannot.

Earlier in this chapter, we saw that student satisfaction with school as a work place was particularly low at five schools: Bradford, Manchester, Fairfield, Laurel, and Newport. If the responses shown in Table 4.17 can be considered one indicator of student satisfaction with school as a social place, we find the lowest satisfaction at the same five schools.

These two aspects of the school, its function as a place where students have work to do and its nature as the site of social interactions of importance to young people, are evidently linked. The quality of one affects the quality of the other. I am not sure which is primary, if one is; I am inclined to suspect that they feed each other, more or less equally contributing to the overall "ambience" of the school.

176

Table 4.17

Many students seem to have negative feelings
about other people in their schools.

	In general, the people at this school can be trusted.	Many teachers at this school don't care about students.	
	% DISAGREE	% AGREE	GRADE
Dennison	7.1%	5.4%	B+
Euclid	10.1	14.2	B
Woodlake	24.3	20.2	B
Atwater	30.1	24.0	C+
Rosemont	33.4	31.9	B
Crestview	45.0	34.7	C+
Palisades	46.2	36.9	B-
Vista	47.8	37.2	C+
Newport	48.0	47.1	C+
Fairfield	48.1	41.4	C
Laurel	51.3	42.5	C+
Bradford	57.9	45.7	C
Manchester	74.6	47.7	C-

Summary: students view the school as a social place

Many students at all of our schools chose "my
friends" as the one best thing about school. At the
more vocationally-oriented schools, this response was
much stronger than it was at the more academically-
oriented schools. At schools where there are a lot of
distracting problems and considerable student and
teacher dissatisfaction, also, students placed more
value on "my friends" and on "sports." At Crestview,
for example, these two categories accounted for a
whopping 62.3% of the total student responses to the
"one best thing" question. At Rosemont, by contrast,
these two categories accounted for only 29% of the
student choices, while "good student attitudes," "the
classes I'm taking," and "variety of class offerings"
claimed 37%. At Crestview, these three more specifically school-oriented categories accounted for only
16.7% of the student choices.

At the high school level, athletes win the popularity contest, no doubt about it. Good-looking students place second in popularity at most schools. Smart students aren't considered popular by most of the students in our sample.

Most of the students in our Study felt that it was easy to make friends at their school, and not many felt afraid of other students or in danger while at school. Over one-third of those who attended urban schools, however, did feel somewhat nervous about walking to and from school alone.

Students at six schools considered alcohol and/or drug use to be a fairly serious problem at their schools. Large discrepancies between the views of teachers and students on this issue, however, suggest that what level of "use" constitutes a "serious" problem is very much an open question. The views of parents, too, need further study. It would be particularly interesting to try and pin down the degree to which parent perceptions of problems like drug/alcohol use and school violence are a function of rumor and media influence as opposed to first-hand knowledge or personal experience.

At twelve of our thirteen schools, students themselves rated "student misbehavior" as a minor problem, and did not feel that teacher discipline of students was lax.

Our data suggest that high school students can recognize racial and ethnic prejudice when they see it, and that white students as well as nonwhite students in most schools agree that some student and teacher prejudice does exist. The degree to which prejudice exists in any given school is, as we saw in the cases of Laurel and Bradford, a function of that school's particular background and circumstances. As a rule, however, the high school students in our sample felt that regardless of prejudice that might exist, students of all races and ethnic groups get an equally good education at their school. There was also strong agreement that students of different races and ethnic groups should attend school together. This support for school integration is, I suspect, based on a strong sense of justice and fair play often found in students of high school and junior high school age. We have already seen this quality displayed in the Global

178

Education Substudy data: the students in our sample were proud of their country, but at the same time were generous and responsible in their attitudes towards other countries, especially poorer nations.

Lest I make our students sound like paragons of virtue, however, we also found that when it became a matter of being personally involved in helping school integration to happen, everyone--students as well as teachers and parents--was much more negative. Obviously it is easier to voice support for an ideal than to work to make the ideal become a reality.

We found a surprisingly high number of students-- two-thirds or more, at every school--involved in extracurricular activities. At those schools where a greater percentage of students were involved, they also tended to participate in more than one kind of activity. At such schools, students seemed more satisfied both with the school in general and the school as a work place, suggesting an organic linkage between the curricular and extracurricular functions of schooling and the overall ambience of the school.

Though we found that most students recognize the principal when they see him, they rarely have any personal contact with him and, at several schools, they do not know if he is friendly or helpful.

Many students seemed to have negative feelings about other people in the school, adults in particular: overall, more than one-third felt that many of the teachers at their school didn't care about students.

For many students, then, the social aspects of attending school mean unavoidable but not necessarily pleasant interactions with adults, interesting and potentially important interactions with other students, and the comparative security of being with one's special friends.

IV.

The Disenchanted: a Substudy

During the final months of the Carter administration, the Carnegie Council on Policy Studies published a report entitled <u>Giving Youth a Better Chance</u>. Noting a national high school dropout rate of 23% and observing that high school is "an alienating experience" even for many students who do not drop out, the Council recommended a number of basic changes for America's high schools.

One newspaper's coverage of the Carnegie Report commented that "the recommended changes would cost the government $1.4 billion to $1.9 billion, but that would be offset by "reduced social costs," including lower crime and welfare rates, the report said.[22] In view of policy changes implemented by the Reagan administration in the years since then, increased funding seems unlikely.

And yet, the problems identified by the Carnegie Council were real--and they are still with us. The alienation felt by many young people who do not have successful, encouraging experiences in school ultimately causes a tremendous waste of potentially productive lives.

With this social issue in mind, I examined A Study of Schooling data for clues that would tell me more about the isolated or alienated student. As it turned out, I did not have far to look: patterns showed up almost immediately.

One of the questions asked of both junior high and high school students was, "If you had to choose the <u>one best</u> thing about this school, what would it be?" Twelve response choices followed. Of 11,767 students responding, by far the largest number selected "my friends" (4,103). "Sports" (1,579) and "Good student attitudes" (1,334) were next.

The fourth most frequently selected response, however, was "Nothing." 941 students were unable to find <u>anything</u> good about school, even the fact of having friends there. 568 of these were high school students; this number constituted over 8% of the 6,828

180

high school students who responded to this question. Seven per cent of the 2,806 girls and almost ten per cent of the 2,742 boys in the sample selected this discouraging answer ("Nothing") over the eleven other possible choices.

Table 4.18 shows how many students at each high school were in this group. It is surely no coincidence that the schools at which higher percentages of students selected "Nothing" were schools at which overall student satisfaction was generally low; conversely, overall student satisfaction was high at Dennison, Euclid, and Woodlake.

Table 4.18

High School students who chose "Nothing" as their response to the question, "What is the one best thing about this school?

	% say "Nothing"	N say "Nothing"	Total N
Dennison	1.8	1	55
Euclid	3.4	8	235
Woodlake	3.6	20	563
Vista	5.5	42	768
Atwater	6.6	18	273
Rosemont	6.6	47	712
Palisades	7.2	49	679
Fairfield	7.5	49	655
Crestview	8.3	45	539
Laurel	8.5	18	212
Bradford	8.7	56	645
Newport	9.7	70	723
Manchester	18.9	145	769
	8.3	568	6828

Students who selected "Nothing" when asked to identify the one best thing about their schools tended to have lower academic self-concepts, and fairly low self-concepts in-relation-to-peers when compared with students who selected one of the eleven other possible responses. Their general self-concepts, however, were about average--neither very high nor very low--compared with students who chose one of the other answers.

These findings should not be surprising. Students who chose "Nothing" specifically elected not to choose "My friends;" the rather low self concept in relation to peers makes sense when viewed in this way. Here is a hint that such students may be isolates, but whether by choice or by circumstance we cannot tell.

And as we shall see, students who selected "Nothing" weren't experiencing much academic success in school; hence the low academic self-concepts. The better general self concept is a hopeful sign, however--perhaps these students have been able to retain a sense of themselves despite their relatively solitary existences in a school which doesn't provide them with many positive experiences as far as school-work is concerned. Indeed, the fact that they did choose "Nothing" suggests a certain healthy belliger-ence. I wonder how many lives would be changed if teachers and administrators made a deliberate effort to identify these students and give them special atten-tion, helping them to have some success in their school work. The problem is, of course, that by high school these students are often the "hardest to love" and frequently resist any offers of help, however subtly extended. Such an effort would have to be made much earlier in the child's schooling.

What else can we learn about the attitudes and feelings of the students who chose "nothing?" Listed below are all the other possible choices:

    fair rules and regulations
    my friends
    the classes I'm taking
    teachers
    little or no prejudice or racial conflict
    the variety of class offerings
    sports activities
    extracurricular activities other than sports
    the campus, buildings, and equipment
    good student attitudes (friendly, good school
      spirit, cooperative)
    the principal and the other people in the
      office who run the school

When the responses of students who selected one of these other choices (from now on, I will refer to them as group 2) are compared with the responses of students who selected "nothing" (group 1), the patterns--on a

182

wide variety of questions--are consistently depressing, as Table 4.19 shows.

Students in group 1 were less likely to feel that people at their school could be trusted, and more likely to feel that teachers at their school didn't care about students. They were less likely to be happy with how well they were doing in school, and less certain that having gone to school would make their lives better in the future. As we have already noted, their self concepts were lower in regard to academic work. Evidently considering themselves to be average, or perhaps even below average students, they tended to agree that "average students don't get enough attention at this school." As we shall see, a smaller percentage of these students than group 2 students expected to go to college, and a larger percentage told us that they planned to drop out of high school or that they didn't know what they would do in the future. They were more likely to agree that the school discriminated in favor of the college-bound students.

Higher percentages of students in group 1 than group 2 told us that they disliked science, social studies, and English. Interestingly, the percentages of both groups that said they disliked math were about the same. In fact, group 1 students were more negative about all the subject areas, even PE and Vocational subjects. They also were far more likely to give their schools a "grade" of D or F, and far less likely to give them an A or B.

Group 1 students were less likely than group 2 students to participate in extracurricular activities, and more likely to identify "gang members" as the most popular students in the school. Their estimates of the percentage of students who were on drugs while at school were higher than those of group 2.

Interestingly, most students in both groups 1 and 2 told us that the vocational function of schooling was the most important as far as they were concerned. In both groups, too, the largest percentage of students identified drug/alcohol use, student misbehavior, and how the school is organized as the biggest school problems. There are some areas of school experience, then, in which both groups of students--so different in other ways--do see eye to eye.

183

I have already mentioned the differences between the two groups regarding their future plans. Table 4.20 presents the actual percentages of the major categories.

Again, the general negativity of the students in group 1 can be seen: they are more likely to say they'll probably drop out of school, or that they don't know what they'll do.

Motivation to learn is usually seen as an individual characteristic, and indeed, the discussion up to this point has reflected this attitude. Most of us assume that, by high school, some students are motivated while others are not--or, at best, are difficult to motivate. This is one of the assumptions which underlies the system of tracking.

But few of us stop to consider the role of the school environment in motivating students. Barker and Gump were able to show that motivation is related to the ecological setting in which the individual is located. Marginal students in small schools felt pressure to behave responsibly, while marginal students in large schools were "...a group apart, a group of outsiders. These findings indicate that the academically marginal students had very different experiences in the two ecologies."[23]

A Study of Schooling findings point in the same general direction. For example, of the 568 students in our sample who chose "Nothing," 304 (about 54%) were from the four large schools: Vista, Rosemont, Newport, and Manchester. Only 45 (8%) were from the four small schools. The remaining 38% were from the five medium-sized schools in the Study.

We shall discuss other findings related to school size in more detail in chapter 7. The point being made here is that marginal students are likely to be proportionately more numerous in large schools than in small schools because of the type of environment which exists in a large school. It is possible for a student to go through four full years of schooling in a large high school without becoming well known to a single teacher in the school. This type of anonymity does not lead such a student to feel involved with or responsible for the welfare of the school.

Table 4.19

Attitudes towards school: a comparison of the responses of two groups of high school students. Group 1 chose "nothing" when asked to identify the best thing about their school. Group 2 students chose one of eleven more positive response options.

	% DISAGREE	
	group 1*	group 2**
In general, people at this school can be trusted.	69	44
I am satisfied with how well I am doing in school.	55	41
I like school.	48	25
It is easy to make friends at this school.	35	18
What I'm learning in school will be useful later in life.	30	16
It is worth going to school because it will help me in the future.	23	9

	% AGREE	
	group 1	group 2
Average students don't get enough attention at this school.	58	48
Many teachers at this school don't care about students.	57	34
If you don't want to go to college, this school doesn't think you're very important.	43	25
A person is foolish to keep on going to school if he or she can get a job.	23	16

* group 1 (N=568) Those who chose "nothing" when asked to identi- fy the one best thing about their school.

** group 2 (N=2,260) Those who chose one of the eleven other possible responses.

Table 4.20

Comparison of two groups of student responses to a
question about what they "will probably" do
in the future. Group 1 chose "nothing" when
asked to identify the best thing about their
school. Group 2 students chose one of
the eleven more positive answers.

	quit, or don't know	finish high school	trade school or jr. college	4-year college or univ.	N
group 1	16%	29%	24%	25%	564
group 2	9%	25%	23%	36%	6208

The disenchanted: from another angle

Now, let's look at the data on students' future
plans a bit more closely. We asked all the students in
our sample three questions about their future plans:
what they'd like to do, what their parents would like
them to do, and what they thought they probably would
do. Most students gave the same answer for all three
questions. I have chosen, therefore, to focus on the
third question, because it was intended to direct the
student's thinking to what was most realistically
probable. 7,014 students answered this third question.
The largest percentage told us they "probably would" go
to a four-year college or university (34.4%). About
one-fourth said they would just finish high school (and
presumably go right to work, though we didn't ask this
specifically). Twelve per cent expected to go to a
trade or technical school and almost the same percentage said they'd probably go to a junior college. Seven
per cent anticipated going beyond a baccalaureate
degree and into graduate work.

But almost two percent told us that they would
probably quit school before graduating, and eight per
cent said they didn't know what they would do. These
two groups, combined, make up almost ten per cent of
the sample: 677 of the 7,014 students who responded to
this question about probable future plans.

Differences between the sexes were, perhaps suprisingly, quite small. A slightly higher percentage of boys (11%) than girls (8%) said they didn't know, or expected to drop out. A slightly higher percentage of boys, too, told us they would probably go to a trade or technical school. But girls were a little more likely to say they would probably just finish high school (27.3%) than boys (23.9%). Girls were slightly more likely to expect to go to college, but the difference was only 2½ percentage points--basically, not much of a difference at all. Nevertheless, despite the fact that about the same percentage of boys as girls expected to go to college, boys overall were more likely than girls to agree that "if you don't want to go to college, this school doesn't think you're very important."

There were no major differences in the way students of different ethnic groups responded to the questions about future plans. About 1.5% of each ethnic group sampled same they would probably drop out of school, and about 7.5% of each group told us they didn't know what they would do. Mexican-American students, however, were less likely to view going to college as a possibility and more likely to indicate that they just wanted to finish high school. They were also a bit more inclined to believe that their school discriminated in favor of the college bound student, but the black students ran them a close second and the white students weren't far behind (31% of the Hispanic students, 29% of the black students, and 25% of the white students agreed that "if you don't want to go to college, this school doesn't think you're very important").

The strongest pattern relative to this question about probable future plans emerged when I examined the self-concept scores of the students in each group. As Table 4.21 shows, the students who planned to drop out, who didn't know what they were going to do, or who just planned to finish high school but go no further had lower self-concepts (of all three types) than those students who planned on some form of higher education.

Furthermore, students whose future plans did <u>not</u> include some form of higher education were more likely to <u>agree</u> with the statement, "If you don't go to college, this school doesn't think you're very important."

This pattern raises some interesting questions about how school feels to those students who evidently, for whatever reasons, haven't had enough success in school throughout the years to want to continue their education beyond high school. That improved self-concept is a _result_ of success, rather than a precondition for success, is a point made by Scheirer and Kraut in their 1979 review of the self-concept literature.[24] Conversely, then, it seems to follow that _reduced_ self-esteem would be a likely result of _repeated_ academic failure. The lower self-concept scores of students who do not plan on going to college suggest, therefore, that these students have experienced failure or, at any rate, have not experienced much success in school.

Table 4.21

Mean self-concept of five groups of students with differing plans for the future. For all three types of self-concept, the differences between the mean scores were statistically significant at the .001 level.

	Group mean self-concept scores			
Future plans	General	Peers	Academic	N
Quit	2.50	2.91	2.46	116
Don't know	2.62	2.92	2.64	559
Finish H.S.	2.62	2.95	2.69	1796
Junior college	2.68	3.02	2.73	1629
4-year college	2.81	3.12	2.93	2896

We know, of course, that the system of schooling in this country, with its roots in the competitive ethic, ensures--in fact, requires--that some students fail. Inevitably, then, there is always a population of students who have discouraging experiences in school, who develop low self-esteem and who ultimately come to view the schools as existing for the benefit of _others_, the successful ones.

The picture becomes yet more complex when we look at student self-concept scores in terms of family

income level and the educational level of the students'
parents. Using matched pairs of students and parents,
we were able to establish that students from wealthier
families had consistently higher self-concepts, of all
three types, than students from families that were less
well off. Likewise, students whose parents had
completed college had higher self-concepts than those
whose parents had not.*

Family income and parent educational level were
also related to the future plans a student might have.
Students from poorer families were more likely to say
they would probably just finish high school and less
likely to expect to go to college. The possible demise
of student loan programs under the Reagan administration will make it even more difficult for students from
poor families, however bright they might be, to get to
college.

Students whose parents went to college were much
more likely to anticipate going to college themselves.
And so the vicious circle closes--those who get a
college education are those who can afford it, and they
are the ones most likely to send their children to
college. The dark side of this coin: young people
whose parents didn't go to college are less likely to
have access to the money they would need to go to
college themselves, and if they can't go to college,
their chances of breaking out of the cycle are dim. So
much for the American myth of equal opportunity for
upward mobility.

We learned that students who planned to drop out of
high school, or who didn't know what they were going to
do, were more likely than other students to disagree
that what they were learning in school would be useful
to them later in life, and that having gone to school
would help them in the future. They were less likely
to agree that "it is easy to make friends at this
school," and more likely to give their school a lower
"grade." Only 56.8% of these students told us that
they liked school, while over 80% of the students who
were planning to go to college said they liked school.

---

* The differences between both sets of mean scores were statistically significant at the .001 level for all but the academic
self-concept by family income, and it was significant at the .05
level.

As one would expect, the students who weren't sure or who thought they'd probably quit were less likely to be satisfied with how well they were doing in school and more likely to agree that their school discriminated in favor of the college bound. They tended to dislike all of the more academic subjects--English, math, science, social studies--in which they were less likely to be having successful learning experiences.

Table 4.22

Relationship of students' future plans to their parents' income and educational level.
Note the inverse pattern.

parent income	finish high school	go to a 4-year college
under $5,000	36.2%	22.2%
$5,000-$9,999	32.7	30.4
$10,000-$14,999	23.7	33.5
$15,000-$19,999	23.7	36.9
$20,000-$24,999	20.7	40.0
$25,000 or more	10.	52.4
parent education		
some HS or less	34.4	24.5
finished HS	28.6	32.1
some college	18.9	39.7
college graduate	8.4	55.4

Most students, no matter what their future plans were, agreed that athletes and good-looking students were the most popular ones in the school. But the third largest percentage selected by college-bound students was "smart students," while the third largest percentage selected by non-college bound students was "gang members."

The same split showed up when we asked the students which function of schooling was the most important to them. Those who planned to quit, to just finish high school, to go to a trade or technical school, or who

190

didn't know what they would do were more likely to select the Vocational function as the most important. Those who expected to go to a junior college, a four-year college, or on to graduate school were more likely to identify one of the other functions--Social, Personal, or Intellectual--as the most important.

All sampled students, regardless of their future plans, were similar in their estimates of how many students were on drugs while at school. There was also agreement on the biggest school problems: student misbehavior, drug and alcohol use, and how the school was organized.

*   *   *

Out of a total of 6,772 sampled students, 109 told us they'd probably quit, 797 said they'd probably go to a trade or technical school, and 1,724 expected to finish high school but go no further. All in all, then, 39% of our sample were not college bound. And if we make the assumption that the 537 who didn't know what they were going to do probably wouldn't go to college either,* that figure jumps to 47%--nearly half.

The most endangered students, I suspect, and the ones for whom we should all be concerned are the ones who selected "nothing" and indicated they'd probably quit or didn't know what they would do in the future. In our sample, there were 89 such students: borderline dropouts, uncertain about their own futures, who felt that nothing was good about their school. Less likely to be academically successful, less likely to have friends, more likely to regard school as a hostile environment, more likely to have low self-concepts, more likely to come from poor, less well-educated families--these young people had three strikes against them before they were even 18 years old. This is the real waste, in human terms, of our society. And it is morally inexcusable, in a nation such as ours which has such wealth and resources at its disposal. Unfortunately, social responsibility has never been a major operational concept of the American system. The notion of laissez-faire, open competition ensures that there will be losers as well as winners, and this concept has

---

* Such an assumption would need to be tested in a longitudinal study, of course.

191

long been taken for granted in the social sphere as well as in the economic sphere.

Table 4.23

Future plans of the students who chose "nothing" as the best thing about their school. 58% were not expecting to go to college. 15.8%--89 students--were borderline drop-outs or uncertain about their future as well as being negative about their school.

	%	N
finish high school or go to a trade or technical school	42.0	137
go to a junior college or a 4-year college or university	35.6	201
quit, or don't know	15.8	89
go to graduate school	6.6	37
		564

Education, too, has become structured in such a way that it is virtually impossible for all children to be successful in school. As we shall see in chapters 5 and 6, despite new understandings about how people learn, the dominant mode of instruction at the high school level is the whole-class lecture, followed closely by monitored seatwork. In essence, all students are given the same assignment, information, and materials and are expected to complete the assignment by the same deadline. Then they are tested, and it is taken for granted that some will do better on the tests than others.

Two assumptions underlie this process. The first is that students should be given an equal chance to succeed--"equal chance" having been interpreted as meaning that all students should be presented with a common set of experiences: reading the same chapter, hearing the same lecture, and so forth.

A second, related assumption is that not all students will or can succeed, but that that is not the school's responsibility. It has done its job by simply giving everyone the same chance.* Up to a point, our society wants all its members to master certain "basics," but no one seriously questions the common belief that <u>there have got to be losers</u>.

Against this deeply-rooted belief, the rhetoric of individualization, mastery learning, and "meeting each child's learning needs" has made hardly a dent. At the high school level in particular, as we shall see in the next two chapters, classroom instruction proceeds much as it always has, ever since the emergence of the comprehensive high school. And in the process, the disenchanted students drop by the wayside.

---

* Actually, as we shall see in the section on tracking (chapter 6), schools <u>don't</u> even give every student an equal chance.

CHAPTER IV, NOTES AND REFERENCES

1. At tiny Dennison, tracking was minimal--but it existed.

2. The differences between boys' and girls' mean scores on these five items were statistically significant.

3. The Antecedents of Self-Esteem, by S. Coopersmith (San Francisco: W.H. Freeman, 1967).

4. These figures combine the percentages of students who selected "4-Yr College" and those who selected "Grad School."

5. Full time equivalent teaching positions.

6. B.J. Benham, An Analysis of Curriculum Materials Submitted by Teachers Who Took Part in A Study of Schooling (Unpublished Technical Report, 1978).

7. See Rosemont profile, Chapter 2.

8. Academic FTE at Fairfield was 47%.

9. Bette C. Overman, Functions of Schooling: Perceptions and Preferences of Teachers, Parents, and Students (Technical Report No. 10, 1980) pp. 58-68.

10. B.J. Benham, The One Biggest Problem at This School, As Perceived by Teachers, Parents, and Students (Unpublished Technical Report, 1979).

11. The Foreign Language percentages are low in comparison with the other subjects because relatively few students were enrolled in Foreign Language courses.

12. Curriculum materials were submitted by 599 teachers.

13. B.J. Benham, Curricula: Intended, Taught, Experienced (Unpublished Technical Report, 1980). Pages 49-50.

14. Bette C. Overman, Functions of Schooling: Perceptions and Preferences of Teachers, Parents, and Students (Technical Report No. 10, 1980) pp. 58-68.

15. Not much has changed in the years since James Coleman found similar patterns in ten high schools he studied. Social Climate in High Schools (HEW, 1961) and The Adolescent Society (Free Press, 1961).

16. At the three remaining schools--Laurel, Dennison, and Palisades--drug/alcohol use didn't even place in the top three, which may possibly be surprising at suburban Palisades, but is not at all surprising in the case of small, rural, isolated and conservative communities such as Laurel and Dennison.

17. B.J. Benham, Responses of Students, Teachers, and Parents to Four Questions About Racial/Ethnic Prejudice in Their Schools, (Unpublished Technical Report, 1979).

18. In Milliken vs. Bradley, 1974, the Court established a basis for future city/suburb busing. To qualify, both the city and the suburbs would have to be found to be clearly in violation of the Constitution--that is, maintaining racially segregated schools.

19. School by school agreement with this statement ranged from a low of 64% at Vista to a high of 90% at Dennison. For a school like Vista, though, 64% is a fairly high percentage on a question like this.

20. School size and student NONparticipation: rho = .80. School size and average number of activities per student: rho = -.62.

21. There are occasional exceptions. Large Rosemont, for example, usually earns "high satisfaction" responses from its students, while small Laurel often gets "low satisfaction" responses.

22. Los Angeles Times, November 28, 1979, p. 19.

23. Big School, Small School: High School Size and Student Behavior, by R.G. Barker and P.V. Gump (Palo Alto: Stanford U. Press, 1964):133-135.

24. Review of Educational Research, Winter 1979.

CHAPTER V

IN THE CLASSROOM: ACTIVITIES AND MATERIALS

> The monasteries helped to give human enterprise
> the regular collective beat and rhythm of the
> machine; for the clock is not merely a means of
> keeping track of the hours, but of synchroniz-
> ing the actions.   -- Lewis Mumford [1]

In the seventh century, Mumford tells us, the Pope
decreed that the bells of the monastery be rung seven
times in the day, to mark the hours of devotion and to
ensure discipline and regularity within the community.
It is not really a coincidence that today, thirteen
centuries later, six or seven bells also measure out
the work days of teachers and students.   To run a
school without a clock and bells would--we assume--be
unthinkable, so the teaching and learning process must
conform to the imposed pattern of measured time.

One of the early lessons a child encounters upon
first entering school is that learning cannot be
allowed to run its natural course from interest, to
exploration, to understanding and mastery.   It must be
confined instead within a prescribed time frame.   The
kindergartener must leave the toy in which he is
absorbed, because it's nap time.   The third grader who
becomes intrigued by something encountered in the
science lesson may be told to save her questions for
tomorrow's science class, for right now it's time to go
on to social studies.   By the time a student reaches
high school, this lesson of segmented learning within
the school context has been well internalized.

Teachers, too, learn to pace their lessons according to allocated time.   A large part of skilled classroom management involves having just enough activity
planned to fill the available time precisely.

Our data on the use of time in the high school
classroom suggests that, during an average 55-minute
period, about eleven minutes are devoted to routines of
one sort or another, one minute is spent by the teacher

attending to student misbehavior, and forty-two minutes are devoted to actual instruction.[2] As Table 5.1 shows, these data from our observation instruments are very similar to the estimates provided by the teachers themselves, especially insofar as time spent on actual instruction is concerned.

Table 5.1

Estimates by teachers of how time is spent
in their classrooms weren't very different
from impressions obtained from the observation
instruments; in minutes

	FMI[3]	Teachers[4]
Instruction	42	40
Behavior	1	5
Routines	11	7
Socializing	1	--

Teachers estimated that five minutes, on the average, would be spent on student behavior but the observers did not record that much.[5] They did record that more time was spent on routines than was estimated by the teachers. For our purposes, however, the close agreement on the amount of time spent on actual instruction is more important than the relatively small discrepancies in the other two areas.

*   *   *

Thirty seconds to the bell. The halls are clearing as students get to their classrooms. Teachers chatting outside the rooms break off their conversations and move toward the doors as the bell rings. Two or maybe three breathless stragglers burst through the door just as the bell stops ringing and slide into their customary places with varying expressions of apology or triumph or belligerence. Depending upon the "personality" or climate of each individual classroom, the students will readily or reluctantly stop talking with their friends and give their attention to the teacher.

A few minutes may then be taken up with passing out books, papers, or materials and equipment, and with sharpening pencils. Before too long, however, the class has more or less settled down and the approximately forty minutes of instructional time begins.

What happens during this crucial forty minutes? What takes place in the encounter between a teacher and students in the high school classroom? The purpose of this chapter is to paint a picture of the American high school classroom, using data from 716 teacher questionnaires and 479 interviews, 11,051 student questionnaires, observation records from 525 observed classes, and curriculum materials provided by 599 teachers. It will be subdivided into two sections. First, we will take a brief look at the observation data on all classrooms, for as we shall see, the overwhelming message of our observation data is that all classrooms are discouragingly similar. In the second section we will examine student and teacher data subject by subject, for some differences between classrooms do have their origins in the differences between subject areas.

The kinds of questions we will be addressing in this chapter include: how much variety is there in the activities and materials used in high school classrooms? What chances are there for students to make choices and decisions, to express themselves, and to be pro-active in the teaching/learning environment? Do teachers and students share similar views of what goes on in class? And what about "the basics"--are they really being neglected?

A General Picture

Desks or tables all face the same direction--usually a chalkboard. Though movable, their position is rarely altered. Whether structural arrangements determine class activities or the nature of class activities determines structural arrangements, there seems to be a fundamental relationship between the physical arrangement of the high school classroom and the activities which students experience in those classrooms.[6] In the classes we observed, the configuration of activities most often found was combination of frontal presentation by the teacher and individual student desk work.[7]

More specifically, we found the teacher instructing or explaining to the class as a whole while students listened and sometimes responded (we found that students seldom initiated interactions), followed by some time during which students would be working alone while the teacher either monitored them or worked at his/her desk. We rarely observed teachers asking open-ended questions, giving helpful feedback or suggestions for improvement, responding to students, or giving encouragement and praise.

The kinds of activities students experienced were both traditional and passive, for the most part: a lot of listening, some asking of questions, and a fair amount of work on written assignments. As we shall see, such written assignments tended to be rather low-level cognitive activities involving primarily recall skills. We rarely saw students working in small groups or with audiovisual materials, or involved in structured learning games such as simulations or role playing. We didn't often see students simply reading, either--even in language arts classes.

Classroom decisions in virtually all areas were made by the teacher, although in some classes, students were allowed to decide where they would sit.

The emotional atmosphere of the classes we observed was overwhelmingly neutral and "flat." There was little in the way of laughter, and even less anger. As Wright suggests,

> ...the generally low levels of either praising or reprimanding students and the resulting neutral atmosphere of classroom life which seems to emerge from our data may be psychologically necessary. To respond to students with a great deal of feeling, be it positive or negative, or to frequently suggest ways that students' work can be improved requires a lot of energy. Perhaps it is too much to expect one individual to constantly respond at a heightened level to large numbers[8] of students six hours a day, five days a week.

Wright also notes the similarity of our findings to those of Dunkin and Biddle, who concluded in 1974 that basic teaching practices and classroom structures have changed little over the years.[9] What we found happening in the classrooms we observed seemed fairly well suited to the development of basic skills--although we found discouragingly little real intellectual challenge existed in the low cognitive level of most classroom activity--but notably unsuited to the personal and social development of students.

As the reader may recall, we defined instruction for personal development as "instruction which builds self-confidence, creativity, the ability to think independently, and self-discipline." Instruction for social development is "instruction which helps students learn to get along with other students and with adults, prepares students for social and civic responsibility, and develops students' awareness and appreciation of our own and other cultures." We found that teachers, parents, and students all believed that the social and personal areas, as well as the intellectual and vocational areas, should be developed by schooling experiences. In this respect, the clients of schools do not seem to be getting all of what they say they want from their education.

Tables 5.2, 5.3, and 5.4 contain some of the data upon which these statements about observed classroom activity and teacher/student interaction have been based.

In Table 5.2, data from the Five-Minute Interaction (FMI) part of the observation instrument--the part that focused on interaction--reveals that teachers dominated the verbal exchanges of the classroom, primarily through instructing or explaining to the whole class. The teacher also fairly often interacted verbally with individual students. Open questions, corrective feedback, and praise were kinds of verbal interaction which were rarely observed.

Tables 5.3 and 5.4 provide different views of the same set of variables. Table 5.3 shows the dominant grouping patterns of classroom activities. Well over two-thirds (71.2%) took place in a whole-class grouping context. Even work on written assignments, although "directed" by each individual student (Table 5.4), was done as a whole-class unit; that is, everyone did it at the same time, even though each student was, technically, working "alone." Very likely they were all also doing the same thing, as well as doing it at the same time. It is strange to realize that for some people,

such uniform and synchronized classroom activity passes
for "individualization."

Table 5.2

Selected FMI Variables descriptive of student/teacher
observed classroom interaction patterns during
instruction in classes at the high school level

Variable	Mean % of FMI Frames Within Instructional Context
Verbal Interaction	57.6
Total Teacher:	44.7
-- to one student	18.9
-- to group(s)	5.9
-- to whole class	19.8
Total student:	12.9
Teacher-to-Student "Whats"	
Direct questions	5.1
Open questions	0.5
Response to student(s)	3.4
Instruct/explain	28.3
-- to one student	7.7
-- to group(s)	4.6
-- to whole class	16.0
Imperative commands	3.7
Acknowledgment/praise/encouragement	2.4
Correction with or without guidance	1.3
Monitor/observe	8.8

Table 5.4 shows who was "in charge," or directing,
the various activities. Over half of the total observed time, the teacher was seen to be in charge;
slightly over one-third of the time the students worked
independently. Only 11% of the activity was cooperative; that is, involving two or more students in
interaction with each other. This would fit in with
our overall finding that the typical configuration of
classroom activity was a mixture of frontal

202

presentation by the teacher to the whole class, and individual student desk work. Listening and writing, listening and writing; sometimes, but not often, asking a question—this is what the students we observed were doing in their classes, day after day.

Table 5.3

Selected Snapshot variables descriptive of activity observed in high school classrooms, according to type of grouping pattern being used.

	Mean % Students Involved			
	Group Type			
Activity	one student	small group	med/lge group	whole class
Preparation for assignments or instruction; clean-up	0.2	0.6	0.7	11.6
Explain, lecture, or read aloud	0.3	0.4	1.3	23.8
Demonstration	0.1	0.2	0.2	1.3
Discussion	0.0	0.2	0.3	4.7
Simulation/role play	0.0	0.1	0.0	0.1
Reading	0.2	0.2	0.5	0.9
Work on written assignments	0.7	2.3	4.3	7.9
Practice/perform (psychomotor)	1.2	4.4	3.9	6.8
Practice/peform (verbal)	0.1	0.6	0.5	3.3
Taking test or quiz	0.1	0.2	0.9	4.4
Using audiovisual equipment	0.1	0.1	0.1	2.7
Teacher disciplining student(s)	0.0	0.0	0.0	0.1
Student non-task behavior or teacher social interaction with student(s)	0.7	1.6	1.5	3.6
group type totals:	3.8	10.9	14.2	71.2

Table 5.4

Selected Snapshot variables descriptive of activity
observed in high school classrooms, according to who
was in charge of directing the activity.

| | Mean % Students Involved | | |
| | Group Type | | |
	Teacher	Cooperative	Independent
Preparation for assignments or instruction; clean-up	11.1	0.2	1.9
Explain, lecture, or read aloud	24.4	1.4	N/A
Demonstration	1.5	0.2	N/A
Discussion	5.0	0.2	N/A
Simulation/role play	0.2	0.0	N/A
Reading	0.1	0.2	1.6
Work on written assignments	1.7	1.3	12.2
Practice/perform (psychomotor)	4.3	3.8	8.3
Practice/peform (verbal)	3.2	0.6	0.6
Taking test or quiz	1.2	0.0	4.4
Using audiovisual equipment	N/A	1.2	1.7
Teacher disciplining student(s)	0.1	N/A	N/A
Student non-task behavior or teacher social interaction with student(s)	1.5	1.7	4.2
director type totals:	54.3	10.9	34.9

*　　　　*　　　　*

It will be apparent to the reader by now that one of the major strengths of this Study was its in-depth examination of classrooms. This involved not merely surveying students and their teachers; it also included the analysis of curriculum materials, an extremely sensitive and detailed observation instrument used by carefully trained observers, and teacher interviews. Classrooms were studied in depth and 525 of them were high school classrooms. Because secondary schooling in the U.S. has become departmentalized, these were single-subject classrooms, of course. Eighty-three were English classes, 71 were math, 76 were social studies, 65 were science, 27 were foreign languages, 65 were fine arts, 105 were vocational subjects, and 33 were physical education.

It is possible to merge the findings across subject areas, to get a general picture of what goes on in classrooms. But this would wash out some of the interesting--and potentially important--differences between the various subject areas. Instead we'll <u>first</u> take a look at some of our classroom findings subject by subject. <u>Then</u> we'll see if there are any generalizations that seem to hold true across all subjects.

This section is concerned primarily with curriculum questions such as the following: what learning activities, materials, and grouping patterns do teachers say they use most often? How do the students feel about these--are there other activities, materials, and ways of working that they also enjoy? Do students feel that what they do in class is interesting? difficult? Do they believe that what they are learning will be useful to them later in life? What is the most common <u>content</u> of courses in the various subject areas? Do teachers feel the materials available are appropriate for students of differing interests, abilities, and ethnic backgrounds? Are teachers satisfied with the amount of control they have over what goes on in their classrooms? What sources of influence affect teachers' classroom decision-making?

The rest of this chapter is devoted to a subject-by-subject examination of the data relevant to these questions. A summary at the end of the chapter will discuss the implications of the patterns which emerge from these findings.

English/language arts

Eighty-three English classes were sampled in the thirteen high schools.[10] On the average, the students told us that they believed that what they were learning in these classes would be "somewhat" useful to them both now and later in life. Only 16.1% said that they felt that the work was difficult, and 68.5% said they found that what they were learning was interesting. This latter percentage doesn't seem too bad--after all, it's more than two-thirds of the responding students. But it was in fact the lowest percentage of students in any of the subject areas who said that "What I am learning in this class is interesting" (see Table 5.5).

The English teachers in our sample told us that they considered it very useful for their students to work either alone or as a whole class, and these were the grouping patterns they said they used most often. Small-group work, they said, was "somewhat useful," and they claimed to use the small group mode "often," though less often than the other two.

The students, however, clearly preferred working in small groups to both working alone and working with the class as a whole. Nearly half (47%) told us they liked working in small groups very much, while only about one-fourth said they liked working "alone by myself" very much (26.8%) or with the whole class (25.7%).

We asked the students in all of our sampled classes whether they did certain activities and used certain materials in those classes; the response to this series of questions was a simple yes or no. Then we asked them to tell how much they liked each of the activities or types of materials, even if they didn't actually do those activities or use those materials in that class. To this series of questions, the students could select one of four possible responses: like very much, like somewhat, dislike somewhat, and dislike very much.

The teachers were given the same lists of activities and materials, and asked to indicate how often the students did or used them (always, often, not very often, never) and how useful the teachers considered each one to be for student learning (very useful, somewhat useful, somewhat useless, very useless).

Table 5.5

Percent of students who said that what they
were learning in the sampled class was <u>hard</u>,
and percent who said it was <u>interesting</u>.

How are or easy <u>for you</u> is what you are learning in this class?		How interesting or boring <u>for you</u> is what you are learning <u>in this class</u>?	
	% hard		% interesting
Science	27.8	Arts	86.8
Math	26.0	Phys. Ed.	85.1
Foreign Language	24.2	Voc. Ed.	83.4
English	16.1	Foreign Language	80.6
Social Studies	15.9	Math	69.3
Arts	9.3	Social Studies	69.0
Voc. Ed.	9.1	Science	68.6
Phys. Ed.	7.8	English	68.5

Since the Study staff was interested in whether
classroom activities were of a low or a high level (in
terms of Bloom's taxonomy in the cognitive domain), we
asked teachers and students another set of questions
about classroom activities. Some of these questions
concerned "low-level" activities requiring simple
recall of facts; others described much more complex
activities requiring analysis, synthesis, and/or
evaluation. Both teachers and students responded to
each activity on two four-point scales, one indicating
how often the activity was perceived to be done (teachers) or how much the activity was enjoyed (students).

In the English classes we sampled, large percentages of students reported that they actually did listen
to the teacher, take tests, write answers to questions,
do research or reports, and have class discussions. Of
these, many liked listening to the teacher and having

class discussions; but many also liked going on field trips, reading for fun or information, and having guest speakers--three activities which far fewer students indicated they ever actually did in class.

The English teachers told us that their students often listened to them, had class discussions, did research or reports, wrote answers to questions, took tests, and read for fun or information. With the exception of reading, these were the same activities the students reported doing.

Interestingly, the English teachers told us they that they never had their students make films or recordings, or go on field trips; on the average, however, the teachers agreed that such activities would be somewhat useful as learning experiences. But there was a large standard deviation on both items, suggesting a wide range of teacher opinion on the value of field trips and the making of films or recordings.

When it came to the cognitive levels questions, we found the students and teachers didn't always agree. For example, in our sampled English classes, the students told us that they often had to remember facts, dates, words, names, or rules. They said they didn't very often (1) tell in their own words what they have read, seen, or heard; (2) write their own stories, plays, or poems; or (3) tell how stories, people, and ideas are the same or different. Interestingly, the students told us that they liked "somewhat" these three activities, but "disliked somewhat" the activity that they actually did: remembering facts, dates, words, names or rules.

Teachers agreed that their students didn't often write their own stories, plays, or poems. But they said their students often did the other three kinds of activities, and they believed that all four activities were useful for student learning.

There was quite a noticeable difference between the kinds of learning materials the students told us they'd like to use and what they actually do use in English classes. The largest percentages said they do use textbooks, other books, and worksheets. What they said they'd like to use were films, filmstrips, or slides; television; newspapers or magazines; other books; tape recordings or records; and games or simulations.

English teachers told us they often used textbooks, other books, and worksheets. Although they considered films, TV, newspapers, tapes, and games to be somewhat useful, they admitted that they didn't use them very often.

"Other books" appear to be very important to English teachers, even more important than textbooks. They consider textbooks somewhat useful, but other books, they said, are very useful--and they reported using them often. Students told us that they liked using "other books." It's too bad that English Department budgets often limit the available supply of other books, forcing teachers and students to work primarily from textbooks, whether they want to or not. Some schools manage to get around this problem by requiring students to pay for some of the paperbacks they use in their English classes, but such a policy can create a different kind of problem, by embarrassing the poorer students who cannot pay for extra books.

Most students told us that they "sometimes" were able to choose their own books and learning materials in their English classes. Nearly forty percent, however, said they never could do so.

English teachers indicated to us that they were only mildly satisfied with the amount of control they had over the selection of materials for their classes. In fact, teachers generally have to make do with the books and materials which are already available. When new books are ordered, the decisions are usually made by a committee rather than left to the individual teachers.

We asked the teachers to tell us whether the content and materials in their subject were appropriate for students of differing interests, abilities, and ethnic backgrounds. On all three measures, the English teachers indicated that content and materials were, in fact, inappropriate for some students.[11]

As far as the actual content of courses was concerned, we asked each participating teacher to provide us with a package of "curriculum materials" used in the sampled class. These were to contain (1) a list of topics taught in that class, (2) a list of skills taught in that class, (3) a list of textbooks and major supplementary materials used in that class, (4) samples of tests and quizzes used and (5) samples of worksheets used in that class. In all, we received 657 such packages; 94 of them were from high school English or language arts teachers.

From the analysis of these materials,[12] we were able to learn that, as far as course content is concerned, the most common English course was a combination of grammar, language mechanics, and literature study. The second most common course seemed to be literature study only, and the third was grammar study only. These formed the core of required English courses. The remainder were special-interest language arts offerings such as speech, journalism, and creative writing. We found a strong emphasis on the basics of grammar and composition reflected in the teachers' lists of topics and skills taught in our sampled English classes. On the other hand, we found little or no fiction writing, etymology study, or media literacy being taught in these classes.

As we have seen, the English teachers in our sample were mildly satisfied with the amount of control they had over the selection of content and materials for their classes. The students didn't feel that they had much of a voice in classroom decisions about what and how they would study. Our observation data, as well, indicates that teachers were firmly in control of classroom decision-making. And, finally, when we asked the English teachers what most influenced their decisions about what they would teach,[13] they told us that their own backgrounds and students' interests and abilities had the most influence on them. Textbooks, district curriculum guides, other teachers, and commercial materials had, they felt, only moderate influence, while district consultants, state curriculum guides, parent advisory councils, state equivalency exams, and teachers' unions had little or none.

479 of the 664 high school teachers who participated in the Study of Schooling were interviewed. One of the interview questions was, "What are the most critical things you want the students in your class to learn this year?" Most of the 479 teachers interviewed provided a list of three or four things they wanted their students to learn, for a total of 1,809 separate items. These responses, when analyzed, were found to fall into one of nine categories, as shown in Table 5.6. By far the most of the learning goals listed by

Table 5.6

Teacher responses to the interview question,
"What are the most critical things you want the students
in your class to learn this year?"
Figures shown for each subject area are the
actual number of responses given in each category.

	Eng	Math	SS	Sci	FL	Arts	VocEd	PE	total	% of total
Subject mastery	178	168	146	176	82	149	260	69	1228	67.9%
Personal development	52	20	27	15	3	34	44	17	212	11.7%
Respect, value, appreciation of others	10	5	14	3	11	1	7	2	53	2.9%
Social/political awareness	14		12	5					31	1.7%
Social interaction skills	10	6	10	8		8	12	20	74	4.1%
Citizenship and responsibility	6	9	23	9		5	16		68	3.7%
Critical thinking skills	28	12	16	6		1			63	3.5%
Good study habits	10	12	9	9	2	1	4		47	2.6%
Obedience	2	3	2	5		2	15	4	33	1.8%
	310	235	259	236	98	201	358	112	1809	99.9%

teachers as "most critical for my students to learn" had to do with mastery of specific subject-based knowledge and/or skills. The student's personal development placed a distant second, and the other seven goal categories drew only a small percentage of the total responses.

There were, however, some differences between the subject areas. For example, note the emphasis on social interaction skills in Physical Education, on critical thinking skills in English, and on citizenship and responsibility in Social Studies.

It is interesting to note the similarity between these interview responses and teachers' answers to the survey question about the proper function of schooling. When asked "Which function do YOU think this school should emphasize?" by far the largest percentage selected the Intellectual function, as Table 5.7 shows. As was the case with the interview responses, the Personal Development function drew the second-largest percent of responses.

Turning to the words of the teachers themselves, we can see in the following small sample some of what the English teachers had in mind when they responded to the interview question, "What are the most critical things you want the students in your class to learn this year?"

"To increase their vocabulary and improve their spelling."
"To be able to give reports."
"To be able to use the dictionary in all capacities."
"The ability to detect half-truths and think through conflicting statements."
"To be able to follow instructions."
"Enjoy reading and improve their reading level."
"To see a relationship between history and English."
"To write effective compositions."
"Originality--not saying things in cliches."
"To THINK: begin to deal with ideas and abstractions."
"To be able to use the library effectively."

Table 5.7

"Which function do YOU think this school should emphasize?"
Percentage of each group that selected each function.
The three data sources seem to have differing views
of what is important.

	Intellectual	Personal	Vocational	Social	N
Teachers	25.6%	29.7	14.8	9.9	656
Parents	46.5	19.3	25.5	8.7	4065
Students	27.3	25.6	31.1	15.9	6670

Math

Seventy-one math classes were sampled in the
thirteen high schools. On the average, the math
teachers said that what the students were learning was
"somewhat" useful now and would be somewhat useful to
them later in life as well. Perhaps this diffidence on
the part of math teachers (why did they not say "very"
useful, as the English teachers did?) stems in part
from the fact that many of them see math as a conceptual, rather than an absolutely practical, tool.

The students sampled in math classes also told us
that what they were learning in math was somewhat
useful now. But they seemed to feel that it would be
slightly more useful to them later in life. Just over
one-fourth told us they felt that the work in their
math classes was difficult, but nearly seven out of
every ten said they thought that what they were learning was interesting (see Table 5.5).

The math teachers in our sample indicated that
working alone was the most useful grouping mode and was
the one they used most often. Interestingly, they told
us they believed that the small group mode, too, was
very useful but that the whole class mode was only
somewhat useful. They reported using the whole class
and small group modes less often. Observers, however,
saw quite a lot of whole-group instruction going on in
these math classes (see Tables 5.8, 5.9).

213

Table 5.8

Summary by subject of the more frequently
occurring FMI variables at the high school level

SUBJECT AREA

Variable	Eng.	Math	Soc.St.	Sci.	For.L.	Arts	Voc.Ed.	P.E.
Instructional Context total	73.6	79.3	75.2	77.5	83.1	75.2	74.1	78.2
Teacher talk	49.4	57.9	52.4	55.2	52.7	46.2	49.3	40.9
Student talk	15.6	16.4	14.8	16.7	23.1	14.1	15.0	10.4
Teacher working alone	14.0	10.4	13.8	10.8	7.5	9.0	14.2	8.1
T to S direct questions	5.7	7.6	5.2	7.0	8.9	3.4	5.2	2.5
T instruct/ explain	28.2	36.6	35.4	33.6	22.2	28.5	30.8	19.7
T monitor/ob- serve	11.0	7.0	8.3	7.5	6.7	8.6	10.3	26.7
Students responding	8.2	9.5	6.9	8.7	16.5	8.3	7.9	9.0
General neutral affect	78.8	84.9	77.7	82.6	83.6	80.8	78.9	82.1
Sample size (N of classes)	83	71	76	65	27	65	105	33

Table 5.9

Summary by subject of selected snapshot activities observed in 525 high school classrooms.

SUBJECT AREA

Activity	Eng.	Math	Soc.St.	Sci.	For.L.	Arts	Voc.Ed.	P.E.
Preparation or clean-up	13.8	11.5	12.6	15.6	8.2	14.2	12.9	15.4
Explain, read aloud, lecture	27.2	35.3	36.9	31.7	21.9	12.8	19.0	5.2
Demonstration	0.7	3.0	0.2	3.2	0.0	2.3	2.1	1.0
Discussion	9.7	2.2	10.2	4.7	6.0	0.9	3.5	0.8
Simulation or role playing	0.3	0.0	0.0	0.3	0.1	0.2	0.0	0.0
Reading	6.1	0.4	3.2	1.0	1.3	0.4	0.8	0.5
Work on written assignments	18.4	27.2	15.2	13.2	15.2	1.4	17.7	2.6
Practice or perform (psychomotor)	1.8	3.3	1.1	12.3	1.9	43.4	29.6	53.5
Practice or perform (verbal)	1.3	0.8	1.0	1.8	26.7	15.3	2.2	3.7
Take test or quiz	9.1	8.5	7.1	8.9	5.9	0.2	3.9	2.4
Use audio-visual equipment or materials	4.1	0.0	5.8	1.0	2.7	2.2	1.9	3.5
Teacher disciplining student(s)	0.0	0.0	0.2	0.1	0.0	0.0	0.2	0.0
Student non-task behavior or teacher social interaction with student(s)	7.2	7.6	6.2	5.7	9.9	6.3	5.8	11.0

That math teachers seem to believe quite strongly in the value of small-group work but seldom use it in their own classes is, perhaps, related to the structural arrangements found in math classrooms as well as to the traditions of math teaching. It has not been considered a subject which readily lends itself to cooperative learning experiences.

Students sampled in these math classes, however, indicated a clear preference for small group work: nearly half said they very much liked working in small groups, while only approximately one-fourth said they very much liked working either alone or with the class as a whole.

In the math classes we sampled, large percentages of students (94-96%--nearly everyone in the sample) reported that they actually did listen to the teacher, take tests or quizzes, and do problems or write answers to questions. Of these, many said they liked listening to the teacher and doing problems, but not as many said they liked taking tests! Activities which many students told us they like but which most of them didn't do in their math classes included taking field trips, having class discussions, and listening to guest speakers.

The math teachers told us that their students "always or most of the time" did problems or wrote answers to questions, "very often" listened to them while they talked or demonstrated how to do something, and "very often" took tests or quizzes. All three of these activities, the teachers felt, were very useful for student learning. They reported using class discussion fairly often, and believed this to be somewhat useful. Guest speakers, though the teachers said they would be somewhat useful, were never used; nor were field trips. Students never, according to these math teachers, did research or reports and presented them to the class. In fact, most math teachers told us they felt that such activities would be somewhat useless (some, however, disagreed; these two items had standard deviations of .92 and .96), and rather low percentages of students said they liked doing research reports and listening to student reports.

Another point on which there was much disagreement among math teachers involved the value ("usefulness") of students' building or drawing things. Most teachers felt that such activity would be somewhat useful, but the standard deviation of .95 indicates that this opinion was not shared by all. Regardless of this activity's perceived usefulness, however, teachers told us they didn't very often have students build or draw things in their math classes. Too bad--because about seven out of ten students sampled told us that they would <u>like</u> to build or draw things, but that they didn't <u>do</u> so in their math classes.

When it came to the cognitive levels questions, teachers and students in our math classes seemed to agree on which activities took place most often: the lower-level ones--remembering facts, rules, or operations and doing number problems. Doing word problems or telling how rules, operations, and problems are the same or different happened less often and "telling in their own words what they have learned" was the least frequent of these types of activities, according to both students and teachers.

Although math teachers, on the whole, considered all five of these kinds of activities to be very useful or somewhat useful, the students weren't terribly enthusiastic about any of them. They said they liked only "somewhat" having to remember facts, doing number problems, and telling how problems are the same or different. And they told us that they actually somewhat <u>disliked</u> doing word problems or telling in their own words what they had learned. That they don't do these very often, then, is probably quite acceptable to the students. However, it is also possible that if they did them more often, they'd learn to like them more. It is not always clear what may be a cause and what may be an effect.

Textbooks and worksheets are what students say they use in math classes and interestingly enough, these are also what they say they like to use. They also like to use things like slide rules, calculators, and computers, but few ever have an opportunity to actually do so. Films, TV, and teaching machines are also popular with many students but are virtually never used.

Math teachers told us they always used textbooks and often used worksheets and that these were very useful, but that they <u>never</u> used TV, tapes or records, films or filmstrips, teaching machines, or newspapers.

217

Learning kits, games or simulations, and things like slide rules, calculators, and computers, they said, were not very often used although they considered them to be somewhat useful for student learning. Computers are more commonly used now than they were in 1977 when the Study data were collected.

Most students in our sample indicated that they were never able to choose their own books, materials, and equipment in their math classes. This was more true of math than of any other subject area, as Table 5.10 shows.

Table 5.10

Student responses by subject to the question, "How often can you choose your own books, materials, and equipment in this class?"

	% Never	$\overline{X}$	N
Math	75.2	1.29	1586
Science	57.5	1.48	1307
Foreign Languages	56.6	1.47	525
Social Studies	53.1	1.53	1745
English	38.8	1.74	1791
Vocational Subjects	34.8	1.86	1722
Physical Education	32.3	1.87	764
Fine Arts	28.1	1.95	1471

Response format:
1.0 - 1.49	Never
1.5 - 2.49	Sometimes
2.5 - 3.0	Whenever I want to

On the whole, math teachers seemed to be fairly satisfied with the amount of control they had over the selection of learning materials for their classes, although a standard deviation of .83 indicates a spread of opinion on this issue, as Table 5.12 shows. As we have remarked earlier, teachers generally must make do with what is already available. This would likely be even more true of a subject such as math, in which textbooks and worksheets are by far the most often-used materials. Textbook selection committees in most school districts, after all, meet to choose new materials only about once every four or five years for any given grade level.

Like the English teachers, the math teachers in our sample indicated that the content and materials in math were sometimes inappropriate for some students of differing interests, ability levels, and ethnic backgrounds.

Seventy-seven packages of math curriculum materials were submitted by math teachers who participated in the Study of Schooling. From the analysis of these materials and of master schedules from each school, we were able to learn that all schools, regardless of size, provided a standard range of math courses, from remedial work through algebra and geometry. Several went further, offering calculus, trigonometry, and computer programming.

Furthermore, it was clear that math is still taught by the textbook. In fact, when asked to provide us with a list of the topics taught in their classes, many math teachers submitted a Xerox copy of the table of contents of the textbook they used. Math curriculum materials across the whole sample revealed nothing unusual or outstanding--math programs are comprehensive and homogeneous, far more alike than different, with a heavy emphasis on basic computation skills.

We did notice, however, that students in high-ability math classes were not receiving any instruction in what might be termed "basic math survival skills." These, often presented in fairly sophisticated ways, were only available to students in lower-track classes. Thus, it seems we are educating a generation of "bright" students who know little or nothing about balancing their checkbooks, reading bank statements, installment buying, income tax laws and how to fill out federal and state income tax forms, computing FICA and withholding taxes, insurance, borrowing money, household bills, depreciation, or comparison shopping.

Math teachers, like English teachers, reported that their own backgrounds and their judgment of students' interests and abilities were the primary sources of influence on their own decisions about what to teach. Other teachers, commercial materials, state and district curriculum guides, and state and district textbooks, they said, had a moderate influence on their curriculum decisions. District consultants, parent advisory councils, state equivalency exams, and teachers' unions had little or none.

Teachers want to teach and, at the high school level, they want to teach their subjects. As Table 5.6 shows, math teachers, like teachers of the other subjects, named learning goals that were primarily subject-based when they were asked to identify the "most critical things" they wanted their students to learn. Here, in the words of the teachers themselves, are a few examples:

"Math in relation to farm products."
"Good algebraic foundation."
"How to buy a car, insurance, a home--practical use of money."
"To be comfortable with and enjoy math."
"How to study."
"Learn to work in a competitive atmosphere."
"Ability to take criticism."
"Factoring polynomials."

Social Studies

Seventy-six social studies classes were sampled in the thirteen high schools. On the average, the social studies teachers told us they believed that what their students were learning was somewhat useful at the time, but would be very useful to them later in life. The students, however, weren't convinced that what they were learning in their social studies classes would be of more value to them later in life: they told us they thought it would only be somewhat useful then.

As in math classes, about seven out of every ten students in sampled social studies classes said that what they were learning in those classes was interesting. Only about 16% said that it was difficult (Table 5.5).

The social studies teachers in our sample indicated that they often worked with students as a whole-class group, or else had the students work alone. They considered both of these grouping modes to be quite useful. While they also considered the small-group mode to be quite useful, they said that they didn't use it very often. I find this an astonishing response from teachers of "social" studies, in a way. One would think that small group learning experiences--that is, learning to work cooperatively with others--would be particularly appropriate and important within the context of social studies classes. And yet I believe it is sadly true that students preparing to become high school social studies teachers aren't trained in the use of small group teaching techniques any more than are prospective teachers of other subjects. When they start their first job, then, they are no more likely to be comfortable with small group techniques than are other teachers. Yet I still consider it amazing to find social studies teachers reporting they use small groups less often than do teachers of every other subject! (Table 5.11).

Not only does the substance of social studies seem to lend itself well to small group work, but indeed the students themselves seem to be receptive to working in small groups. The students we sampled in social studies classes indicated a clear preference for small group work over both working alone and working with the class as a whole--46.7% told us they very much liked working with a small group; 30.2% said they very much like working with the whole class and only 25.8% said they very much liked working alone.

In the social studies classes we sampled, large per centages of students (85-95%) told us that they actually did listen to the teacher, take tests or quizzes, write answers to questions, and have class discussions. Of these, many (81-85%) said they liked listening to the teacher and having class discussions, but far fewer said they liked writing answers to questions (55%) or taking tests (52%). Activities which many social studies students told us they enjoyed but which relatively few actually did in their classes included field trips, guest speakers, and reading for fun or information.

The social studies teachers agreed with their students that the activities which the students did most often were listening to the teacher, having class discussions, (both of which, the teachers said, were very useful), writing answers to questions, and taking tests or quizzes (somewhat useful).

Table 5.11

Mean responses of teachers to the question, "How often do the students in your class work in small groups?"

X̄ Frequency

Science	3.20	——————————"high often"
Foreign Languages	2.96	
Math	2.75	
Fine Arts	2.73	
		"low often"
Vocational Subjects	2.73	
English	2.55	
Social Studies	2.48	——————————"not very often"

One might expect that a wide variety of teaching/learning experiences would be found in social studies classes, but this simply wasn't what we found. Activities were limited to the primarily passive and traditional: listening and discussing (as a whole class), and answering questions and taking tests. Although the social studies teachers in our sample agreed that guest speakers, reading for fun or information, doing research or reports, building or drawing things, acting things out, and making films or recordings were all somewhat useful for student learning, they admitted that they rarely used such activities in their classes.

As far as the cognitive levels of social studies activities are concerned, there were some discrepancies between the perceptions of teachers and students. Students reported that they often remembered facts, dates, names or places and told how people, places, and ideas are the same or different. But they said they seldom told in their own words what they had read, seen, or heard, or used what they learned to solve problems. Teachers, on the other hand, said they believed that their students often did all four of these kinds of activities.

Textbooks are what the highest percentage of students (88%) said they actually used in social studies classes, followed by worksheets and films/film-strips (76% each) and things like globes, maps, and charts (68%). Less than half (47%) reported using newspapers or magazines, although these would seem to be a natural for social studies teaching and learning, and over three-fourths of the students said they would like to use newspapers and magazines.

Many social studies students told us that they enjoyed films and filmstrips, which they did use, and would also like TV, which they didn't use. Many also said they would like to use games or simulations, but only 25% said they had used those kinds of learning materials in their classes.

Social studies teachers, like teachers of other subjects, indicated that they must rely on textbooks but that they also often made use of things like globes, maps, or charts, worksheets, films and film-strips, newspapers and magazines, and other books. As we have already seen, relatively few students said they used newspapers or "other books," so here is another point on which student and teacher perceptions differ.

The social studies teachers admitted that they rarely if ever used TV, games and simulations, or tapes and records, although they considered such materials to be somewhat useful for student learning.

Just over half of the sampled social studies students told us that they could never select their own books, materials, or equipment in social studies classes (see Table 5.10). As in the other subject areas, social studies teachers expressed mild satisfaction with the amount of control they had over the selection of content and learning materials, although a high standard deviation (.95) indicates a wide spread of opinion on this issue.

223

Like the English and math teachers, the social
studies teachers in our sample indicated that the
content and materials in social studies were sometimes
inappropriate for some students of differing interests,
ability levels, and ethnic backgrounds.

Seventy-four packages of curriculum materials were
submitted by social studies teachers who took part in
the Study. From the analysis of these materials and of
master schedules from the thirteen schools, we discovered enormous differences between schools in the range
of social studies courses offered. The extremes are
represented by Fairfield, where the social studies
curriculum consisted entirely of four one-year required
courses with no electives; and Vista, where students
were able to choose from a huge assortment of 55
quarter courses, any 16 of which would make up a
student's four-year social studies requirement. The
other eleven high schools fell somewhere between these
extremes, with the small schools usually, though not
always, having a more limited selection than the
medium-sized or large schools.

Regardless of these differences, all thirteen
schools offered--indeed, most of them required--the
"basics:" American History and Government. Ten of the
thirteen schools offered World History and nine offered
World Geography. Eight offered Sociology, seven
offered Psychology, five offered Economics, and two
offered Anthropology. Manchester and Palisades had
Black Studies and Rosemont had a course in Mexican,
Black, and Indian History. Rosemont and Northmont both
had courses in Third World Studies, in which the focus
was on Asia, India, Latin America, and Africa.

So, as we see, there were many different kinds of
courses included under the general rubric of "social
studies." But regardless of what course they were
taking, the students were all doing basically the same
things: listening to the teacher, having class discussions, writing answers to questions, taking tests, and
occasionally seeing films or filmstrips.

As far as actual course content is concerned, the
basic and required courses were nearly identical across
all thirteen schools. U.S. History begins with the
colonial era and moves through certain topics (more or
less predictably skimming very lightly over others, or
omitting them altogether), up to the 1960s. U.S.

Government includes the Constitution and the three branches of government, and often covers state and local government as well as the federal system. Yet students never visit a local courtroom to observe the judicial process, nor does the local congressperson ever come to speak to the class.

Like math and English teachers, social studies teachers reported that their own background and their judgment of the students' interests and abilities had the highest influence on their decisions about what to teach. Textbooks, district curriculum guides, commercial materials, and other teachers had a moderate influence. District consultants, state curriculum guides, parent advisory councils, state equivalency exams, and teachers' unions had little or no influence.

When the social studies teachers were interviewed and asked "What are the most critical things you want the students in your class to learn this year?" the greatest number of responses concerned subject mastery (see Table 5.6). Responses that had to do with the students' personal development or with their becoming responsible citizens placed a distant second and third. What is surprising is that responses having to do with social interaction skills and the development of mutual respect, value, appreciation and trust, when combined, accounted for only 9% of the total of 259. One really is forced to consider the possibility that "social studies" may be a misnomer for this group of courses: there isn't much about them that is truly involved with the development of social awareness and interaction skills. Perhaps we should call a history course a history course, and leave it at that.

"Map reading skills."
"Better understanding of their own and other people's behavior."
"Ability to collect and organize information-- library and research skills."
"To be informed consumers."
"To develop some sense of historical perspective."
"Awareness of how mass media affect them."
"Understand how the criminal justice system works."
"To know more about local politics and officials, be aware of local problems and how to do something about them."

225

These are just a few of the more interesting of the goal statements listed by teachers of social studies in response to the question "What are the most critical things you want the students in your class to learn this year?" This handful of examples does not reflect the overwhelming preponderance of goals related solely to subject mastery, however.

Science

Sixty-five science classes were sampled in the thirteen high schools. Science teachers, in general, felt that what their students were learning in science was "somewhat" useful immediately, and would be somewhat useful to them later in life as well. I suppose perhaps that science teachers would only say their subject was "very" useful for students if they knew that those students would be continuing on into science-related careers. At the high school level, however, science must be geared as a general introduction for all students. For most people, what they learn in their high school science classes becomes part of the general knowledge in the background of their lives--not, then, "very" useful but, more modestly, "somewhat" useful.

The students who were sampled in these 65 science classes seemed, on the whole, to feel that what they were learning would be slightly more useful to them later in life than it was right then. The difference was small, however, and does not indicate enormous faith in the future value of science knowledge.

Interestingly enough, alone of all the subject areas it was the science teachers who told us that the small group mode was very useful and that they used small groups very often in their classes. Teachers in other subject areas agreed that small group work was useful for student learning, but that they didn't use small groups as often as the science teachers did (see Table 5.11).

Working with the whole class and working individually were both somewhat useful for student learning, science teachers said, and they used them often but not as often as they said they used the small group mode.

This somewhat unexpected emphasis on small group work in high school science classes may be due to the structural arrangements of many science rooms—in particular in lab rooms, there are generally six or eight well-equipped work areas, consequently the class which uses that equipment is more than likely to be subdivided into six to eight work groups. Too, often budget limitations require that students share limited materials, such as microscopes or fetal pigs. Thus we find in high school science, perhaps more than in any other subject area except vocational education, <u>cooperation</u> as a necessary aspect of the classroom experience. And evidently this situation is quite acceptable to the students, who indicated a clear preference for the small group mode: 55.7% of the students sampled in science classes told us that they very much liked working in small groups, whereas only 20.4% and 22.5%, respectively, said they very much liked working alone or with the whole class.

In the science classes we sampled, large percentages of students (92-96%—nearly everyone) reported that they did listen to the teacher, watch the teacher demonstrate how to do something, take tests or quizzes, and write answers to questions. These activities are just what students did most of in other subject areas. But fairly large percentages of science students also reported that they do preplanned experiments or projects (74%) and have class discussions (70%). Just over half said they also do research and write reports. Most science students told us that they like watching and listening to the teacher, having class discussions, and doing planned experiments. Not so many said they like taking tests, writing answers to questions, or doing research and reports.

Activities which many science students said they like but which few said they ever actually did in their classes include going on field trips, doing their own (rather than pre-planned) experiments, and making films or recordings. Listening to guest speakers and building or drawing things were also fairly popular science activities but only 40-45% of the students said they ever did these.

The science teachers told us that doing pre-planned experiments, listening to the teacher and watching the teacher demonstrate something, taking tests, class discussions, and field trips were all very useful for student learning. Of these, they reported that they often did the first five, but were not often able to take their classes on field trips. Other activities for which these science teachers responded "not very often" or "never" included guest speakers, student reports and research, building or drawing things, making films or recordings, and doing their own experiments.

While it is true (and not just in science) that many activities are out of the question simply because there isn't enough money for the necessary supplies (e.g., making films or recordings) or, in the case of field trips, for transportation and a substitute teacher, it remains to be tested whether, given an unlimited budget, teachers would use it for these less-frequent kinds of activities. I would venture a guess, and here again, I am not speaking only of science teachers, that the money would be used for more books and more equipment or supplies of the kind already being used. Force of habit is strong; and "things as they are" in classrooms are familiar and under control--why disrupt life by trying lots of new or different kinds of learning activities?

And I hasten to add that this situation is not entirely the teachers' fault. In fact, our whole educational system seems to support a very conservative approach to classroom activities. Within a specified range considered appropriate for each subject area, classes are supposed to be more or less quiet and orderly. Insofar as they are, the school as a whole hums along, just as it is "supposed to." A guest speaker in one class wouldn't be a problem, but building or drawing things, making films or recordings, or class discussions that get more heated than usual-- these might tend to raise the decibel-level above the "appropriate" limit. And taking just one class group on a field trip can send ripples of disruption through the whole school. For reasons of money, then, as well as of what we might call tradition and sometimes because of the structural arrangements of the classrooms themselves, learning activities in most subjects remain confined to a fairly narrow range.

Teachers and students weren't too far apart in their perceptions of which cognitive levels activities happened most often in science classrooms. Five types of activities were mentioned for science: (1) remember

228

facts, names, or rules; (2) tell in their own words what they have read, seen, or heard; (3) use what they learn to solve science problems; (4) tell how facts, things, and rules are the same or different; and (5) do experiments, take things apart or create new things. Teachers felt that all five of these kinds of activities occurred often in their science classes. Basically, students agreed, although the students felt that "remembering facts, names, or rules" happened a little more often than the others and that "doing experiments, taking things apart or creating new things," didn't happen very often, though it was the one kind of activity of the five which the students seemed to enjoy the most.

What students evidently used in science classes are textbooks, lab equipment and materials, and worksheets. Many students (65%) also said they used films, filmstrips, and/or slides, and just over half told us they used things like models, charts, and pulleys. These student views tally more or less exactly with those of the science teachers, the only difference being that the teachers add "other books" to the list of materials their students use often.

Science teachers reported that they never used tapes or records or television, and seldom used learning kits, games or simulations, newspapers or magazines, and things like plants and animals. This is too bad, because a great many students (from 62-85%) told us that they would like to use such materials in science classes.

On the average, the students sampled indicated that they were never able to select their own books, materials, or equipment in science classes (see Table 5.10). The science teachers made the decisions about what materials the students would use, based on what was available. But the science teachers weren't particularly satisfied with the amount of control they themselves had over the selection of instructional materials for their classes; as Table 5.12 indicates, teachers in five other subject areas expressed more satisfaction in this regard than did the science teachers.

Like the teachers in the other academic subject areas (English, math, and social studies), the science teachers in our sample admitted that the content and

229

materials in science were not always appropriate for students of different interests, ability levels, and ethnic backgrounds. One wonders whether the science teachers themselves would act to correct this situation if they had more "control" over the selection of materials. This is posed as a rhetorical question, really; science teachers, like all teachers, work within severe budget restraints which generally make a rich variety of learning materials, appropriate to all students, an impossible dream.

Table 5.12

Teacher satisfaction with control over
selection of classroom learning materials

	$\bar{X}$	sd	N	
Vocational Subjects	3.26	.75	133	
Physical Education	3.16	.68	51	
English	3.14	.77	123	high mildly satisfied
Fine Arts	3.07	.73	57	
Math	3.02	.83	85	
Science	2.94	.78	77	
Social Studies	2.90	.95	84	low mildly satisfied
Foreign Languages	2.83	.89	29	

Sixty-eight curriculum materials packets were submitted by the science teachers who took part in A Study of Schooling. From the analysis of these materials and of master schedules at each of the thirteen schools, we were able to learn that all schools offered the "science basics"--general or Physical Science, Biology, Chemistry, and Physics. Seven of the thirteen high schools also offered a range of science electives, such as Aviation, Oceanography, Astronomy, Entomology, and Ecology.

On the whole, the actual content of the basic science courses was highly similar across schools partly, I would assume, because so many schools used the same or highly similar textbooks: one publisher, for example, dominated the science curriculums in eleven of the thirteen schools.

There were, however, a few less common topics in a handful of the science courses across the sample. "Cryogenics, biophysics, and astrophysics" were units included in the Physics course at Fairfield; "science and society, current scientific literature, and careers in science" were part of a Biology 2 course at Palisades. Oddly enough, transactional analysis was part of a Chemistry course at Rosemont. And in the Entomology course at Atwater, one unit was "insects and genetic research." It is my hypothesis that these unusual topics were inserted into science courses on the personal initiative of individual teachers who happened to be especially interested in these topics themselves, or who believed them to be important. This, of course, would need to be tested by further investigation.

Science teachers, like teachers of all the other subjects, told us that their own backgrounds and their judgment of the student' interests and abilities had "high" influence on their decisions about what to teach. Unlike teachers in English, math, social studies, the arts, and physical education, however, science teachers said that commercial materials--supplementary publications, worksheets, and workbooks--also had a high influence on their curriculum decisions. This should come as no surprise, for we have already noted that both teachers and students reported that worksheets were used very often in science classes.

Textbooks, district curriculum guides, and other teachers had "moderate" influence on science teachers' decisions about what to teach, but district consultants, state curriculum guides, parent advisory councils, state equivalency exams, and teachers' unions had little or no such influence, according to the science teachers in our sample.

Most of the learning goals mentioned by science teachers when they were interviewed ("What are the most critical things you want the students in your class to learn this year?") were involved with mastery of the subject matter (see Table 5.6). The personal development of their students drew only 6% of the responses, and the other seven categories drew even less. Like teachers of other subjects, then, science teachers are primarily concerned with whether or not their students learn the subject matter.

"Working knowledge of the metric system."
"Ability to find information either from books or other sources."
"Learn how physics and chemistry apply to photography."
"To know about the human body and how it functions."
"Awareness of environmental problems."
"Knowledge and use of scientific methods."
"Working in groups."
"Self discipline, cooperativeness, and responsibility."
"Learn to live with change."

Foreign Language

Twenty-seven foreign language classes were sampled in twelve of the high schools (no foreign languages were taught at Dennison). On the average, foreign language teachers said they believed that what their students were learning was somewhat useful now and would be somewhat useful to them later in life as well. The students tended to feel that what they were learning might be a little more useful to them later in life than it was just then.

Just under one-fourth of the students sampled in foreign language classes told us they felt that what they were learning in those classes was difficult, but a large majority--80%--said that what they were learning was interesting (Table 5.5).

The foreign language teachers indicated that they believed all three grouping modes (alone, small group, whole class) were very useful, but that they most often worked with the whole class. Small group work was the next most frequent, according to the teachers, followed by students working by themselves. The students reported a strong preference for working in small groups: 64% of them told us that they very much liked working in this way, whereas just 31% said they very much liked working with the whole class and only 20% said they very much liked working alone.

In the foreign language classes that we sampled, almost all the students told us that the activities they did included practice in speaking the language they were learning (95%), writing answers to questions (96%), listening to the teacher (97%), and taking tests (99%). Seventy-nine percent also told us they had class discussions. Two activities that many students said they would enjoy but which few said they actually ever did in their classes were taking field trips and making films or recordings. Many also said they would enjoy listening to guest speakers, but only 37% indicated that they ever had guest speakers in their classes.

Nevertheless, many of the activities that students told us they do in foreign language classes were things they said they enjoyed doing: 90% said they like to practice speaking the language they were learning, 88% said they enjoyed class discussions, and 87% told us they enjoyed listening to the teacher.

And it's lucky that they do, because according to the teachers, "listen to me" was what their students did most often. That, and practice in speaking the language were the activities which the teachers considered most useful and which were also the most frequent. Taking tests, writing answers to questions, class discussions, and acting things out were also considered very useful by the teachers, who told us that these activities were often done by the students in their classes (interestingly, only about one-third of the students indicated that they had ever acted things out in their foreign language classes).

The teachers admitted that their students didn't often go on field trips, make films or recordings, hear guest speakers, or do research and listen to each other's reports, despite the teachers' feeling that such activities would be useful learning experiences.

In foreign languages, students and teachers were asked about six kinds of activities at different cognitive levels:

233

1. Remember words, sentences, names, or places
2. Translate from one language to another
3. Read in the language being studied
4. Speak in the language being studied
5. Write in the language being studied
6. Tell how places, people, and ideas are the same or different

Students told us that they liked "somewhat" all six of these kinds of activities and that they often did the first five.

The foreign language teachers, however, distinguished between remembering, reading, and speaking on one hand (these, they felt, students did always or most of the time) and translating, writing, and making comparisons which were done by students slightly less often. Translating, the teachers indicated, was somewhat useful as a learning activity, but less so than the other five types of activities, which the teachers considered to be very useful.

The learning materials most students said they use in foreign language classes are, first and foremost, textbooks. Worksheets and tapes or records are also used by many students, but that's about it. As it happens, many students said they like using the textbooks. But just as many--or even more--say they would like to use learning materials that they seldom or never do use: films, TV, games or simulations, and newspapers or magazines. Foreign-language newspapers or magazines would seem to be a natural for these classes, but only about half of the students sampled said they had ever used them.

The foreign language teachers' views of the materials used most often in their classes were the same as those of their students: textbooks; and then tapes/records and worksheets. What the teachers said were never used were TV, teaching machines, and learning kits. Newspapers, other books, games or simulations, films or filmstrips, and things like globes, maps, clothing and art works from another culture were seldom used, although the teachers did acknowledge that such materials would be useful for student learning.

Most foreign language students indicated that they never had the chance to select their own learning materials in their foreign language classes (Table

5.10). Foreign language teachers, too, were less than completely satisfied with the amount of control they felt they had over the selection of learning materials for their classes. In fact, foreign language teachers were less satisfied with this aspect of their teaching than were teachers in all other subject areas (Table 5.12). The reason for their dissatisfaction, however, is unclear. Evidently they were not unhappy with the materials they did have, for unlike teachers of other academic subjects, the foreign language teachers said that the materials they used were generally appropriate for all students, regardless of ethnicity, interest, or ability level.[14] So it must have been what they actually said it was that bothered them: that they'd had little control over the original choice of these materials. It would be interesting to investigate all the various aspects of the relationship between teachers and the materials they use, but this would require another study.

Twenty-eight packets of curriculum materials were submitted to the Study staff by the foreign language teachers in our sample. From the analysis of these materials and from the school master schedules, we were able to learn a good deal about the foreign language curriculums at the twelve high schools which offered programs in languages other than English.[15]

Spanish seems to have been the foreign language most widely taught; of the twelve schools offering foreign languages, only one did not offer Spanish. In fact, at two (Laurel and Euclid) Spanish was the only foreign language taught. Rosemont and Palisades were at the other extreme, offering five: in addition to Spanish, students at Rosemont and Palisades also had the opportunity to study French, German, Latin, or Russian.

Rosemont, Palisades	S-F-G-L-R
Newport, Bradford	S-F-G-L
Vista, Woodlake	S-F-G
Atwater, Manchester	S-F
Fairfield	S-G
Crestview	F-G
Laurel, Euclid	S
Dennison	--

We found, however, that all foreign language courses were taught in basically the same way and that the content of a Spanish course, for instance, was much like the content of a French or a German course. This must surely be in large part due to the nature of the textbooks and supplementary materials used, for these are highly standardized across languages. First-year French, German, and Spanish texts produced by the same publisher usually have identical contents (readings, exercises, vocabulary lists, and tests); only the language and the cultural settings differ.

What the teachers themselves said they emphasized in their courses seemed to depend on whether a teacher's basic approach was literary (i.e., oriented to reading and writing) or conversational (oriented to speaking). All foreign language teachers stressed "listening, speaking, reading and writing" as the skills they teach, but when asked about the topics they teach, some emphasized grammar while others stressed conversational fluency. Both included familiarity with the other culture as an important aspect of learning a foreign language.

We have already noted that, according to both teachers and students, textbooks were the most frequently-used materials in foreign language classes, followed closely by recordings and worksheets. It doesn't come as a surprise, therefore, that the foreign language teachers told us that state and district texts and commercial materials had a high degree of influence on their decisions about what to teach. Like teachers of other subjects, the foreign language teachers also said that their own background and the students' interests and abilities had a high influence as well.

District consultants, state curriculum guides, parent advisory councils, state equivalency exams, and teachers' unions all had little or no influence on their curriculum decisions, foreign language teachers indicated. District curriculum guides and other teachers had some influence. But what the foreign language teachers relied on most on was their own training, their judgment of student needs, and the textbooks and commercial materials they taught from.

Foreign language teachers' goal statements (when asked, "What are the most critical things you want the students in your class to learn this year?") were almost exclusively subject-based (Table 5.6), although about ten percent of the goal statements were concerned with the development of mutual respect, value, and appreciation of others. For example:

"To develop more tolerance of different customs and different peoples."
"International understanding."
"Conjugate verbs."
"Listening, speaking, reading, and writing."
"Being comfortable attempting to speak another language."
"To understand and say basic conversation if they travel."

Fine Arts

Sixty-five fine arts classes were sampled in the thirteen high schools. There was a great deal of difference in the range of arts courses available at the various schools. At Laurel High, only chorus and two visual arts classes were offered while, at the other extreme, Woodlake High offered nine different music courses, nine visual art courses, and drama. The other eleven schools fell between these extremes, but all offered at least one vocal music course and at least two visual art classes.

On the average, teachers of arts subjects said they believed that what their students were learning was somewhat useful now and would be somewhat useful to them later in life also. The students sampled in arts classes were less optimistic: they felt that what they were learning was somewhat useful then but would be slightly less so later in life.

Only a relative handful of students (9%) said that what they were learning in their arts classes was difficult. (We do not know for sure, but I would make a guess that these might have been primarily instrumental music students). Most arts students, therefore, felt that what they were learning was easy; most (87%) also told us that they found it interesting and not boring (see Table 5.5).

The arts teachers in our sample indicated that they believed that working with the whole class group was somewhat useful, but that it was even more useful for students to work either by themselves or in small groups. They told us that they often use all three

237

grouping modes. I suspect, however, that within the various arts subjects there may well be some differences as far as most common grouping modes are concerned. For example, in a band or chorus class students would be less likely to work alone, while in a drawing class they would work alone most of the time. A drama teacher might be more likely to use small groups. These differences wash out when all the arts subjects are considered together, unfortunately, and this is true of student as well as teacher data.[16] Despite this limitation, however, we can see some patterns worth noting.

Just over two-thirds of the students sampled in arts classes indicated that they liked working alone, and the same percentage said that they liked working with the whole class. A much larger percentage (89%) told us that they liked working in small groups.

Strange as it may seem, the activities which most arts students said they do in class were surprisingly passive: listen to the teacher (95%), watch the teacher show how to do something (93%), and look at art works or performances, or listen to music (80%). Only about two-thirds of the students told us that they practice art skills and "make art works, sing, play instruments, dance, act, or write stories or poems," that is, actually do the arts activities themselves.

Conditioned to predominantly passive classroom activities by the whole of their schooling experience, perhaps, the students we sampled didn't seem to mind that their most common experiences in arts classes were also passive: over 80% told us that they like listening to the teacher, watching the teacher show how to do something, and looking at art works or performances. However, eighty percent or more also said they liked doing the arts themselves (practicing arts skills; making art works, singing, playing instruments, dancing, acting, or creative writing).

Many arts students indicated, however, that they would like to do various kinds of activities which relatively few of them ever did: go on field trips (89% like this, only 35% did it); look at films or filmstrips (77% liked this, only 41% did it); listen to guest speakers (74% liked this, only 48% did it); and have class discussions (73% liked to do this, only 53% did it). As far as students are concerned, then, there

238

is room in arts teaching for more use of class discussions, guest speakers, films, and field trips. All of these seem appropriate for the arts--as, indeed, for all subject areas--but, as has already been mentioned, school routines and limited budgets often make field trips next to impossible. Films, often available from school district offices, guest speakers (a teacher who is alert to arts activities in the community can often find some good ones), and class discussions should be much easier to incorporate into curriculum planning.

The arts teachers' perceptions of the activities which were most useful for student learning in the arts were the same ones that most students said they actually did in their classes: listen to the teacher, watch the teacher demonstrate something, look at art works or performances, practice art skills, and "make things, perform--" and so on. The teachers agreed that these were what their students did most often. They also agreed that the students seldom went on field trips, had the chance to hear guest speakers, saw films, or participated in class discussions, although the teachers themselves admitted that such activities would be quite useful for student learning in the arts.

The exploration of cognitive levels in arts activities consisted of seven items:

1. Remember names, rules, or ways to do things.
2. Follow directions.
3. Finish each project that is begun.
4. Tell what is seen, heard, or felt when looking at art works or performances or listening to music.
5. Use what is learned in doing other projects or performances.
6. Make projects or performances express what is felt or thought.
7. Decide what is good about one's projects or performances, what needs to be made better, and why.

Students in sampled arts classes told us they liked all of these kinds of activities somewhat, and that they did all but the fourth one quite often. Arts teachers agreed that students did the fourth type of activity less often than the other six; they also indicated that they felt it was slightly less useful for student learning than the other six. Nowhere in

239

the high school curriculum, not even in the fine arts, do students really have genuine opportunities for self-expression.

Due to the wide range of arts classes in the sample, we did not ask questions about what materials were used in these classes. We did, however, ask the students how often they could select the materials they would use in their arts classes, and as Table 5.10 shows, the mean response was "sometimes." Only 28% said they never could choose their own materials--a far different situation than that found in, for example, math classes.

We also asked the arts teachers how satisfied they were with the amount of control they had over the selection of learning materials in their classes, and their responses indicated that they were fairly satisfied with this aspect of their teaching (Table 5.12). They also told us they felt that the arts materials used were generally appropriate for all students, regardless of differences in interests, ability levels, or ethnic backgrounds.

We do know, from the analysis of curriculum materials submitted by arts teachers, that very few arts courses have textbooks or any books which are used by the whole class. Books and materials listed by teachers were generally "one of each," and often were the sources used by the teacher rather than by the students. When arts teachers refer to being fairly satisfied with the amount of control they had over the selection of materials for their classes, then, they were not usually (unlike teachers of other subjects) referring to textbooks. An exception to this, of course, might be a course in music appreciation or one in art history.

Fifty-six packets of curriculum materials were submitted by arts teachers in the sample. Topics taught in arts classes, as one would expect, varied according to the different kinds of arts. In visual arts, "topics" were usually taken to mean the different kinds of media used (i.e., silkscreen, batik, lithography, linoleum-block, etc.). In music classes, "topics" were usually the different types of music techniques used. "Performance and rehearsal discipline" was also listed as a topic in some music classes.

240

Skills listed by arts teachers ranged from the very general ("develop imagination") to the very specific ("stretch and prepare canvas"). Most skills mentioned had to do with the mastery of techniques.

Arts teachers, like teachers of other subjects, told us that they relied most heavily on their own background and on their perception of student interests and abilities in deciding what to teach. Other teachers and commercial materials, they said, had a moderate influence on their decisions, but all other possible sources of influence--including textbooks, district consultants, and state or district curriculum guides-- had little or none.

As Table 5.6 shows, most of the goals listed by arts teachers were subject-based. Some were personal self-development goals, however. The list below includes a few of each kind:

"Read music."
"Patience and persistence."
"Fun, and the satisfaction of creating something."
"Use mistakes to learn from."
"Technical skill in performing their instrument."
"To be able to appreciate and evaluate their own work."
"Knowledge, care, and use of materials."

Vocational/Career Education

One hundred and five vocational or career education classes were sampled in the thirteen high schools. The diversity of courses included under the general heading "voc ed" was even greater than that of those grouped under "fine arts." It included a variety of different courses in home arts (not only cooking and sewing, but child care, consumer education, family living, and "single survival"), industrial arts (auto mechanics, wood shop, mechanical drawing, electronics, drafting, etc.), office practices (typing, shorthand, accounting, bookkeeping, etc.) and agriculture (horticulture, livestock). At some schools, there were also certain specialized courses such as cosmetology, hospital occupations, upholstery, architecture, aviation, marketing, business law, food management, building construction, commercial photography, and print shop.

241

Finally, most of our high schools provided some kind of work-study program in certain vocational areas.

Not surprisingly, teachers of the vocational subjects told us they felt that what their students were learning was very useful now and would be very useful to them later in life as well. The students were similarly enthusiastic--they told us they felt that what they were learning was somewhat useful to them immediately, but would be even more useful to them later in their lives. Only 9% of these students felt that what they were learning in vocational classes was difficult, and 83% thought it was interesting (see Table 5.5).

The vocational education teachers as a group indicated that working alone was the most useful grouping mode and was the one they used most often in their classes. They felt that small groups and whole-class activities were somewhat useful, and said they also used these grouping modes quite often.

As far as the students were concerned, more of them said they liked working in small groups (89%) than working alone (70%) or with the class as a whole (60%). To a certain extent, as in science classes, grouping modes used in the vocational subjects are determined by the type of class, the structural arrangements of the classroom, and the availability of materials and equipment. One cannot well imagine a typing class in which there would be much in the way of small group activity, for example, while small groups would be the most frequent pattern one might expect to find in a cooking class (like science labs, most Home Economics rooms have a half dozen or so work-cluster areas) or for auto mechanics.

I find it interesting that despite the variety of courses in vocational education and what seems to be a "hands-on" emphasis in these courses, what the students reported that they actually do in vocational education classes is very much like what they do in other subject areas. Above all, the students listen to their teacher, take tests or quizzes, and write answers to questions. Just over two-thirds also indicated that they use the equipment appropriate to the class in which they were sampled. And although many students told us that they like to listen to the teacher and to use the equipment, just as many also said they like to go on

242

field trips but only 17% said they ever did so. Other activities which students in vocational education classes told us they would like to do but which far fewer said they actually do included making films or recordings, building or drawing things, and interviewing people. The activity which most students said they dislike was doing research and/or reports (65% said they disliked this). Evidently research and reports are rarely assigned in vocational education classes, however, because seven out of every ten students told us that they didn't do this activity in the class in which they were sampled.

Teachers of vocational subjects, on the average, told us that their students never made films or recordings and seldom interviewed people, went on field trips, listened to guest speakers, and did research or reports. Like their students, the vocational education teachers perceived that the most frequent classroom activities were listening to the teacher, using the equipment, taking tests, and writing answers to questions. Unlike their students, teachers also perceived that class discussions occurred quite often.

Questions designed to examine the cognitive level of most classroom activities in vocational education classes had to be stated very generally in order to be applicable to the wide variety of courses being sampled. Only three types of activities were included:

1. Remember facts, names or things, or ways of doing things.
2. Show in some way that I really understand what I am learning.
3. Use what I have learned in doing other projects or assignments.

While the teachers in our sample felt that all three were very useful and said they often used all three in their classes, students had slightly different perceptions. The students in our sampled vocational education classes seemed to feel that they did the first kind of activity more often than the second, and that they did the third kind the least often. However, they told us that they liked the third kind best and the first kind--remembering facts, names of things, or ways of doing things--least. In other words, what the students indicated they liked most was what they did

243

least often, and what they liked least was what they did most often.

Due to the wide range of vocational classes in the sample, we did not ask questions about what materials were used in these classes. We did, however, ask the students how often they could select the materials and equipment they would use in their vocational education courses, and as Table 5.10 shows, the mean response was "sometimes." About 35% said they never could select their own materials or equipment. It is likely that most of these students were in certain kinds of courses, such as typing, in which there is not a great deal to choose from in the way of materials.

We also asked the vocational education teachers how satisfied they were with the amount of control they had over the selection of learning materials for their classes, and we discovered that the vocational education teachers expressed a higher level of satisfaction in this area than did the teachers of any other subject (see Table 5.12). The vocational education teachers also told us that the materials used in their classes were generally appropriate for all students, regardless of differences in interest, ability level, or ethnicity.

From the analysis of curriculum materials submitted by vocational education teachers, we also learned that commercially-produced materials and learning kits were used a great deal in vocational courses, particularly in office practices and home economics classes. Just three publishers seemed to dominate the vocational education materials market --a type of monopoly not found to such an extent in most other subject areas.

It is, therefore, hardly surprising that when teachers of vocational subjects were asked what most influenced their decisions about what to teach, they said that their students' interests and abilities, their own backgrounds, and commercial materials all had a high influence on those decisions. Other teachers, textbooks, and state and district curriculum guides, they told us, had a moderate influence while district consultants, parent advisory councils, state equivalency exams, and teachers' unions had little or none.

One hundred and nineteen packages of curriculum materials were submitted by high school teachers of vocational subjects who participated in the Study. They revealed a great similarity of topics taught in some courses, especially those which were most dependent upon commercially prepared materials. Allowing of course for differences in teacher style and personality, a shorthand class in one school is likely to be virtually identical to a shorthand course in a school in another part of the country, largely because the students are very likely to be using precisely the same workbook. This is also often true in home economics and many of the industrial arts/shop classes.

Skills listed by vocational education teachers tended to be primarily technical and manual in nature: proper use of tools, materials, and techniques are the skills they say they teach. On the other hand, when teachers of vocational subjects were asked "What are the most critical things you want the students in your class to learn this year?" many mentioned personal self-development and social interaction skills (see Table 5.6). The few examples listed below include all three types:

"Use of hand and power tools."
"Appreciation for craftsmanship."
"Learn the language of the industry."
"Facts about junk food."
"Type 45-55 words per minute."
"Follow directions and listen."
"Learn how to do a tune-up on a car."
"Be aware of different opportunities for careers in this field."
"Be able to look at both sides of an issue."
"Making choices."
"Sense of responsibility."
"Basic skills of sewing."

Physical Education

Thirty-three P.E. classes were sampled in the thirteen high schools. On the average, the P.E. teachers said they believed that what their students were learning was somewhat useful then and would be somewhat useful to them later in their lives as well. The students themselves seemed to share this view.

P.E. students strongly preferred to work in small groups, and were content to work with the class as a whole, but somewhat disliked working individually. We did not ask the P.E. teachers which grouping mode they used most often, but our observation data showed that most of the P.E. classes that were observed were using the large group mode.

What nearly all sampled P.E. students said they do in class is listen to the teacher (94%). Approximately seven out of every ten P.E. students sampled told us that they also practice P.E. skills and play team games. Sixty percent said they did exercises. Less than half (48%) told us that they played an individual sport such as tennis, archery, track, or gymnastics. Most, however--70% or more--said they <u>liked</u> to do all these things.

The P.E. teachers said that listening to the teacher, playing both individual sports and team games, and practicing skills were all very useful, and that their students did all four often. However, there was a very high standard deviation for the frequency of team games (1.04), which indicates a wide range of teacher responses--evidently in some of the sampled classes teachers said their students <u>never</u> played team games, while in other classes the students <u>always</u> played team games. The mean response across all P.E. classes, however, was that students "often" played team games. This seems to be a good example of extreme responses cancelling each other out. It also reveals the potential problem with measures of central tendency--namely, the chance that they will mask important differences. The same pattern was found for individual sports (sd = .92); that is, some teachers said their students <u>never</u> did these kinds of activities in class, while others said they always did them. All of this makes sense when we note the nature of the P.E. classes that were sampled: very few were general in nature. Most P.E. courses offered in the thirteen high schools which participated in the Study were limited to one sport (e.g., swimming) or to a cluster of sports (e.g., track; self-defense; kickball/volleyball/basketball).

Since P.E. classes are primarily concerned with student development in the psychomotor domain, we asked no questions about the cognitive level of P.E. activities. And since so many different kinds of P.E. classes were sampled, as in fine arts and vocational education, we did not ask questions about classroom materials.

246

We did learn, however, that most students were sometimes able to select the materials and/or equipment they would use in their P.E. classes. Only 32.3% said they never could do so (see Table 5.10). P.E. teachers, for the most part, retained ultimate control over equipment and materials and were fairly satisfied with this aspect of their jobs (Table 5.12). The P.E. teachers in our sample indicated they believed that the content of their classes was generally appropriate for all students regardless of differences in interest, ability levels, and ethnic backgrounds.

Forty-one packages of curriculum materials were submitted by P.E. teachers who took part in the Study. From the analysis of these materials, we learned that "topics" taught in P.E. were generally considered to be the particular sport or sports which were the focus of each course. Sportsmanship, teamwork, and a positive mental attitude were also listed as topics by a few P.E. teachers. The skills which P.E. teachers said they taught in their classes were almost exclusively psychomotor performance skills. And when asked, "What are the most critical things you want the students in your class to learn this year?" P.E. teachers tended to give answers like these:

"How to follow instructions."
"Know the rules of the game."
"Sportsmanship and manners."
"Physical conditioning."
"Working together as a team."
"Acquire lifetime sports skills."
"Self-discipline of staying with an activity until it is mastered."
"How to care for equipment."

In deciding what to teach, P.E. teachers--like the teachers in all other subject areas--relied on their own background and on their own judgments of students' interests and abilities. Other teachers and district curriculum guides, they indicated, had some influence on their curriculum decisions, but other possible sources of influence had little or no impact on their decisions about what to teach.

Summary: A Pervasive Sameness

The cumulative impact of these classroom data is remarkable. Students, teachers, and observers agreed that classroom activities in all subjects are primarily passive and traditional; that teachers talk and students listen and write;[17] and that learning materials used in most subjects are discouragingly limited in variety. Observers recorded little or no open-ended questions, praise, or helpful feedback by teachers. Students noted a preponderance of memorization activities and an almost total absence of systematic opportunities for self-expression or decision-making.

In general, there was little in the way of small-group activity, although students indicated a strong preference for working this way and teachers agreed that small-group activities are useful for student learning. Only 10.9% of the total observed classroom time spent on instruction was spent in small-group work, and from our student and teacher survey data in the various subjects we can assume that most of this 10.9% was observed in science and vocational education classes.

The overwhelming majority of time which students spend in high school classrooms they spend either listening to and interacting with the teacher as a whole-class group, or working individually at their desks. Listen to the teacher, write answers to questions (on worksheets, or at the end of the chapter in the textbook) and taking tests or quizzes are the dominant classroom activities according to both teachers and students in almost every subject area. Table 5.13 provides a summary of the activities which teachers in every subject told us happen "often."

The teachers said that class discussions also happen often, but careful examination of our observation data suggests that what passes for "discussion" is usually a matter of fairly simple oral review of the subject matter which has just been covered. Teachers rarely ask open-ended questions, or provide opportunities for students to express themselves and to articulate their thoughts, feelings, or opinions. Students rarely initiate verbal interaction with the teacher. For the most part, they confine themselves to reacting. In short, the elements necessary for true discussion were missing from most high school classrooms that we observed.

Table 5.13

Activities used often, as reported by teachers
in the various subject areas

English	$\bar{X}$	sd	Social Studies	$\bar{X}$	sd
Listen to teacher	3.38	.58	Listen to teacher	3.30	.49
Class discussions	3.09	.69	Class discussions	3.07	.73
Write answers	2.88	.76	Take tests	2.86	.54
Take tests	2.73	.64	Write answers	2.62	.71
Write reports	2.73	.84			
Read	2.63	.70	Science		
			Listen to teacher	3.15	.54
Math			Watch teacher	3.08	.67
			Do experiments	2.95	.79
Write answers	3.55	.58	Take tests	2.87	.53
Listen to teacher	3.42	.61	Write answers	2.85	.63
Take tests	3.02	.56	Class discussions	2.74	.60
Class discussions	2.52	.80			
Foreign Languages			Vocational Subjects		
Listen to teacher	3.54	.58	Listen to teacher	3.38	.57
Practice speaking	3.48	.80	Use equipment	3.25	.89
Take tests	3.11	.51	Class discussions	2.88	.73
Write answers	3.11	.58	Take tests	2.71	.58
Class discussions	2.74	.76	Write answers	2.66	.79
Act things out	2.68	.75	Build or draw	2.64	1.19
Fine Arts			Physical Education		
Practice skills	3.55	.66	Listen to teacher	3.37	.56
Make things, etc.	3.42	.96	Practice skills	3.08	.76
Listen to teacher	3.23	.63	Indiv. sports	3.04	.92
Watch teacher	3.20	.70	Play team games	3.00	1.04
Look at art, etc.	2.98	.73	Do exercises	2.73	.83

One of the findings that bothers me the most is the degree to which the students in our sample seemed quite contented with the passive nature of their classroom experiences. Of course, it could be that they are so thoroughly conditioned by the time they reach high school that they really don't expect anything else. We have evidence that they would respond quite positively to a wider variety of classroom activities, however--in every subject, many students told us that they'd like to do a number of activities which relatively few ever did have a chance to do. One of these would be to listen to guest speakers. This is an activity which, admittedly, requires some advance planning on the part of the teacher, but it is one that could greatly enrich the curriculum of every subject area; and it doesn't cost anything.

The interesting thing about the findings on the cognitive level of classroom activities is the discrepancy between the views of teachers and students. On the average, teachers in all subjects seemed to feel that activities at all cognitive levels took place often in their classes. The students, however, indicated that activities requiring simple recall ("remember facts, names, ways of doing things," etc.) happened more often than did activities requiring more complex cognitive processes. The students also told us that they liked "remembering things, etc." less than some of the other kinds of activities.

I have long believed that people learn something most thoroughly if they have to explain it in their own words to someone else. I know that I have learned best those topics which I have had to teach to others, and students of mine who have tutored other students have achieved greater mastery than students who only sat in class, listened, and fed back information on a written test. The teaching-learning process could be far more successful than it presently is, I suspect, if teachers systematically required students to explain what they were learning in their own words rather than merely to recall what the book or the teacher said. And yet this was one of the kinds of activities that happened least of all, according to the students in most of the classrooms we sampled.

The materials most used by students in the five academic subject areas[18] were rather limited. Textbooks and worksheets were the old reliable standbys in every subject area, though there is some additional variety in materials reported used by social studies and science teachers, as Table 5.14 shows.

Many students in our sample indicated that they would like to use other kinds of materials if they could: films and filmstrips, tapes and recordings, games and simulations, learning kits, television, and newspapers, for example. The teachers admitted that such materials would be useful for student learning but in general, they said, they used only a few of them often. Why? Didn't they _have_ such materials? Had inflation already so decimated school budgets by 1977 that the use of appropriate magazines, for instance, was out of the question? Budget limitations are chronic in areas such as the arts, science, and vocational subjects, in which materials and supplies are consumed in great quantities. And in recent years every subject area has been hit by budget-cutting. This may be one reason why materials in most subject areas are so limited in variety. If so, what a shame: we are shortchanging our children and impoverishing their learning experience.

Or could it be that teachers, in general, haven't learned _how_ to use a wide variety of materials in their pre-service or in-service programs? How many college "Methods of Teaching? courses include a unit on the use of games and simulations? Where are the in-service workshops on using the newspaper as a teaching tool?

Perhaps another reason for the limited variety of learning materials used in many subject areas is the often-cumbersome process involved in getting equipment, films, tapes and so forth from the media center. And as for television--in many schools I have visited over the years, the TV stands in a corner. Often it is broken and has been broken for months.

But I believe that tradition and force of habit are the real culprits, when all is said and done. Textbooks and worksheets fit right in with the passive student behavior which is considered appropriate in most subjects. And we should bear in mind that some teachers must deal with up to 40 students in each class--and not all of them are cooperative or interested in learning. Simply keeping on top of the situation is as much as many teachers can manage in such scandalously overcrowded conditions.

Another finding about classroom materials which should be noted is the tendency of English, math, social studies, and science teachers to acknowledge

251

that the materials available for use with their classes are not always appropriate for all students. Frequently, teachers in schools which served large numbers of Hispanic or black students reported that materials and content were appropriate for only about 50% of the students in their classes. This was more true of schools serving Hispanic students. Conversely, teachers in schools which served predominantly white students reported that materials and content were appropriate for almost all students in their classes when the criteria of ability and ethnicity were applied but not when the criterion of interest was applied. This would seem to lend credence to the argument which states that not enough attention is yet given to the development of materials and content for minority students.[19] I might add that although many publishers have made considerable improvement in this area, part of the problem could be that school districts weren't in 1977 yet purchasing the new books in quantities sufficient to make a difference for teachers and students.

Data on content reported in this chapter suggest that "the basics" were alive and well in the high schools we studied in 1977. Curriculum materials submitted by teachers revealed that in English, the emphasis was on grammar and composition, and in math, it was on mastery of the four basic computation processes. In social studies, U.S. history and government, and often state history and government as well, were required of all students. We found, too, that the goals stated most often by teachers had to do with basic mastery of subject matter. And we know that when teachers were asked what they considered to be the most important function of schooling, the largest percentage said that the intellectual function (instruction in basic skills in mathematics, reading, and written and verbal communication; and in critical thinking and problem-solving abilities) was the most important. There is little evidence in our data to support the conservative argument that American high schools have strayed from their central mission of schooling students in the basics of reading, writing, computation and citizenship. If the students don't seem to be learning as they "used to," that is another question, one to which there is surely no quick and simple answer.

252

Last but definitely not least, the data we have examined in this chapter clearly shows that the teachers we sampled dominated their classrooms. They dominated classroom interaction: teachers talk, students listen; students write, teachers monitor. They, and not the students, selected the content to be taught and the materials and activities which would be used. In making these decisions, the teachers told us that they relied most heavily on their own background and training, and on their own judgments of the students' interests and abilities.

Table 5.14

Materials used often, as reported
by teachers of academic subjects

Math	$\bar{X}$	sd
Textbooks	3.54	.84
Worksheets	2.75	.74
English		
Textbooks	2.96	.96
Other books	2.84	.77
Worksheets	2.63	.94
Foreign Languages		
Textbooks	3.59	.64
Recordings	2.81	.98
Worksheets	2.67	.73
Social Studies		
Textbooks	3.19	.92
Maps, etc.	2.99	.73
Worksheets	2.73	.81
Filmstrips	2.69	.65
Newspapers	2.66	.81
Other books	2.51	.81
Science		
Lab equip.	3.00	.77
Textbooks	2.97	.87
Models, etc.	2.90	.65
Worksheets	2.82	.67
Filmstrips	2.61	.69
Other books	2.52	.70

The data presented in Table 5.15 confirms the views of the teachers in our sample that they were very much in control of all aspects of planning for and teaching their classes:

Table 5.15

Teacher responses to the question,
"How much control do you feel you have over decisions about each of the following areas of your planning and teaching?"

Response options: 4.5 - 5.0 "Complete"
3.5 - 4.4 "A lot"
2.5 - 3.4 "Some"
1.5 - 2.4 "Little"
0.0 - 1.4 "None"

	X	% who said "complete"	narrative explanation
Grouping students for instruction	3.61	34.8%	a lot
Scheduling use of time	3.63	30.1%	a lot
Selecting materials	3.86	32.9%	a lot
Use of classroom space	3.98	46.2%	a lot
Selecting content, topics, and skills to be taught	4.29	49.2%	a lot
Setting goals, objectives	4.32	46.2%	a lot
Selecting activities	4.47	59.6%	complete
Evaluating students	4.54	63.2%	complete
Selecting teaching techniques	4.56	65.3%	complete

In addition to looking at teachers' responses for each element of their planning and teaching, we also averaged each teacher's responses across all the elements to generate a teacher control scale. Analysis of these scale scores by Joyce Wright revealed statistically significant differences between the means for the different subjects as well as for the different schools.[20]

Briefly, the data in Table 5.17 show that teachers of all the subject areas said, on the average, that they felt they had "a lot" of control in their classroom. However, teachers of the more academic subjects had lower scale scores, indicating slightly less perceived control. The difference between these mean scale scores was significant (.001), even though they do not look very large as shown in the table.

The data in Table 5.18 reveal that the teachers at Dennison High felt they had <u>complete</u> control, and that the teachers at the other twelve schools, as a group, felt they had "a lot" of control over their in-class curriculum decisions. However, teachers at Newport, Laurel, Fairfield, and Manchester--all "less satisfying" schools on the teacher satisfaction index[21]--had slightly lower mean scale scores. Again, though the actual differences in these school means seem small, they were found to be statistically significant (.001).

The observation booklets included a daily summary which, among other things, asked observers to rate the locus of classroom decision-making, based on a variety of factors. As Table 5.16 shows, the only element over which teachers did not dominate was the issue of where students would sit. In other words, in about half of the observed instances, the students were permitted to select their own seat in the classroom.

Again, it is possible to average these responses to obtain an overall scale score which can then be examined by subject and by school.

Table 5.19 shows that observers recorded higher percentages of control being exercised by teachers of the more academic subjects. This is interesting, for it does not tally with the <u>teachers</u>' perceptions: as we have seen, teachers in the more academic subjects felt they had slightly <u>less</u> control over classroom decisions than did the teachers of the arts and physical education (Table 5.17).

Table 5.16

Observation data: daily summary shows
teachers in control of most
classroom situations

	% controlled by teachers
Seats	49.4%
Grouping	100.0
Content	95.2
Materials	87.4
Space	83.5
Time	93.0
Activities	95.0

TEACHER VIEWS OF THEIR OWN CONTROL
OVER CURRICULUM DECISIONS IN THE CLASSROOM

Table 5.17

Rank order of teacher control
scale scores, by subject

	$\bar{X}$	sd	N
Arts	4.35	.55	57
Physical Educ.	4.31	.59	52
Foreign Lang.	4.21	.58	30
Vocational Ed.	4.20	.65	133
English	4.16	.52	121
Social Studies	4.11	.67	86
Science	3.97	.71	77
Math	3.92	.76	85

Table 5.18

Rank order of school means
for teacher control scores

	$\bar{X}$	sd	N
Dennison	4.50	.36	10
Woodlake	4.40	.45	52
Atwater	4.35	.51	24
Euclid	4.31	.53	23
Palisades	4.27	.67	59
Bradford	4.20	.59	47
Rosemont	4.16	.65	111
Vista	4.12	.50	84
Crestview	4.11	.52	44
Newport	4.10	.77	76
Laurel	4.06	.72	17
Fairfield	4.05	.65	42
Manchester	3.72	.79	63

OBSERVER VIEWS OF TEACHER
DECISION-MAKING IN THE CLASSROOM

Table 5.19

Percent of classroom decisions observed
made by teachers, by subject

Foreign Language	89.4%
English	89.0
Science	89.0
Social Studies	88.3
Math	87.4
Physical Education	86.2
Vocational Education	79.0
Arts	77.4

Table 5.20

Overall percent of observed teacher decision-making, rank order of schools

Woodlake	95.0%
Manchester	90.8
Vista	87.7
Bradford	87.5
Rosemont	85.9
Fairfield	85.3
Atwater	85.1
Laurel	82.8
Crestview	82.5
Newport	79.7
Euclid	77.9
Palisades	77.7
Dennison	74.5

Likewise, the amount of teacher control over classroom decisions recorded by observers at each school, shown in Table 5.20, bears little resemblance to the views of teachers themselves as shown in Table 5.18. While the teachers at Manchester High, for example, had the lowest mean scale score on perceived control of decisions, observers found the Manchester teachers to be in control of their classroom decisions almost entirely. Only the Woodlake teachers were observed to have a higher percentage of decision-making power. We must remind ourselves, however, that at all of our schools, teachers agreed that they had a lot of control, and that is also basically what we see in the observer data shown in Table 5.20.

In conclusion, decision-making in the high school classroom seems to be pretty solidly in the hands of the teachers. When students were observed making decisions, the elements they had some control over were usually seating, use of space, or materials. Decisions about grouping, content, use of time, and learning activities appear to have been made predominantly by teachers.

The almost total absence of any opportunities for students to make some meaningful decisions about their classroom learning experiences means that we keep our young people in a dependent and subordinate position until they are seventeen or eighteen. There are those who would defend this aspect of the school's role but as far as I am concerned it is indefensible. It would be far healthier for our society, I believe, if students were expected to accept more responsibility for participating in their own education, and teachers should be trained and encouraged to include more student decision-making within the curriculum of every subject area. This is one of several recommendations to emerge from the data covered in this chapter. It, and others, will be discussed further in chapter 7.

CHAPTER V, NOTES AND REFERENCES

1. Lewis Mumford, _Technics and Civilization_ (NY: Harcourt, Brace, and World, 1934).

2. In the thirteen high schools, 525 classes were observed for three class periods each within a two-week period. For details, see P. Giesen and K.A. Sirotnik, _The Methodology of Classroom Observation in a Study of Schooling,_ (Technical Report No. 5, 1979).

3. FMI = Five Minute Interaction, a section of the observation instrument in which the observer records classroom activity at regular intervals, coded according to whether the activity is taking place in an instructional, behavior, routines, or socializing context.

4. Do not add up to 100% because teachers were asked to account only for class time spent in these three categories.

5. Data have been converted into minutes based on a 55-minute class period.

6. The argument about whether form follows function or vice versa is not a new one, but its application to the field of education is relatively new. See, for example, _Tasks and Social Relationships in Classrooms_ by S.T. Bossert (New York: Cambridge University Press, 1979).

7. Data presented in this section come primarily from K.A. Sirotnik, _What You See is What You Get: A Summary of Observations in Over 1000 Elementary and Secondary Classrooms._ (Technical Report No. 29, 1981).

8. Joyce Wright, _Teaching and Learning._ (Technical Report No. 18, 1980), p. 56.

9. _The Study of Teaching_ by M.J. Dunkin and B.J. Biddle (New York: Holt, Rinehart, and Winston, 1974).

10. "Sampled" means a class was observed, its teachers interviewed, its students and teacher were questionnaired, and the teacher was asked to submit a package of curriculum materials used in that class. 525 high school classes in the thirteen schools were sampled in this way.

11. Due to time, personnel, and money constraints, content analysis of textbooks was one of a number of analyses that could not be tackled by the Study staff.

12. B.J. Benham, An Analysis of Curriculum Materials Submitted by Teachers Who Took Part in A Study of Schooling (Unpublished Technical Report, 1978).

13. M. Frances Klein, Teacher Perceived Sources of Influence on What is Taught in Subject Areas. (Technical Report No. 15, 1980).

14. Of course, students who take foreign languages tend to be an elite group, by the very nature of foreign languages as a college-prep elective. They are less likely, perhaps, to have a wide range of ability levels, interests, or even ethnic backgrounds.

15. It should be remembered that Newport and Rosemont also had sizeable--and necessary--ESL programs. These classes were excluded from our sample, however.

16. A separate book about the Study of Schooling findings in the arts area is being prepared by Joyce Wright. The interested reader will be able to find a much more detailed analysis of these data in that book, since it will differentiate between the various arts subjects in a way that is not possible in this high school volume.

17. 16,409 high school seniors who formed the baseline sample group for the National Longitudinal Study estimated that they had spent 83% of their class time in listening to the teacher. National Longitudinal Study of the Class of 1972: A Capsule Description/Base-Year Survey. USOC/NCES and the U.S. Department of Health, Education and Welfare (U.S. Gov't Printing Office, 1974), p. 7.

18. We did not ask about materials in arts, vocational education, or PE classes.

19. Kenneth Tye, Teacher Perceptions of the Appropriateness of Content and Materials. (Unpublished Technical Report, 1979).

20. Joyce Wright, Teaching and Learning. (Technical Report No. 18, 1980).

21. See chapter 3.

261

CHAPTER VI

IN THE CLASSROOM: ASPECTS OF INTERACTION

In chapter 5, we looked at what goes on in the high school classroom--how time is spent, what students and teachers were observed doing, and the activities and materials that were being used. We compared the perceptions of students, teachers, and observers, and we took a look at each subject area to see how it differed from the other subject areas in regard to activities, materials, and grouping patterns used.

In chapter 6, we will look at the high school classroom from another angle. Our focus now will be on patterns of classroom interaction. Class "climate"--that elusive quality that makes each class "feel" different from all others--will be examined in considerable detail. The relationship of class climate (as perceived by students) to teaching practices, to teachers' educational beliefs, and to overall student satisfaction will be investigated. It may be that we will be able to learn something about a constellation of interrelated factors which seem to produce a "happy" or an "unhappy" classroom.

In chapter 5, we saw that there was little individualization in high school classes. For the most part, instruction was to the whole group, with students listening to the teacher and doing written work at their desks. In chapter 6, we will explore the general absence of individualization in more detail. We'll also look at the evaluation methods used by high school teachers, and how the students feel about them.

A Study of Schooling found clear evidence that students in high and low-track classes had very different schooling experiences. These findings will be discussed, and an alternative to tracking will be proposed.

Exploring classroom climate

During 1974-75, when instruments for A Study of Schooling were being developed, the decision was made to include a comprehensive "class climate" measure in the secondary student questionnaire.[1] After field-testing and intensive statistical analysis, a final form of this measure was determined which contained 100 items and 18 scale dimensions. These 18 dimensions of "climate" are listed below, along with the number of items in each:[2]

Teacher Concern (8)	Peer Esteem (7)
Teacher Punitiveness (6)	Student Decision-Making (8)
Teacher Authoritarianism (8)	Class Dissonance (3)
Teacher Favoritism (3)	Student Competitiveness (4)
Teacher Enthusiasm (3)	Student Cliqueness (3)
	Student Satisfaction (4)
Teacher Clarity (4)	Student Compliance (4)
Feedback (4)	Student Apathy (4)
Task Difficulty (4)	
Organization (11)	Class Physical Appearance (2)

The 18 clusters of items, or scales, are approximately evenly divided between dimensions having to do with teacher behavior and dimensions having to do with student behavior. Only one, Classroom Physical Appearance, fits neither category.

Among the nine dimensions which focus on student perceptions of teacher behavior, five have to do with generalized teacher attitudes, while four are more closely related to clusters of teacher practices apart from affective considerations. Teacher concern, punitiveness, authoritarianism, favoritism and enthusiasm all fall into the former category while teacher clarity, feedback, task difficulty, and organization belong in the latter group.

Each of the eight dimensions which focuses on student perceptions of their own behavior and that of their peers seems to measure a unique aspect of class climate. Unlike the nine teacher-focused dimensions, the student-focused dimensions do not seem to cluster into subcategories which are conceptually logical. We shall, therefore, consider them individually.

Although much is lost when classroom data are aggregated across schools or across subjects, nevertheless some interesting differences in climate by school and by subject do emerge in our findings. An analysis by Gerald Engstrom established that a number of intriguing relationships may exist between the class climate dimensions and various student, teacher, and observer variables. Finally, I have done some analyses of my own to see if it may be possible to develop a picture of "good teaching" from the student's viewpoint, by exploring variables that correlate highly with the Student Satisfaction subscale of the climate instrument. We will be examining all of these patterns in the next several pages.

By school

When it comes to atmosphere, each high school class is a world in itself, different from every other in the school and even changing within itself from day to day. Some classes are happier places than others; some are more productive in terms of time spent on actual teaching and learning. We found evidence that happiness and productivity are related. Because, as we saw in chapter 5, the teacher is such a dominant force in the classroom, each teacher's personality, educational philosophy, pedagogical skill and daily state of mind combine to affect the kind of environment in which each of his or her classes takes place. Every high school has happy teachers who are satisfied with their work and enjoy young people. Every school also seems to have some unhappy teachers, who regard teaching as a constant battle and students as the enemy.

The students, of course, contribute their share as well. What kinds of people they are, how they relate to each other and to the teacher, and their daily state of mind (both individually and collectively) add to the positive or negative atmosphere. No two class groups are exactly alike, even if they have the same teacher.

Because every school contains a range of personalities and, in effect, a wide assortment of "class climates," one would not expect to find major differences between schools in this area. In other words, within-school differences between classes would be expected to be much greater than between-school differences on class climate measures. Aggregating climate

265

scale scores school by school, then, would be likely to wash out the extremes and leave all schools looking rather similar.

Up to a point, that is what we found. To take one of the 18 climate scales--Teacher Authoritarianism--as an example: when class scores for each school were aggregated and school means were calculated, all school scores fell within the range that indicated that students "mildly disagreed" that their teachers were authoritarian in their behavior.

However, when the school means for Teacher Authoritarianism are rank-ordered from highest to lowest, one can see that Laurel High School had the highest$_3$ mean score, and Woodlake High School had the lowest. In other words, students sampled in classes at Laurel were more likely than students sampled at Woodlake to perceive their teachers as authoritarian.

The interesting thing about this finding is that the pattern repeats itself again and again in the class climate findings: Laurel had the highest mean for Teacher Punitiveness, Woodlake had the lowest. Laurel had the highest mean for Class Dissonance, Woodlake had the lowest. Laurel had the highest mean for Student Apathy, Woodlake had the lowest.

Conversely, Laurel had the lowest mean for Teacher Concern, and Woodlake had the highest. Laurel had the lowest mean for Teacher Enthusiasm, Woodlake had the highest.

Against all expectations, aggregations of class climate data school by school seem to suggest that Laurel High was a more negative place and Woodlake High was a more positive place. This was a noticeable pattern, and it fits with what we learned about Laurel and Woodlake in chapters 2, 3, and 4. We saw, for example, in chapter 2, that teacher satisfaction was low at Laurel and high at Woodlake for a variety of reasons. Similarly, students seemed more satisfied at Woodlake and less so at Laurel. I am forced to acknowledge that Woodlake seemed to have a greater number of "happy" classrooms than Laurel. This, combined with higher teacher and student satisfaction on other measures, suggests that Woodlake's overall school atmosphere was probably more positive than Laurel's.

In effect, schools are <u>not</u> the same. They <u>feel</u> different, and those who spend their days in them act (and react) accordingly. It would be fascinating to arrange some student and teacher exchanges between Laurel and Woodlake, and to document these with a program of before, during, and after interviews. I am certain that the participants would be able to talk very perceptively about the differences they experienced in the two schools.

By subject

When the 525 sampled high school classes are grouped by subject area rather than by school, another sort of pattern emerges. Although once again the differences are not extremely dramatic, still we find that the foreign language classes show up rather well, relative to the other subjects, and the science classes show up rather less well.

Foreign language classes had the highest mean score for Teacher Concern; science classes had the lowest. Foreign language had the highest mean for Teacher Enthusiasm, and science had the lowest. Foreign language had the highest mean for Student Compliance (cooperation), science had the lowest. Conversely, foreign language classes had the <u>lowest</u> mean scores for Student Apathy, Teacher Punitiveness, and Teacher Authoritarianism while science classes had the highest means on all three of these scales. In addition, science classes had the lowest means for Teacher Clarity, Organization, and Student Satisfaction, and the highest mean score for Task Difficulty. Foreign language classes had the highest means for Feedback and Peer Esteem, and the lowest mean score for Classroom Dissonance.

All in all, it seems that the foreign language classes in our sample were relatively happy places, and that the science classes in our sample were less so. Students in foreign language classes seemed to view their teachers as slightly more enthusiastic and concerned, less punitive and authoritarian, and more likely to give helpful feedback than teachers of other subjects. Students in foreign language classes also seemed to see themselves as more cooperative and less apathetic than students in the other subjects saw themselves.

267

Students in science classes viewed their teachers as slightly more authoritarian and punitive, the work as more difficult, and themselves as more apathetic as compared with the views of students sampled in other subjects. Science students also seemed to feel that their teachers weren't always clear in giving information and instructions, and that the goals of the classes were not always clear.

As the data in Table 6.1 suggest, students in foreign languages and students in science classes didn't feel very different about how difficult their classes were. 46% and 47%, respectively, told us the work was "just right." And yet, as we have just seen, the responses of these two groups to the climate measures reveal that they must have had very different kinds of experiences in class. A moment's reflection on the nature of these two subjects and their places in the American high school curriculum suggests some possible reasons for these differences in class climate between science and foreign language classes.

Table 6.1

Percentage of students in each subject who considered what they were learning in class to be "hard," "easy," or "just right."

	% Hard	% Easy	% Just Right	N
Science	27.8	25.2	47.0	1313
Math	26.0	28.3	45.7	1587
Foreign Language	24.2	29.8	46.0	526
English	16.1	32.3	51.6	1793
Social Studies	15.8	35.2	48.9	1749
Arts	9.3	45.4	45.3	1474
VocEd	9.1	42.5	48.4	1726
P.E.	7.8	54.0	38.2	768

First and foremost, foreign languages are electives, and are usually chosen by achievement-oriented, college-bound students. While it is also true that these are the same kinds of students most likely to be found in upper-level science courses, still the

students sampled in science classes were more heterogeneous than those sampled in the foreign language
classes. This is largely because entry-level science
courses are mandatory for all students; in some states,
two full years of science are required for high school
graduation.

Foreign language was rarely mandatory for all
students. The sampled students in foreign language
classes were therefore much more likely to be a more
nearly homogeneous group in terms of ability and,
because they selected foreign language as their elective, they are likely to be more motivated to learn, as
well. It was also often true that foreign language
classes are quite small in size compared to classes in
other subjects. I suspect that these three factors
exerted an enormous positive influence on the teachers
(after all, who wouldn't enjoy teaching bright, motivated students?) and, therefore, on the classroom
atmosphere in general. This would account for the
higher positive class climate scores over all foreign
language classes relative to the other subjects.

While foreign language classes may have had twelve
or fifteen students, required classes in science may
easily have had double that number, or even more. We
have already noted in chapter 5 that because of the
physical arrangement of many science rooms, science
teachers often had students work in small groups. The
fact that communication may be more difficult with the
small group mode could account for the relatively lower
rating that science students gave their classes on the
dimension "Organization." That a large class of
students working in small groups is also likely to be
more difficult to manage may account for the relatively
higher rating that science students gave their classes
on the dimension "Teacher Authoritarianism." This does
not mean, however, that confusion reigned or that
students in science classes were unhappy. (Remember
that the differences between the means of the various
subjects were not very large; all we are really pondering here is the tendency of foreign language and
science classes to fall at opposite ends of the rankings). In fact, 68.6% of the students sampled in
science told us that what they were learning was
interesting, and 72.2% told us that what they were
learning was either "easy" or "just right." These
responses hardly suggest a strongly negative atmosphere
in science classes.

269

By sex

Thus far, we have looked at class climate scale scores by school and by subject. In each case, we found some patterns which suggested real differences between schools and between subjects.

When we look at class climate scores by student gender, we find another pattern. In a way, this finding seems even more dramatic than the previous two: briefly, girls had higher mean scores than boys on the more "positive" scales--Teacher Concern, Teacher Enthusiasm, Teacher Clarity, Student Compliance, Organization, Feedback, and Peer Esteem. Boys had higher mean scores than girls on the more "negative" scales: Teacher Punitiveness, Teacher Authoritarianism, Teacher Favoritism, Class Dissonance, Student Apathy, Task Difficulty, and Student Competitiveness.[4]

Elsewhere in the student data--that is, on items other than those in the class climate instrument--I was able to find further evidence of sex differences. For example, we asked all students to respond to the statement, "Average students don't get enough attention at this school." On the average, the boys agreed and the girls disagreed with this. In response to "I like school." the girls' mean score was higher--that is, more positive--than that of the boys. The same was true of the girls' responses to "I am satisfied with how well I am doing in school:" it was more positive than that of the boys.[5]

It certainly looks as if the girls felt better about their experiences in school than the boys did, at least in the high schools we studied (and we have no reason to believe that they were much different from other American high schools).

There is a good deal of literature and recent research to suggest that this pattern is far from coincidental. Girls and boys have internalized their "proper" sex roles long before they reach high school. By then, what society expects of each sex in the way of behavior is taken for granted as the way things ought to be. We are all far more culture-bound than we realize, and most of us are too timid or perhaps too lazy to examine the assumptions that shape our own behavior. As Maxine Greene has put it, "There has been a bland taken-for-grantedness about such notions as males do the important work of the world and females who seek jobs for the sake of fulfillment are in some sense unfeminine. People who believe these things seldom remark that this is the way they have learned to interpret experience. They...are convinced they are making judgments about what is objectively true." And again, "...it is profoundly important for teachers themselves to subject their own assumptions to searching criticism, using whatever tools they have at their disposal (precisely the tools their students need, if they are to learn) and avoiding the one-dimensional vision that freezes, fixes, and constrains."[6]

A number of studies have suggested that schools as they are presently structured tend to reward behavior we have all learned to regard as "feminine"--passivity, cooperation, and obedience, for example. What interests me about our class climate findings as far as gender differences are concerned is the support they seem to provide for the notion that teachers do, in fact, relate differently to girls than to boys in the classroom. Without even realizing it, certainly without doing the hard work of self-awareness proposed by Greene, they contribute to maintenance of the status quo--a situation, I might add, which is quite as constraining for boys as it is for girls, though in different ways. Young people of both sexes are shaped by social expectations, and boys are no more free to become ballet dancers or kindergarten teachers than girls are to become electricians or veterinarians.

The extent to which boys actually expect to dislike school and don't even mind feeling this way is suggested by their positive responses to the items which constitute the Student Satisfaction subscale of the class climate instrument. Overall, both boys and girls expressed mild agreement with items such as, "I feel good about what happens in this class," and there was no significant difference between their mean scores on the four-item Student Satisfaction scale. Furthermore, while the girls in our sample did have higher academic self-concepts, the boys had higher general self-concepts, so evidently they were not being too badly damaged by their school experiences (chapter 4). Both boys and girls agreed that "This school gives students a good education," and there was no significant difference between their responses. But boys' means were significantly more positive for "It is easy to make friends at this school," which suggest that boys learn

271

to find other satisfactions in schools to compensate for the negative experiences they feel they have in some of their classes.

I have a feeling that these data on gender differences are only the tip of the iceberg. Secondary analysis of A Study of Schooling data bank would, I suspect, yield many more insights into the differing perceptions of boys and girls concerning their school experiences.

By SES and ethnicity

Engstrom, using parent income data as a measure of student socioeconomic status, found no relationship between this variable and any of the class climate dimensions. He therefore proceeded to analyses which focused on another student background variable--ethnicity.

Three high schools and three junior highs were used for this analysis. Fairfield Junior and Senior High Schools had a fairly equal mix of Hispanic and white students, while Palisades and Laurel Junior and Senior High Schools had a fairly equal mix of black and white students. Engstrom discovered that "...when there were significant differences between groups on a climate scale, it was generally the minority group that had the more positive score...the exception to this generalization was that both minority groups perceived their classes as being more difficult than did the white students."

This finding of positive responses to the climate dimensions by black and Hispanic students isn't as surprising as it may seem at first glance. (Many Americans assume, I suspect, that minority students always have less positive experiences in schools than do white students). We have already had occasion to hypothesize (chapter 4) that minority students value schooling as the path to success in a way that white students no longer seem to do. One may speculate as to whether our society is as capable now of absorbing ethnic minorities as it has been in the past, and one may hope that it is; for if not, our hopeful young Hispanic and black students may be in for a tremendous disappointment if they find that schooling no longer guarantees advancement as it once did. In the

272

meantime, our findings suggest positive attitudes towards schooling on the part of many minority students, including evidence that large percentages of them intend to continue on to college.

Teaching practices

Among the 18 class climate dimensions, there were five which focused on the teacher's personality and four which focused on the teacher's pedagogical skills. It is interesting to notice that, in the views of students, these cannot be separated. For example, there was a high correlation (.79) between Teacher Concern (a "personality" dimension) and Teacher Clarity (a pedagogical dimension).

Nor can teacher dimensions necessarily be kept separate from student dimensions, as we shall see. And finally, many of these class climate dimensions are evidently closely connected, in the students' minds, with other variables descriptive of the teacher or of the students themselves. The classroom is indeed a complex creature.

In examining the relationships among the climate dimensions and between the climate dimensions and other pertinent variables, however, a number of patterns can be found which, I believe, are worthy of further reflection and research.

1. Our findings suggest that the teacher who is seen by students as being both concerned (friendly, fair, and interested in students) and enthusiastic about teaching
    -- gives clear, understandable information and instruction
    -- gives corrective feedback
    -- is well organized, and communicates the goals of the class clearly
    -- does not show favoritism
    -- is not punitive
    -- is willing to try different ways of doing things

When these teacher characteristics are present in the classroom, students find the class more interesting and seem more willing to leave decision-making in the hands of the teacher.

Student satisfaction and cooperation are high and student apathy is low.

2. In contrast, the teacher who is regarded by students as authoritarian is punitive; shows favoritism; doesn't communicate class goals clearly; is unwilling to try different ways of doing things; is difficult to understand, or unclear in giving information and instructions; and is not likely to give much helpful feedback.

When these teacher characteristics are present in the classroom, student satisfaction is low and apathy is high. Students find the class less interesting, and express a stronger desire to be involved in making decisions about what happens in class.

Table 6.2 on the next page contains the correlation data upon which the above summaries are based. It seems to me that these data offer some helpful guidelines for the conscientious high school teacher. Improvement of the atmosphere of the classroom is linked to improvement of teaching practices and of the affective, or emotional, relationship that exists between the teacher and the students.

Do I give my students enough helpful feedback, or do I just pass back their papers and go right on to the next topic or assignment?
Do I make the goals of the class clear? Do I take the time to explain why what we are doing is important?
Am I willing to try different ways of doing things? When was the last time I really did try something different in my classes?
Do I show favoritism?
Do I really listen to my students, and encourage them to express their opinions and feelings?
When was the last time we all had a good laugh together?

Questions such as these are helpful self-awareness tools for any teacher, and may well stimulate some personal goal-setting. If our findings do in fact reflect classroom reality as I believe they do, improvement in basic teaching practices such as these is likely to lead to an increasingly positive classroom atmosphere for students and teacher alike.

Table 6.2

Correlations of various variables with the Teacher Concern,
Enthusiasm, and Authoritarianism scales of the
class climate instrument. These represent student
perceptions of the teacher and the class.

	Teacher Concern	Teacher Enthusiasm	Teacher Authoritarianism
How interesting or boring is what you are learning in this class?	.70	.63	-.56
The teacher is willing to try different ways of doing things.	.73	.60	-.67
I would like to be able to make more decisions about what goes on in this class.	-.61	-.52	.66
TEACHER PUNITIVENESS	-.62	-.58	.74
TEACHER FAVORITISM	-.62	-.51	.62
TEACHER CLARITY	.79	.65	-.67
ORGANIZATION	.79	.74	-.66
FEEDBACK	.69	.67	-.57
TASK DIFFICULTY	-.55	-.44	.58
STUDENT APATHY	-.68	-.65	.63
STUDENT COMPLIANCE	.50	.49	-.43
STUDENT SATISFACTION	.81	.69	-.69

...even the most satisfied students have their
complaints, and the least satisfied their
pleasures.   --Philip Jackson[8]

The teacher who is regarded by students as concerned and enthusiastic has certain attributes and the
teacher who is regarded as authoritarian has certain
attributes, and in each case the type of teacher is an
important determinant of other aspects of class climate. But there are other variables which also contribute to student satisfaction or dissatisfaction in the
classroom. Without losing sight of Jackson's pertinent
reminder, we now turn to some data which allow us to
explore correlates of student satisfaction a bit
further.

The four items which constituted the Student
Satisfaction subscale of the climate instrument were
these:

1. I feel good about what happens in this class.
2. Students feel good about what happens in this
   class.
3. After class, I usually have a sense of satisfaction.
4. I don't like coming to this class.

Responses to the fourth item were reversed when the
scale scores were computed. Table 6.3 shows some of
the variables which correlated highly with the Student
Satisfaction subscale.

The happy classroom

Table 6.3 suggests, then that student "satisfaction," as defined by the four items in the satisfaction
subscale, was high in classrooms where the teacher was
concerned, enthusiastic, willing to try different ways
of doing things, and well organized. The teacher in
such classes would also be one who gave helpful feedback and clear information and explanations, and who
made the goals of the class clear. Such a teacher
would not be perceived by students as authoritarian.
Finally, the students would find what they were

learning to be interesting, and would not be bored or apathetic.

Table 6.3

Correlates of Student Satisfaction
subscale of the class climate instrument

	r
How interesting or boring for you is what you are learning in this class?	.870
Teacher Clarity subscale	.843
Organization subscale	.842
Teacher Concern subscale	.812
Feedback subscale	.743
This teacher is willing to try different ways of doing things.	.730
Teacher Authoritarism subscale	-.693
Teacher Enthusiasm subscale	.689
Student Apathy subscale	-.639

This is what I learned from my own investigation. But Engstrom's analysis enables us to go further, and in fact provides a link between our class climate findings and Sirotnik's work with the observation data.[10] For what Engstrom discovered was that students in classes where more time was spent on Instruction responded more positively to the climate scales. He found evidence, in other words, that students perceive the climate of their classes to be more harmonious, enjoyable, and productive when more time is spent on Instruction rather than on Behavior or Routines.[11] A moment's reflection will show that this is entirely consistent with the correlation findings displayed in Table 6.3. Everything ties together: the teacher who is organized, who gives helpful feedback, and who gives clear information, explanations, and instructions is engaged in teaching behaviors--that is, in instruction. Students in such classes report that they are not bored or apathetic, but "feel good about what happens in class."

Their teachers, too, feel good about what happens in class: Engstrom also found that students whose teachers expressed satisfaction with and enjoyment of their careers responded more positively to the climate scales. Let's link this finding together with the one cited earlier: students who responded positively to the class climate dimensions had teachers who (1) were satisfied with their work, and (2) spent more class time on instruction. Sirotnik discovered that teachers who spend more time on instruction were also the ones who were more likely to be involved in professional activities--taking extra coursework, attending work-shops, serving on committees, and the like. A teacher who is unhappy in his or her work is unlikely to spend extra time on professional activities, it seems to me. And we come full circle again when we recall that student satisfaction was highly correlated with the "Teacher Enthusiasm" dimension of class climate--a dimension which consisted of items like "This teacher seems to like being a teacher."

We have established connections between student satisfaction, teacher satisfaction, positive class climate, good instructional practices, and time spent on instruction. But there is more still. For example, teachers who believed that the intellectual function of schooling is the most important (as compared to the social, personal, or vocational functions) were more likely to spend more class time on instruction. Teachers who had small classes were more likely to spend more class time on instruction. Teachers who spent more class time on instruction were less likely to have a lot of disruptive behavior on the part of the students. Teachers who spent more class time on instruction were more likely to use the whole group and small group modes of instruction, and less likely to have students working alone at their desks. And finally, teachers of high-ability-track classes were more likely to devote more class time to instruction. In fact, track level was found to be the single best predictor of time spent on instruction.[12] The implications of this finding will be discussed at length later in this chapter. For now, my purpose has been simply to bring together the many various bits of data which seem to contribute to a description of the happy classroom.

The unhappy classroom

In our investigation, apathy seemed to describe the feelings of students who were not satisfied or happy with the classes in which they were sampled. The Student Apathy subscale of the class climate instrument contained the following four items:

1. Failing in this class would not bother most of the students.
2. Most of the students pay attention to the teacher.
3. Students don't care what goes on in this class.
4. I don't care what goes on in this class.

For the purposes of this discussion, then, these four items define what we will refer to as "student apathy." This unhappy feeling was, we found, characteristic of classes in which the teacher was perceived as being disorganized or unclear, more inclined to show favoritism, less likely to give helpful feedback, or less willing to try different ways of doing things.

These classes were also seen by students as ones in which the most time was spent on student behavior rather than on instruction; class dissonance, or disruption, was more likely to be perceived as fairly common and student compliance, or cooperative with the teacher, was seen as low. Students in such classes told us they like the subject matter less and found the class boring and the work more difficult. They also wished they could be involved in making some of the decisions about what would happen in class.

Teachers in such classes, too, were less than content. They were less likely than teachers of happier classes to feel satisfied with the amount of control they had over various aspects of their planning and teaching. And they were more likely to report that the materials available for their classes were less than adequate for all of their students on at least one of the three specified criteria: interest, ethnicity, or ability level. What we have here is a hint that these less happy classes were more likely to have been lower-ability-track classes. We already know that more time was spent on instruction in higher-track classes, and we also found that Student Apathy correlated negatively (-.63) with time spent on instruction. In other words, students were more likely to be apathetic

279

in classes where less time was spent on instruction. It isn't fair to conclude that these were always and invariably lower-track classes; however, track level was found to be an indicator of time spent on instruction. We will pursue this aspect of our findings later in this chapter, in the section on tracking.

Engstrom also found that students were more negative on the class climate dimensions in classes where the teacher had a strong belief in being completely in control of the class and where, in the students' opinion, the teacher didn't allow any student decision-making but in fact did retain the complete control they professed to believe in.[13]

Teachers' Educational Beliefs

A moment ago, we noted Engstrom's finding that students were more negative on the climate dimensions in those classes where the teacher had a strong belief in being completely in control. What Engstrom did was to investigate the relationships that might exist between the climate of a class--as perceived by the students--and the educational philosophy of the teacher in charge of the class. At the high school level, 397 sets of matched teacher and classroom data were available for these kinds of analyses.[14]

What the Study staff termed the "Teacher Educational Beliefs" measure was a subsection of the Teacher Survey. It consisted of four clusters of items. These four clusters formed scales, and each teacher's combined responses to the items in each cluster constituted that teacher's score for that scale. The four scales were:

"Traditional" scales (Disciplinarian)
1. Teacher Discipline and Control. A scale composed of items measuring the degree to which teachers believe that strong discipline and tight control is necessary in the classroom (seven items).
2. Basic Subjects and Skills Emphasis. A scale measuring the teacher's opinion of the importance of basic skills and subjects (three items).

"Progressive" scales (Humanitarian)

3. Student concern. A scale measuring the teacher's opinion of the importance of personal contact with students (two items).
4. Student Participation. Measures whether teachers feel that students should participate in deciding about various classroom options (five items).

We found that teachers who held disciplinarian beliefs were viewed more negatively by their students. The relationship, however, was not a strikingly strong one.[15]

The absence of any stronger--or more positive--relationships between the class climate data and the teacher educational beliefs data may be due to some ambiguity in the teachers' responses to the items of the educational beliefs measure. This, in itself, is an interesting finding. Specifically, we found that teachers tended to agree with many statements which seemed to contradict each other. They strongly agreed with statements about teacher control, for example, but they also agreed with statements about student participation.[16] This finding--that teachers tended to agree simultaneously with what might be considered both "traditional" and "progressive" belief statements--reflects, I suspect, a sincere belief that it is possible to have both in the classroom.

First and foremost, of course, is control. Everyone, including the students and the teachers, and certainly parents and administrators, expects that the class will be kept under control. That is a large part of what teaching is understood to be all about, as the overwhelming anxiety of student teachers to master classroom management skills shows. When the teacher is in control of his or her class, other things--such as student participation--may be allowed to happen. But this will be stopped at once if students become disruptive or undermine the teacher's control of the situation.

Co-existing with this concern for control, however, is the general belief in teaching as a humane profession, one in which the really good teacher is interested in, and supportive of or concerned about the students. We found this belief demonstrated in the highly positive responses to each of the two items in the Concern for Students scale, "Learning is enhanced when

281

teachers praise generously the accomplishments of individual students," and "The best learning atmosphere is created when the teacher takes an active interest in the problems and affairs of students."

Unfortunately, we found evidence to suggest that some of these beliefs do not necessarily find their way into actual classroom practice. The statement about the value of praise is a case in point. 517 of the 654 high school teachers who responded to this item expressed quite vigorous agreement with it.[17] Our observation records of these same teachers and classrooms, as we saw in chapter 5, however, revealed a striking <u>absence</u> of praise of any kind. Evidently, when it came to praise, the teachers in our sample didn't practice what they preached.

This distance between what teachers believe in and the way they think they behave, on one hand, and the different perceptions of students or observers on the other is, for me, one of the most intriguing findings of the Study. It reinforces my belief in the school as a place of multiple realities. Perception is a personal and idiosyncratic phenomenon, as we now know--psychological studies have shown that different people observing the same event will give different accounts of what happened. Our teachers no doubt believed they gave more praise than they were perceived to do by observers. But professional growth may result from recognizing these kinds of discrepancies, and one of the great values of instruments like our class climate measure is their use as self-evaluation tools by teachers. It may be a help to a teacher to realize that his students find his explanations unclear. Another teacher may be dismayed to discover that her students feel she shows favoritism. Yet another may find that his students don't think he enjoys being a teacher, and who knows? He may thus come to admit it to himself for the first time. Teachers secure enough--or curious enough--to seek such feedback about their classroom behavior from their own students are sure to be rewarded with some useful data upon which they can act to improve their own teaching and, because the two are connected, the climate of their classes. They are also likely to receive some pleasant surprises. Teachers are often happily surprised by student responses which are more favorable than the teachers themselves expect.

*   *   *

Before we move on into another subset of data, it may be of interest to note a difference in the responses of male and female teachers to the four educational beliefs scales. Male teachers, as a group, had higher mean scores on the two "traditional" scales-- Teacher Discipline/Control and Basic Subjects/Skills Emphasis. Female teachers had higher mean scores on the two more "progressive" scales--Student Concern and Student Participation.[18] I'm not convinced that this difference in responses to these item clusters, however, reflects any observable differences in the actual teaching practices of the two sexes. We have already seen that a strongly expressed belief in the value of praise is not necessarily linked to praise-giving behavior in the classroom. And all teachers, regardless of sex, work to maintain control of their classes.

Whether teachers' classroom behavior is or is not consistent with their expressed beliefs is an interesting question regardless of gender. But these responses to the educational beliefs questions do conform to familiar expectations of the two sexes in our culture. Women are to be more empathetic and nurturing, and men are to be more assertive. These sex roles were reflected in the expressed educational beliefs of the teachers we sampled and, to a limited extent, they were also reflected in the students' views of their teachers. We found a tendency for students in classes with male teachers to be a little less positive in their responses to the class climate dimensions, for example.[19]

Further analysis of Study data may reveal additional insights into differences between male and female teachers, as perceived both by students and by the teachers themselves. Such findings might be pertinent to suggestions for change in teacher training. For example, college women preparing to enter teaching might benefit from a certain amount of assertiveness training, and men might gain from training which develops their capacity for nurturing behavior.

Summary: exploring classroom climate

Of the 525 high school classes we studied in depth, some had more positive climates, in the view of the students. In others, the climate was less positive. We found evidence to suggest that some schools have a greater number of what I have called "happy" classrooms while other schools have far fewer. The climate of foreign language classes seemed to be consistently positive, while that of science classes was less so although this pattern wasn't extremely strong and can be explained by the nature of the two subjects and their roles in the American high school curriculum.

A stronger pattern was found when student responses to the class climate dimensions were examined by student gender. Girls seemed to feel a good deal more positive about their classroom experience than did boys, but oddly enough this did not seem to bother the boys very much. They expressed about the same degree of satisfaction with their classes as did the girls, and agreed about equally that their school gives students a good education. The discrepancy between the girls' and boys' perceptions of the climate in their classes is grounded in learned sex role differences and the extent to which these are compatible or incompatible with the structures and purposes of the school. It is interesting to note that male teachers seemed to be more control-oriented in their educational beliefs than female teachers; further evidence that men accept the need for control when they are students, as well as their "rightful" role in maintaining control when they are teachers.

Black and Hispanic students expressed more positive feelings about the atmosphere of their classes than did white students, though at the same time there were indications that the minority students found the work more difficult.

Our findings provide a pretty good set of guidelines for the improvement of teaching practices. From the standpoint of the students we sampled, the teacher who is concerned and enthusiastic gives clear, understandable explanations and instructions and quick, frequent feedback; is well organized; does not show favoritism, and is willing to try different ways of doing things. These are technical skills of teaching which can be learned if a teacher is willing to try.

Furthermore, according to the students the concerned, enthusiastic teacher "seems to enjoy being a teacher." And it was true that these teachers

284

themselves told us in a number of ways that they were satisfied with their work. They also reported being more involved in other professional activities.

The observation data revealed that in classrooms with these positive characteristics, more time was spent on instruction than was true in classes with less positive climates. Classes in which a relatively greater amount of time was spent on instruction also tended to be smaller in size. In this era of fiscal conservatism, this finding has implications for school funding which cannot be ignored. If, as other research has shown, the amount of actual time students spend focused on learning[20] tasks is related to gains in achievement, and our data suggests that smaller classes are likely to spend more time on instruction, the conclusion is clear: we should be putting more money into hiring more teachers, rather than less. The student:teacher ratio at the high school level, if reduced to a maximum of 20:1 could, if coupled with vigorous in-service and pre-service programs aimed at improving the quality of teaching itself, lead to substantial improvement in high school education.

The students in our sample who reported feeling unhappy and apathetic indicated that their teachers were disorganized, showed favoritism, gave unclear explanations and instructions, didn't let them know how they were doing or how to do their work better, and were unlikely to be willing to try different ways of doing things. These students told us that disruption was common in their classes, and that the teacher spent a lot of time dealing with it. They wanted to be more involved in making decisions about what would happen in class, but this was unlikely to happen because teachers of classes such as these tended to have a strong belief in maintaining strict control themselves.

Teachers of these "unhappy" classes tended to be less than satisfied with their jobs. But which comes first? Is the teacher unhappy because of the hard-to-handle class, or is the class hard to handle because the teacher is unhappy and doesn't do a very good job of teaching?

This question, though not easy to answer, has important implications for the improvement of education at the high school level. Some might say: get rid of the teacher, and then the students will be alright.

Others might say: get rid of the students who are the most disruptive, and then the teacher will be fine. Both answers, I believe, are insufficient. The negative environment is an interactive one. Changes need to be made on both sides.

A principal who is involved with his faculty as an instructional leader, one who provides constructive, helpful supervision (rather than one annual class visit, the only outcome of which is a decision about contract renewal), will be alert to class situations of this type and able to help in a variety of ways. For example, it may be possible to re-schedule some of the students to other classes.

Simultaneously, the teacher's pedagogical skills need to be improved. The teacher can make a conscious effort to avoid showing favoritism, and can--with the principal's support and encouragement--try out one or two different ways of doing things. These should, perhaps, not be too dramatic, or the teacher's behavior won't seem authentic to the students. Some studies have suggested that classroom interaction patterns, once set, are extremely difficult to alter.[21] In some settings it might be wiser for the teacher to wait until, at the end of the semester, he or she has a new group of students and can work consciously at establishing a better interaction pattern with them. Two teaching behaviors that can be improved are (1) clarity in giving explanations and instructions, and in presenting--often--the goals and purposes of the class; and (2) frequency of helpful feedback. This latter skill is one that is not often practiced in teacher-training programs, and I would be willing to bet that in every school in the country at least half of the teachers could benefit from inservice workshops designed to help them improve in this area.

Other approaches to improving the negative classroom are possible. The reader who is a school practitioner will be able to think of several in addition to those I have mentioned. This type of effort at the classroom level is, I believe, at the very heart of real educational improvement in our high schools. If the principal doesn't have the skills (or the desire) to provide instructional leadership, the community would be well advised to invest in hiring a staff development specialist, whose sole responsibility would be to serve the teachers in their efforts to improve

286

their teaching. I have believed for some time that every high school should have such a person "in residence," so to speak, as a resource for the teachers and, for that matter, for the administrative staff as well.[22] If real improvement in teaching (and ultimately in student learning and skill mastery) are truly what we are after, this kind of expenditure--one additional salary per year--would be likely to yield more tangible improvement in the long run than anything else the school district could buy.

Finally, in this section of the chapter we took a look at teachers' educational beliefs and found evidence that there may sometimes be quite a gulf between belief and practice. A certain amount of ambiguity characterized most teachers' responses to the 21 educational beliefs items in our survey: they tended to agree with both disciplinarian and humanitarian statements. I have argued elsewhere that this kind of inconsistency is grounded partly in lack of attention paid to the foundations subjects, particularly history and philosophy of education, in teacher training programs.[23] Teachers must learn to think about the connection between what they do, why they do it, and what they believe (or don't believe) about students, about learning, and about the purposes of schools. Of course, it is also true that our culture is not an introspective one, and this kind of self-awareness-building doesn't come easily to any of us.

I suspect most high school teachers would welcome some discussion of their educational beliefs, and that a measure such as our 21-item educational beliefs instrument, or another, similar one, could serve as a very useful starting-point for individual self-awareness-building or for faculty inservice, or both. This could be followed by administration of the class climate inventory to perhaps two or three of each teacher's classes. Student responses in each class should be aggregated to provide a class mean score for each item. Teachers could then see what their students felt about many different aspects of their class, including teaching practices. Juxtaposing these data against their own educational beliefs, the teachers would then be able to locate discrepancies between what they believe and what their students perceive to be their classroom behavior. Each teacher, if provided with data such as these, could--either individually or after discussion with colleagues--set some professional improvement goals. In the absence of instructional leadership (on the part of the principal or a staff development specialist, as discussed earlier), this is one way in which a faculty can get itself started on some professional growth activities. Diagnosis, however, must come first and real data is a good foundation upon which to build.

II.

Individualizing and Evaluating

Individualization of instruction has been a matter of enormous concern in education during the past several decades. Psychological findings about learning combined with the societal forces of the late 60's and early 70's to sensitize educators to the differences both in what young people bring with them to school and in how they learn best once they get to school. Compensatory programs were developed for students whose family background left them at a disadvantage in coping with school and with schoolwork. For a while, curriculum expansion--the addition of new courses--was another means used to accommodate differences in student learning needs. Ability grouping, or "tracking," has been assumed to contribute to individualization, by separating students who learn more slowly or with greater difficulty from those who learn more quickly. And in the realm of actual teaching practice, individualization of instruction was intended to provide the fine-tuning necessary for making each student's learning program optimally appropriate for that student.

As a result of cutbacks in federal funding for education, most compensatory programs have been dismantled and the high school curriculum has reverted to more traditional proportions. Gone are many of the courses in ethnic studies, ecological awareness, and science fiction, for instance.

There is ample evidence in the data from this Study that actual individualization of instruction has never really taken root at the high school level. In chapter 5, we found that teachers usually worked with the class as a whole--in which case the teachers talked, and the students listened--or else they had the students work alone at their desks, using textbooks and/or

288

worksheets. Seldom did students work in small groups, although this is one useful technique for individualizing, especially if each small group is working on a different assignment. Almost never was there any indication that students with different learning styles could use different kinds of learning materials. And students told us that they never, or very seldom had any opportunity to select their own learning materials. Classroom activities were overwhelmingly passive: listening and writing, primarily; and teachers, on the average, tended to <u>disagree</u> that "when given a choice of learning activities, most students generally select what is best for them." Finally, we have seen that teachers control the classroom, allow little or no student participation in classroom decision-making, and are satisfied with it that way.

These findings, discussed in chapter 5, paint a clear picture of the high school classes we studied, a picture based on data from students and observers as well as from teachers. It is not a picture in which individualized instruction can be seen, but one which reveals the classroom as a place in which all students do the same thing in the same way, with a very limited range of learning materials and activities which are mostly passive and traditional.

This picture took shape from data on classroom activities rather than from responses to specific questions about individualization as such. We did, however, ask such questions of both teachers and students. The time has come to examine this aspect of the classroom encounter.

*   *   *

We listed seven ways in which teachers might individualize instruction, and asked the teachers in our sample to tell us how often they actually did individualize in each way. Table 6.4 shows that in most cases, the largest percentages of teachers said that they didn't use <u>any</u> of these strategies very often. About one-fifth said they used each one often. Only approximately 5% of the teachers we sampled told us that they <u>always</u> used these individualization strategies--only one teacher in every twenty. These responses tend to give added weight to the observation data reported in chapter 5, which showed little or no individualized instruction taking place in observed classes.

We also asked our teachers to tell us what information they used in individualizing instruction. Allowing for the fact that few of them were doing much individualizing in the first place, still the responses to this question were interesting. Most of the teachers in our sample told us that they <u>didn't</u> use student aptitude or diagnostic test results. Nor did they pay much attention to student behavior and performance in previous classes. Many said they did take student preferences and the student's grade level into account. But nearly all of them (90%) said they often or always relied on their own judgment about students ("teacher observation of student performance and behavior" and "teacher analysis of student classwork") in making decisions about individualizing instruction.

It isn't surprising that the largest percentage of our teachers said they hardly ever make use of diagnostic test results. At the high school level, few programs being used by teachers have pre-tests and individualizing strategies built in. In my experience, high school teachers rarely begin a unit of study with a pre-test, and virtually never provide different learning experiences for different students based on the results of such tests. Why not? Two possible answers come to mind. Sheer numbers of students, for one thing--up to 150 students a day. Most teachers in such a position remain unconvinced that the mechanics of record-keeping necessary for even a moderate amount of individualization could be manageable.

Then, too, there's the common belief that tracking puts students with the same learning needs and abilities together so that no further tailoring of programs to individual needs, abilities, or learning styles is really necessary. Given a choice between having a class of mixed abilities and having a class of students of differing ages or grade levels but similar ability level, most teachers would choose the latter. In fact, among our sample of teachers, well over half (65%) agreed that "it is good to have students of different ages and/or grade levels in the same classroom." At individual schools, responses ranged from 41% agreement at Laurel, to 74% at Newport.

Table 6.4

Percentages of teachers reporting the frequency
with which they use different ways of
individualizing instruction.

	not very often	moderate amount	often	almost always
Use of different instructional methods for different students	34.7	35.5	23.0	6.8
Use of different activities	39.9	32.6	21.5	6.0
Use of different groupings	44.5	27.8	21.9	5.8
Use of different objectives	44.5	32.7	16.3	6.6
Use of different materials	48.1	27.1	19.7	5.2
Use of different content	48.6	28.6	17.0	5.8
Use of different time schedules	62.9	18.9	12.8	5.3

"Students at this school receive a lot
of individual attention from their teachers."
Average responses from the teachers in
each of the thirteen Study schools.

Mildly Disagree	Mildly Agree	Strongly Agree
Newport	Palisades	Dennison
Bradford	Vista	
Fairfield	Woodlake	
Rosemont	Crestview	
Manchester	Atwater	
Laurel	Euclid	

Only at tiny Dennison did the teachers feel strongly that their students received a lot of individual
attention. The reader will recognize by now that the
six schools in the "mildly disagree" cluster are
basically the same six we have seen at the less

291

positive end of many other variables (see, for example, the teacher and student satisfaction groupings in chapters 3 and 4). One hypothesis that might be tested further is that dissatisfied teachers are less willing to make the extra effort needed to individualize instruction for their students. But we also shouldn't lose sight of the fact that even satisfied teachers did little to individualize. The students at every one of our thirteen schools (including Dennison)--those where teacher satisfaction was high as well as where it was low--agreed overwhelmingly (82-90%) that "I have to do the work the teacher assigns, even if I already know how to do it." One must wonder how much potentially productive learning time is simply wasted because teachers do not use diagnostic techniques and have not mastered teaching methods which include management of even a modest amount of classroom individualization. Instead, they lecture, lead some discussion, and supervise seat work, giving the whole class the same assignment, to be done with the same materials and finished by the same deadline. This familiar pattern begins to look more like a control mechanism than educationally sound teaching. As Goodlad points out in chapter 5 of A Place Called School, "Once more, we see the demands of managing a relatively large group of people in a small place becoming a formidable factor in determining and limiting pedagogy. It is difficult to know how fully teachers are aware of these circumstances and how consciously and contentedly they adapt to them."[24]

Just under one-fourth of our teachers, overall, told us that they often set different learning objectives for different students. But many more teachers felt that using behaviorally-stated instructional objectives was worthwhile, and indicated they used them often, evidently setting the same objectives for the whole class group instead of using them as a tool for individualization. This was especially true of teachers at the larger schools. Interestingly, despite the fact that most teachers thought that behavioral objectives were more appropriate for some subjects than for others, teachers of all subjects reported using them often.

Despite their limitations, behaviorally-stated instructional objectives do have a place in teaching. They have the advantage of being brief, clear, and easily understood by students, and are also useful as

292

evaluation tools for the teacher. It is not surprising, then, that the majority of teachers in our sample had fairly positive attitudes towards the use of such objectives. Three out of every four told us that behavioral objectives were built into the instructional program they used and helped them know "what and how to teach." (Notice: pre-determined objectives, rather than student needs identified through diagnostic techniques, determine not only what will be taught but also how it will be taught.)

Eighty percent of the teachers we surveyed said that behavioral objectives "help me to evaluate my own teaching." And 85% told us that they "assist me in evaluating student progress" and "assist students in knowing what is expected of them."

On the other hand, 55% of the teachers said that behavioral objectives take too much time to prepare, and 40% said that "keeping records of student attainment is too time-consuming," so there was some resistance to the use of behavioral objectives. But on the whole, our teachers seemed to feel that they can be quite worthwhile.

*   *   *

If individualizing is something that happens seldom in high school classrooms, evaluation goes on all the time. But it occurs in only a limited number of forms. We have already seen that the teachers in our sample did not use evaluation as a diagnostic tool. How do they evaluate? And what use do they make of the results of their evaluation?

Evaluation of students can be done in a number of ways, but we learned that teachers of the "academic" subjects (English, math, science, social studies, and foreign languages) relied primarily on tests or quizzes, and on their own evaluation of students' classwork and/or homework. Teachers of the fine and vocational arts, on the other hand, used tests less. They were more likely to evaluate student progress by having students perform or show how to do something, or by having them make projects or do reports. They also expected far less homework.

Overall, 83% of the teachers of academic subjects told us they want students to do one-half to one hour

293

of homework a night. Fifty percent of the teachers of
PE, fine arts, and vocational subjects said they
required no homework, and 36% told us they expected
about half an hour each night. These differences in
the amount of homework teachers are likely to expect
create huge discrepancies in the overall learning
experiences of students. For example, one student,
whose schedule includes English, math, social studies,
PE, art, a vocational course of some kind, and a study
hall will--on the average, based on our data--have 2
hours of homework a night, at least some of which can
be done during study hall. Another student, whose
schedule includes English, math, social studies,
science, PE, a foreign language, and music, with no
study hall, might have 3½ hours or more of homework a
night set by his or her various teachers. Assuming
that such a student actually does do this homework,* in
the course of his or her high school years that student
is spending much more time involved with schoolwork.
Whether "time on task" is spent in or out of school,
one current popular hypothesis is that more of it is
likely to result in more student learning.

I am not, however, arguing for homework assignments
in the nonacademic areas--although perhaps once in a
while that may be a good idea. Rather, I am suggesting
that students may find that they are cheating themselves in the long run by selecting, or allowing a
counselor to select for them, an "easier" schedule of
classes. I also happen to believe that all students,
regardless of their future plans, should experience a
much more balanced program of academic and nonacademic
classes. In other words, I would like to see the
"college prep/non-college prep" dichotomy greatly
reduced.

As Table 6.5 shows, tests are the choice of the
largest percentages of English, science, and social
studies teachers and the second-largest percentages of
math and foreign language teachers when it comes to
evaluating student progress. And indeed, as we saw in
chapter five, tests and quizzes are one activity which
most students reported doing very often.

---

* We did not ask the students how much time they spent on homework. It was also an activity that many of them didn't particularly enjoy, as we noted in chapter 5.

As far as the teachers in our sample were concerned, tests and quizzes are the most useful tool for them in evaluating student progress. Secondarily, teachers also feel that tests and quizzes are useful as actual learning experiences in themselves (Table 6.6).

And what are high school tests <u>like</u>? As part of the curriculum materials task, we asked participating teachers to provide us with samples of the tests and quizzes they use in their classes. We received many tests, quizzes, and worksheets from some teachers and none at all from others. This variability of responses or compliance was typical of the curriculum materials task as a whole. As a result, therefore, it is necessary to be rather cautious in drawing conclusions about these data.

It is possible, however, to <u>describe</u> what we were given by the teachers. And as far as tests and quizzes are concerned, what the teachers gave us was overwhelmingly traditional in both form and content. Very seldom did we see anything other than so-called "objective" tests and quizzes, requiring fine-tuning of memorization skills but not much in the way of critical thinking or the higher cognitive processes such as analysis, synthesis, or evaluation. Even when an essay question or two were included, they usually required only that the student write down a paragraph of remembered facts. Far and away the most common formats were Multiple Choice, Matching, and True/False items.

I would like to believe that teachers would do more higher cognitive level testing if they could find a way of organizing so as to allow for the extra time needed to read and respond to each student's paper. If one teaches 150 students a day one doesn't assign many essay questions, unless one is prepared to spend all night reading them. So it is understandable that teachers test the way they do. Yet even hand-scoring of objective tests takes a lot of time.

It is possible to conceive of an at least partial solution to this dilemma, however. Computer technology may provide a way for teachers to use both objective and higher-level testing. All objective tests should be automatically computer-scored. Then, the time the teacher previously spent hand-scoring objective tests could be spent reading student essays and reports instead. This kind of a system is within reach of most

Table 6.5

How teachers in each subject evaluate student progress

Key: 1 = largest %age of teachers who said they do it this way
2 = next largest %age said they do it this way
3 = third largest %age do it this way
4 = smallest %age said they do it this way

English	math	soc. st.	science	for. lang.	arts	voc. ed.
1. tests	classwork	tests	tests	classwork	show	classwork
2. classwork	tests	classwork	classwork	tests	projects	show
3. projects	show	projects	projects	show	classwork	projects
4. show	projects	show	show	projects	tests	tests

296

schools, I believe. Many district offices and teacher centers offer computer-scoring services for teachers. Often they are not well utilized, however, because teachers have not been trained in their use, and because in some cases tests must first be redesigned so that computer-scorable answer sheets can be used. A school district interested in helping its teachers to improve the quality of their instruction would do well to provide the initial outlay of resources--released time and inservice training--that could help teachers learn to use computer-scored objective tests. Thereafter, the teachers would be expected and encouraged to work in developing and using some essay tests that require the students to analyze, synthesize, and evaluate information and ideas. Both kinds of tests are useful for student learning. Both are needed and, I believe, it is possible for teachers to use both without dying of exhaustion.

Table 6.6

Comparison of teacher responses to two questions
about the usefulness of tests and quizzes.

	How useful in helping to evaluate students?	How useful for student learning?
Math	87.6%	76.4%
Foreign Languages	80.0	67.6
Social Studies	64.8	44.8
Science	63.2	49.4
English	55.7	43.1
Vocational Subjects	44.6	45.4

The students, while they don't really enjoy taking tests, have long since learned that they are an inescapable fact of school life. About 80% told us that "the grades or marks I get in this class are fair," and two-thirds said that "the grades or marks I get in this class help me to learn better." The fact that almost half (47%) said that the grades they got had "nothing to do with what I really know" isn't, perhaps, as contradictory as it may seem at first glance; objective tests alone can't possibly measure all or even most of what students learn in a class.

Aside from tests per se, students indicated a fairly high degree of satisfaction with the amount of corrective feedback they were getting from their teachers. Three-fourths or more agreed that "if I do my work wrong, my teacher tells me how to do it right" and "we know when we have learned things correctly." Nevertheless, as we noted in chapter 5, not much oral corrective feedback was observed in the classrooms we studied. Perhaps students have, over the years, become accustomed to the amount of feedback they do get--little as it may be--and think it is enough.

These, then, were our findings about individualization of instruction and about evaluation of student learning. They are, in both cases, rather grim. We give students little in the way of personal attention, but we test them constantly. We do this primarily to obtain measures of their "achievement," narrowly defined as being what they can parrot back to us relatively soon after we have dictated it to them. And finally, we found that students seem to be well-adjusted to this kind of a schooling experience.

III.

Tracking

Conant's Question

A quarter of a century ago, James Conant posed what then seemed to be one of the central questions of American education: can the comprehensive high school succeed? He wondered "...whether, under one roof and under the same management," it is possible for a school to satisfactorily fulfill three functions: (1) to provide a good general education for <u>all</u> pupils; (2) to provide elective programs for the majority to develop useful skills, and (3) to educate adequately "those with a talent for handling advanced academic subjects." If not, he suggested, then "a radical change in the structure of American education would be in order."[25]

Since then, many more generations of young people have passed through our high schools. These decades have been ones of rapid technological development, but the social response to the accelerated pace of change

298

often seems to have been increased stratification and rigidity in many of our institutions, including schooling. So the answer to Conant's question must be both yes, and no. The concept of a sound general education for all is worthy, and the American high school has succeeded reasonably well in raising the overall literacy of the population. Furthermore, it is true that most high schools today manage to provide a range of coursework sufficiently broad to meet the disparate needs of students with different talents and plans for the future. But in doing so, it has also institutionalized a system of sifting and sorting which is contributing to the development of a class society based not on the Jeffersonian ideal of a true intellectual meritocracy, as we'd like to believe, but on the basis of wealth, privilege and, to some extent, ethnicity.

At the beginning of the twentieth century, most Americans ended their formal education at the 8th grade. The high schools of that time existed primarily to prepare a very small number of students for college. As the century progressed, the country became more urbanized and industrialized, and continued to attract immigrants from all over the world who hoped to find a better life. The pressure to assimilate these new citizens led to the movement towards universal secondary education, and the inevitable diversity of such a population led to the development of the comprehensive high school concept. As Conant observed, the task of such a school was to meet a wide range of needs: in effect, to be all things to all people.

The next step, the idea of grouping students according to ability, was inevitable. If a school is to offer different programs to different students, the organizational question becomes how to decide which students go into which programs. Decisions based on the ability levels of students, established through the use of nationally standardized tests and supposedly free of non-objective considerations, were felt to be fair and appropriate as well as organizationally workable. The possibility that the tests contained hidden biases, and the possibility that "ability" was being rather narrowly defined, were both carefully ignored and until the middle of the 1960s no one said much about the relationship of so-called "ability" to a student's home background, either. The nation had too much of an emotional investment in the myth of equal opportunity to entertain such nagging doubts as these.

299

Now the century is drawing to a close. The ability-grouping of high school students--"tracking"--is a well-entrenched practice. Indeed, it is largely taken for granted as being not only necessary but as right and proper, and a fair way of deciding who goes into the various different programs of the comprehensive high school. In fact, it is far from fair, as we shall see.

There are two traditional justifications for the separation of students by ability. First, it is argued that grouping students together with others of a similar ability level is a better way to meet the differing needs of those students. Fast students can move through material more quickly and tackle more challenging learning tasks without being held back. Slower students can take their time to master the material without feeling pressure.

Two insidious assumptions lie below the surface of this argument. One involves the pervasive belief that a "fast" student is, ipso facto, a "good" student, while a student who learns more slowly is a "poor" student. This judgmental linkage of learning style with personal worth is damaging to individual students and to society as a whole, for through it we lose many good minds--a loss no democratic society can sustain for long if it is to remain healthy. The other assumption is that students will achieve more if they are in a group with others of similar ability. In fact, however, existing research has consistently failed to demonstrate that ability grouping leads to gains in student achievement (see, for example, Persell, 1976),[26] and in fact has shown that it can have negative effects on students placed in average and lower groups (Findley and Bryan, 1970; Alexander, Cook, and McDill, 1978).[27,28]

The second justification of tracking is that it eases the teacher's task by reducing the range of student differences found in the classroom. The teacher can then find appropriate material at the students' level, and teach to the whole class without worrying too much that some students will be bored while others are left far behind. In practice, however, the separation of students into just three or four ability groups is too rough a categorization. As any teacher can tell you, even within the "high" track or the "low" track, and certainly within the "average"

track, one still finds an enormous range of learning
abilities and learning styles. We found evidence of
this in our data from students--in responding to the
open-ended question, "What is the most important thing
you've learned so far in this class?" articulate,
thoughtful responses came from students at all track
levels--and so did inarticulate ones. Here are a few
examples:

From a high-track English class--
    "Well, I think it is our oraginal writtings. But
she corrects it she changes our thoughts then it seems
like she writting it not us."

    "The most important thing, I think, is the vocabu-
lary and spelling techniques. I now understand them
both well."

From a high-track math (Calculus) class--
    "Hardly anything it is to far above me."
    "I guess the most important thing I've learned is
logic and reasoning, and using my imagination with what
I learned and applying it to make problems work."

And a high-track science class--
    "To dismangle animals disect (pigs)."
    "The dissecting. I liked it a lot because I want
to go into medicine."

From a low-track biology class--
    "The metric system, parts of the microscope, the
cell functions and the Cell Theory."
    "Nothing Because it is a hasle if you never Done it
and Don't understand it."

And a low-track math class--
    "We have recently learned how to figure out income
tax. In the past months we learned fractions, percentages and several other types of problems."
    "I have not did nothing very important in this
class at all. And every thing I did learn I don't
think its going to help me in years to come."

    Furthermore, it is not always true that slower
students have a poor attitude towards learning, or that
they aren't fun to teach, though these are widely
shared beliefs among teachers.

301

"I have learned that if you want to be good at something, you have to work. Even if it comes easy for you, you have to work to be really good."

"I have learned more about how to do math problems. The ones I thought would be hard are right easy."

"I have learned from this class, more English words. Trying a second language is hard, but in this class I try to do the best I can by learning always more and more."

The assumption that tracking yields teachably homogeneous groups, then, is patently absurd. In most high school classrooms, whatever the track there are likely to be students functioning at a wide range of levels and learning in many different ways. And yet, we pretend this isn't true. We continue to teach to the whole group, letting students sink or swim as best they can. This was quite clearly the case in the classrooms we studied, as we saw in chapter 5, and it is the really pernicious thing about the mythology of homogeneous grouping.

All in all, the evidence seems to suggest that tracking serves little if any educative function; its primary purpose as an organizational structure is to make life a bit easier for teachers and administrators. The fact that it cannot be convincingly justified as being demonstrably good for the students themselves may account for the common reluctance of school people to discuss openly the policies and practices of tracking which exist at their own schools. This was our experience when we attempted to examine the tracking systems of the thirteen high schools and twelve junior high schools in the Study of Schooling. We found that tracking was not an orderly phenomenon in which school practices are consistent with or even reflective of clearly stated school or district policies. Finding out what really takes place was like putting a puzzle together, and at each school the pieces of the puzzle were different.

I suspect that this reluctance to discuss tracking is based on tacit recognition of the fact that, as now practiced in most high schools, the tracking system is contrary to the American egalitarian tradition. In fact, as it now functions, tracking serves as a way of denying equal educational opportunity to some groups of students. In short, we are kidding ourselves if we claim that tracking is no more than ability grouping.

302

Data from A Study of Schooling show that it also works to separate students by race and by socioeconomic level.

Information on the track level of the high school and junior high school classes we studied was gathered from the schools involved. Each sampled class was identified as being either a high, average, or low track class; or as being heterogeneous in ability levels. Table 6.7 shows how many classes of each type were sampled at each of the thirteen high schools. An estimate of the percentage of courses which were deliberately tracked at each school is also included:

Table 6.7

Number of classes sampled at each track level at each of the thirteen high schools in the Study.

	estimated % of courses tracked *	N of classes sampled at each track level			
		low	average	high	hetero
Woodlake	25%	2	2	8	24
Laurel	33%	4	7	3	10
Vista	44%	6	24	3	15
Euclid	50%	0	8	12	20
Crestview	50%	9	15	8	10
Newport	65%	5	12	8	21
Bradford	65%	5	11	17	15
Palisades	70%	5	6	9	28
Manchester	80%	5	12	7	24
Atwater	90%	5	12	2	3
Rosemont	100%	4	11	5	28
Fairfield	100%	4	11	7	25
Dennison	no estimate provided	3	5	6	5
		57	136	95	228

There was a certain amount of tracking at every school, regardless of size, even at Woodlake, where the principal was openly opposed to the practice of tracking. However, we found a number of differences between the schools when we examined the extent and nature of tracking practices at each school. For example, homogeneous grouping appears to have occurred in only four subject areas at Vista. Classes in the other four subject areas were open to students of any ability level--that is, they were heterogeneous in composition. At Fairfield, Rosemont, and Atwater, on the other hand, students were tracked in all eight subject areas-- including PE, the arts, and vocational subjects.

We also found that the tracking systems at our thirteen high schools varied considerably in the amount of flexibility built into their structure. At some schools, students were literally locked into their entire school program as a result of their track placement. At others, students were placed into track levels subject by subject, and it was quite conceivable that an individual student might be in a high-track English class and an average-track math class, for example.

Less Flexible: Tracking Across Subjects	More Flexible: Tracking Subject by Subject	
Fairfield	Vista	Woodlake
Atwater	Crestview	Laurel
Palisades	Rosemont	Manchester
Bradford	Newport	
No Information	No Formal Tracking	
Dennison	Euclid	

Another interesting point to be made about tracking is that it doesn't always operate at a formal level. Even a school which has no tracking policy and no structured system of placing students in classes according to their ability may in fact have a fairly rigid system of tracking. It is achieved informally, in one of two ways (or a combination of both): first, scheduling requirements may create what are, in effect, tracked classes. For example, if French III is only offered during second period and Trigonometry is only offered during fourth period because there isn't enough student demand for more than one section of each, then the students who take both French III and Trig will not only be in those two classes together, but will also be that much more likely to end up in the same sections of English and social studies during the remaining avail- able time slots.

Second, tracked classes may emerge as the result of self-selection by students who have long since learned which "box" they belong in. For example, students who have learned to think of themselves as slow will be unlikely to want to sign up for what they perceive as more difficult courses, and may also tend to avoid teachers who have a reputation for being more demanding or college-prep-oriented. These two informal processes can lock students into--and out of--certain programs just as effectively as a formal tracking structure, while allowing the school to deny that it tracks its students.

Grouping students by ability could perhaps be pedagogically desirable if it were done on the basis of sound (and frequent) diagnostic testing, and if considerable mobility were built into the system. This would hold true both within and between classrooms. Within a class, the teacher might group and re-group students often in the course of a semester or a year, using various criteria--need, interest, ability--for different learning experiences. A student who understands decimals but just can't catch on to fractions, for example, could be placed in a faster-paced group for the decimals unit and a slower-paced group for fractions. That would be within-class mobility, and frequent diagnosis and regrouping is the key to making it work.

Between-class mobility implies that a student could move up to a higher-level class at anytime during the year that it was determined that he or she was ready for it. Likewise, a student having trouble in a regular class might be put into a slower class for a period of time, to master the competencies in which he or she was lacking. The student might or might not return to the regular class that year, but would certainly have the chance to do so at the end of the year. Again, frequent diagnosis is the key.

Unfortunately, the schools we studied were not set up to meet student needs with the degree of flexibility I've just described. Diagnostic tests were rarely, if ever, used by teachers of any subject; teachers taught to the whole group and seldom used small within-class grouping and regrouping strategies; and students remained at their assigned track level, not only throughout the year, but from one year to the next. When occasionally a student was moved to another track level, it was usually to a lower one rather than to a higher one. In effect, as the system functions, once a student is place in a track he or she is trapped there.

We learned, too, that control of tracking decisions in the schools we studied rested more or less definitively with the school counselor. Sometimes teacher judgment was taken into account, but students and parents were rarely, if ever, consulted.

The experiences and concerns of students in the same type of program are often more similar to one another, even though they are in different types of schools, than they are to those in a different program in the same type of school.[29]

This finding from the High School and Beyond Study was similar to what we found in A Study of Schooling. In effect, students in a high-track class at School A are likely to have more in common with high-track students in School B than with students in a low-track class at their own school. As we shall see, students in low-track and high-track classes are taught different things, and are taught in different ways. Furthermore, since tracking also functions as an instrument of social selection, what the high-track student and the low-track student bring to their classes--their background, aspirations, previous experiences; all the trappings of their family's social status be it high, middle, or low--can be very different.

It is difficult to conceive of a less democratic, less egalitarian system. Students in high tracks feel superior, and those in lower tracks, we discovered, feel inferior; there is little common ground. Among students, friendships are usually formed with others in one's own track level. The tracking system deprives students of the chance to get to know other students who have different needs, learning styles, life goals, values and backgrounds. Carried to its most extreme, a system of tracking in a school can contribute to the perpetuation of misunderstanding and tension between students whose schooling is preparing them to work with their heads and those who are preparing to work with their hands. Since track placement has been shown to relate to the student's ethnic identity and socioeconomic status, tracking does much to enhance a system of social classes in America.

306

```
            *           *           *
```

Jeannie Oakes used a subset of classes from A Study of Schooling to examine the effects of tracking in more detail. Because English and math were the most frequently tracked subjects, she used the 156 English and 141 math classes at the junior and senior high schools in the study as her sample.

Table 6.8

Number of classes sampled at each track level
--high school and junior high English and math

	low	average	high	hetero	total
HS English	12	31	18	22	83
JH English	18	15	16	24	73
HS math	19	20	22	11	72
JH math	17	17	19	16	69

With track level as the independent variable, Oakes looked at such dependent variables as: time spent on instruction, content of instruction, teaching practices, classroom interaction and student attitudes. The patterns she found were dramatic:[30]

1. The topics studied in high-track classes were those traditionally associated with preparation for higher education, while the topics studied in low-track classes were more likely to be related to basic literacy and computation, and "everyday life and work knowledge."

2. Teachers of higher-track classes tended to list activities and skills requiring higher levels of cognitive functioning than did teachers of classes at lower track levels.

3. Teachers of higher-track classes were concerned that their students learn independence and critical thinking, while teachers of lower-track classes seemed to emphasize conformity and obedience to rules and expectations.

307

4. High track classes spent more time on instructional activity during class than did lower-track classes.

5. High track students were expected to spend more time on homework.

6. Instructional practices were distributed among tracks in such a way that students in the lowest groups were the least likely to experience better teaching.

7. Students in the lower tracks were more likely to view the teachers as punitive, while students in the higher tracks tended to view their teachers as concerned and supportive.

8. Peer relationships were reported to be positive by students in higher track classes, less positive by students in lower track classes. Students in lower track classes also reported that they "often felt left out." and they were less positive about their own class participation.

9. High-track classes tended to be characterized by a greater frequency of active learning activities, higher levels of active student participation, and more on-task behavior in the classroom than were lower-track classes.

10. Students in low-track classes had less positive self-concept scores.

All in all, Oakes' findings suggest that the actual classroom experiences of students vary enormously, depending on the track level of the classes in which they are placed. Students in low track classes are likely to have discouraging, alienating experiences while students in high track classes are more likely to have experiences which leave them feeling relatively confident, secure, and optimistic.

Teachers as well as students are affected by the tracking practices in effect at the schools where they work. Traditionally, teachers with more seniority are given the higher-track classes while young teachers fresh out of college must "do their time" with the lower-track classes. The educational wisdom of this pattern is open to question, however. A strong case can certainly be made for the argument that slower students badly need contact with the best and most experienced teachers a school can provide.

Self-fulfilling Prophecy?

During interviews, 47 teachers of high school classes identified as low-track made comments on the climate of their classes. Of the 47, 35 referred to the low ability level of their students and of these, 19 did so in a negative, "put-down" way, revealing a dislike of and impatience with the students.

When asked to rate their class climate from 1 (low) to 10 (high), these teachers' average rating was 6.6, while 82 teachers of classes identified as high-ability rated the climate of their classes, on the average, at about 8.3. Once again we must consider the possibility of a self-fulfilling prophecy at work. Over their years of schooling--often beginning in first grade, with separation into ability groups for reading--students who are slow to grasp concepts, less articulate, or who have undiagnosed and therefore uncorrected learning disabilities are stigmatized. The tragedy is that evidently they soon learn to blame themselves for being inadequate,* when some of the blame must surely rest with an educational system which labels them as failures at an early age and then treats them accordingly for years.

*   *   *

Oakes also found evidence that degrees of curriculum differentiation exist even within track levels, and that these differences are clearly related not to ability but to the students' ethnic identity and socioeconomic backgrounds. For this analysis, she examined the data from the sampled vocational classes. At the high school level, students in high-track classes and those preparing for college rarely take vocational programs, so the populations of these courses are generally average and lower-track students. Oakes found interesting differences in both content and format between the vocational programs of the all-white

---

* As we have seen, Oakes found lower self-concepts among lower track students.

schools and those which had mixed or all-minority student populations.

While all three kinds of schools—white, nonwhite, and mixed—had similar levels of vocational emphasis overall, a closer look at the kinds of courses offered shows clear differences. Vocational programs at all-white schools tended to focus on industrial arts and home economics courses that were appropriate for all students and to which no special stigma was attached. Even students headed for college could learn some woodworking skills, not to mention "bachelor cooking," for instance. Business courses at these schools stressed such topics as management, taxation, and the stock market. Elite courses, such as aviation or marine technology, were sometimes available. And all these courses took place on the school grounds, within the context of the regular school schedule. They were an integral part of the overall school program.

In contrast, vocational programs at mixed or minority schools tended to focus on training for specific and often fairly low-level occupations: building maintenance, commercial sewing, cosmetology, TV repair, and the like. Business courses at these schools stressed clerical skills and retail sales. Many of these courses took place off campus and outside of the school's regular schedule—that is, they were likely to remove the students to another location for up to half a day, thus distancing them from the regular school program and subtly communicating a message that the regular school is not for them. Inevitably, such students may come to feel that they don't really belong to the regular school. Vocational programs such as these are often labelled "work experience" and, as Oakes concludes, the end result

> ...may be that large numbers of predominantly non-white students are channeled early into training for specific low-level occupations, rather than encouraged to continue in more academic programs. These students may be eased out of the school setting through on-the-job training during the school day. They may be likely to leave school early believing they have been trained in a marketable skill, only to find that they cannot translate these skills into occupational advantage.

It is unlikely that employers view graduates of vocational programs, and certainly not early leavers, as successful at school. Students from vocational programs, in fact, may be seen as school failures, unable to succeed in the more academic programs. As a result, employers are likely to prefer non-vocational students who appear to be more certified as trainable. For non-white vocational students, these difficulties may be even more pronounced. For in obtaining any but the lowest-level positions it may be more essential for non-whites to have the appropriate school certification. Because of the historic barriers faced by non-whites in employment, employers may require greater assurance of the desired cultural and personality characteristics in non-white employees. Vocational education program attendance does not appear to supply this assurance.

In view of these findings, school people and policy makers should seriously reconsider the appropriateness of specific occupational training in secondary schools. It is likely that these programs do not serve the democratic ends most Americans wish their schools to achieve.[31]

*   *   *

Conant suggested that if the comprehensive high school cannot succeed in fulfilling its three-part mission, a "radical change" in the structure of American secondary education would "be in order." While it is true that our high schools are providing an education for all Americans, they may be doing so in ways that could have disastrous social consequences, for they separate people instead of bringing them together. A class system directly contrary to our supposed national belief in equality and the worth of every person has been set in place and is becoming more deeply entrenched with every passing year. The tracking system contributes to this stratification of our society because it is not based on ability alone but on social factors such as the student's race, socioeconomic status, and family background.

I am not sure whether Conant would have considered the replacement of tracking practices with a deliberate policy of heterogeneous grouping to be a "radical change," but the findings of A Study of Schooling clearly suggest that secondary schools should be re-organized so that students are no longer separated into so-called "homogeneous" ability or achievement groups.

One of the most exciting findings of A Study of Schooling was the outcome of Oakes' comparison of tracked classes with untracked (heterogeneous, or mixed-ability) classes. For years, the conventional wisdom has held that mixed-ability classes operate at the level of the lowest common denominator. That is, the teachers aim their instruction just below the average of the students in the class. Our findings, however, clearly showed that mixed-ability classes were much more similar, in both content and processes, to upper average and high-track classes. Students in such classes had the advantage of better teaching, more time spent on instruction, and more positive class climate. They had the further advantage of being able to work with students of differing interests and ability levels and home backgrounds and future plans--in short, they were learning in a pluralistic, democratic setting. They were not learning to feel inferior, and they were not learning to feel superior or snobbish. Despite the tendency of teen-agers to be judgmental about each other, the subliminal message learned by kids who experience heterogeneously grouped classes is that differences between people are a natural part of life, and are perfectly all right.

Mixed-ability classes need not be a burden for the teacher. Indeed, in many subjects teachers already work primarily with heterogeneous groups of students. The management techniques for mixed-ability teaching exist, and can be mastered: diagnostic pre-testing, within-class grouping and re-grouping, student-to-student tutoring, and the use of learning centers, for example. And there are still many times when the teacher can and should present material to the class as a whole.

Functioning this way in the high school classroom would be a professional challenge that many teachers would find stimulating. Others might feel threatened, but could adjust if given appropriate encouragement as well as opportunities to learn and to practice the unfamiliar skills. In truth, the change to a policy of heterogeneous grouping <u>would</u> be a "radical" one, in that it runs counter to tracking practices which have become so deeply entrenched that they are rarely, if ever, questioned. It's a truism that "we teach as we were taught," and most teachers experienced some form of tracking themselves, when they were students.

Nor do present pre-service teacher training programs deliberately prepare teachers to work with mixed-ability classes, so non-tracking policies implemented in public schools would call for changes in teacher training, as well. The effects of such a policy change would be far-reaching. But our findings suggest that such a reorganization would be beneficial for young people, pedagogically sound, and ultimately healthier for our society as a whole.

Summary: individualizing, evaluating, and tracking

There is ample evidence in the data from this Study that individualization of instruction has never really taken root at the high school level. Like many curriculum reforms, techniques of individualization remain untried, and life goes on much as it always has, "behind the classroom door."

The teachers in our sample admitted that they didn't individualize their instructional programs much, if at all. To begin with, they told us that they do not use diagnostic or aptitude test results and without the information that such tests can provide, teachers tend to rely upon their own judgment. Teaching to the whole class is the most familiar and comfortable strategy for the great majority of high school teachers, and that is what they do. They told us this themselves, in a variety of ways. Many of these were discussed in chapter 5. Students, too, told us that they work primarily as a whole-class group. And this is certainly what our trained observers recorded in the 525 classrooms that were observed.

Most of the teachers in our sample reported making use of behaviorally-stated instructive objectives, but not as a tool for individualization. Rather, the tendency was to set the same objectives for the entire class and then to use them as a basis for evaluating student progress. The teachers found behavioral objectives quite helpful, when utilized in this way.

We found that "evaluation" in the more academic subjects meant tests, quizzes, and the teacher's judgment of students' classwork and homework. In the less academic subjects, teachers made use of a wider array of evaluation methods, including having students perform or show how to do something, or having them make projects or prepare reports. They also used tests, quizzes, classwork and homework, of course.

Tests and quizzes in every subject area were generally of the traditional, "objective" type. That is, they were a mixture of Multiple Choice, True/False, matching, and so on, requiring fine-tuning of memorization skills but not much in the way of critical thinking or higher cognitive processes such as analysis, synthesis, and evaluation. Even when an essay question or two were included (usually at the end, and often for "extra credit" only), they usually required only that a student write down a paragraph of remembered facts. Computer scoring of objective tests would free teachers to spend more time reading and responding to student essays and questions requiring original thought.

Huge differences in the amount of time that students spend on schoolwork, both in and out of school, are directly related to the type of academic program in which the student is placed. This is one of the many inequities of the tracking system. Students who are placed in "general" or "vocational" programs may find themselves shortchanged in the long run, because in these programs less time is spent on instructional activity in class and less homework is expected. That may be fine with the students, who perhaps enjoy what they perceive to be an easier schedule. But the quality and quantity of their learning is surely affected, and after graduation they may find themselves at a disadvantage.

Contrary to popular belief, there is no evidence that ability grouping, or tracking, leads to gains in student achievement. On the other hand, there is some evidence that ability grouping can have negative effects on the self-esteem of students placed in average and low-track classes, and A Study of Schooling data revealed that students in average and low-track

314

classes were more likely to experience inferior teaching, spend less class time on instruction, have less access to higher-status knowledge, were less frequently expected to function at higher cognitive levels, and were expected to acquire habits of conformity and obedience rather than learning to think for themselves.

Another common assumption about ability grouping is that it reduces the range of student differences in the classroom. While tracking may separate the extremes of student ability, it does not really create homogeneous groups. It is probably safe to say that in every tracked class, one will find a broad range of student abilities as well as major differences in student learning styles. The rhetoric of tracking, however, with its mythology of teachably homogeneous grouping, allows us to continue teaching the same thing to the whole class, just as we have done for so long.

The practice of grouping students by ability is open to serious criticism on two other counts as well. First, evidence in our Study and in research by others clearly suggests that the students' background plays a big part in the track placement decisions made by school counselors. The absence of diagnostic testing means that such decisions in fact must rest on factors other than measured aptitude or ability. They are likely to be made on the basis of what is known about the student's personal background, what track the student was in at previous grade levels (this process can sometimes be traced all the way back to decisions made in kindergarten or first grade!), and on assumptions made about the student's potential based on his or her ethnic identity.

The second fallacy of tracking is that it is a neutral process which has no judgmental impact. The absurdity of this argument is obvious when data showing the discouraging, alienating effect of low-track placement on young people is examined. A Catch-22 situation is created: teachers expect students in low-track classes to be more difficult and less pleasant to teach; they relate to these students accordingly (as Oakes has been able to document so clearly), and inevitably their expectations are met.* I have come to feel that the only workable way to break this vicious circle is to replace the tracking system with a stated policy of heterogeneous grouping. Not only is this educationally justifiable, but it is more socially equitable, psychologically healthier for students, and professionally more challenging for teachers.

---

* An insidious side effect of the tracking system is the part it plays in creating a status hierarchy among the teachers at a school. I believe a healthier work environment would require that all teachers have an equal share in teaching all kinds of students.

1. Further details can be found in Technical Report No. 6, Kenneth A. Sirotnik, Mitchell A. Nides, and Gerald A. Engstrom, Some Methodological Issues in Developing Measures of Classroom Learning Environment (1980).

2. Readers interested in the technical aspects of this component of the Study are referred the Technical Report No. 23: An Examination of the Viability of Class Climate as a Useful Construct in Secondary Schools. G. Engstrom, 1981. Most of the data in this section of chapter 6 is drawn from the Engstrom analysis.

3. The differences between school means for the Teacher Authoritarianism scale were significant at the .001 level.

4. The differences between boys' and girls' means on each of these 14 scales were statistically significant at the .001 level.

5. For all three variables, the differences between the boys' and the girls' mean scores were significant at the .001 level.

6. Landscape of Learning, by Maxine Greene, (New York: Teachers College Press, 1978) pp. 249-250.

7. Engstrom, op. cit., pp. 40-41.

8. Life in Classrooms, by Philip Jackson, (New York: Holt, Rinehart, and Winston, 1968) p. 60.

9. K.A. Sirotnik, The Contextual Correlates of the Relative Expenditures of Classroom Time on Instruction and Behavior (Technical Report No. 26, 1981).

10. According to observers' records as well as to the estimates of the students themselves.

11. Engstrom, Technical Report No. 23, op. cit.

12. Sirotnik, Technical Report No. 26, op. cit., p. 20.

13. Engstrom, Technical Report No. 23, op. cit., p. 55.

14. For various reasons, only English, math, social studies, science, and arts classes were used for this analysis. Engstrom, Technical Report No. 23, 1981, p. 48.

15. Engstrom, op. cit., p. 55.

16. David P. Wright, Teachers' Educational Beliefs (Technical Report No. 14, 1980).

17. In fact, only one other item of the 21 educational beliefs items had a higher mean response, and that--as we might have guessed--was a Teacher Control item: "Good teacher-student relations are enhanced when it is clear that the teacher, not the students, is in charge of classroom activities."

18. In both cases, the differences between the means were statistically significant.

19. Engstrom, Technical Report No. 23, op. cit., p. 52.

20. David D. Berliner, "The Beginning Teacher Evaluation Study: Research to Inform Policy," The Generator, AERA Division G, Vol. 1 No. 1 (Spring, 1979).

21. For example, Bossert 1979, op. cit. chapter 5.

22. B.J. Benham, "How a Staff Change Agent can Help Teachers, Schools," NASSP Bulletin. (November, 1976) pp. 92-97.

23. B.J. Benham, "Thoughts on the Failure of Curriculum Reform," Educational Leadership (December, 1977) pp. 205-208.

24. A Place Called School, by John I. Goodlad. (New York: McGraw-Hill, 1984).

25. The American High School Today by James B. Conant. (New York: McGraw-Hill, 1959).

26. C.H. Persell, Testing, Tracking, and Teacher Expectations: Their Implications for Education and Inequality. (New York: American Jewish Committee, New York Institute on Pluralism and Group Identity, 1976).

27. Warren Findley and Miriam Bryan, Ability Grouping 1970 (Athens, Ga: Georgia University College of Education, 1970) ERIC # ED048382.

28. K.L. Alexander, M. Cook, and E.L. McDill, "Curriculum tracking and educational stratification: Some further evidence." American Sociological Review. (1978) 43:47-66.

29. High School and Beyond, op. cit., p. 1.

30. Jeannie Oakes, A Question of Access: Tracking and Curriculum Differentiation in a National Sample of English and Math Classes, (Technical Report No. 24, 1981).

31. Jeannie Oakes, Limiting Opportunity: Student Race and Curricular Differences in Secondary Vocational Education, (Technical Report No. 28, 1981).

CHAPTER VII

THE OTHER SIDE OF THE FOREST

Complexity of the School

It is almost a cliché, these days, to observe that schools are tremendously complex social systems. Sarason has observed, fairly enough I think, that it is impossible even for an insider to know the culture of the school in all of its dimensions.[1]

And yet it often seems as if most Americans feel that they fully understand what a school is, how it works, and what is needed to make it work better. Indeed, everyone has an opinion. These opinions are based on personal experience as a student, first; later on, as a parent, taxpayer, and community member.

They are also based on information received by way of television, radio, magazines and newspapers. Such information may be complete or incomplete; those who present it may or may not be fully informed themselves, or may hold opinions which affect their treatment of the subject of schools. Regardless of whether schools are fairly or unfairly represented in the communications media, the information is interpreted by each listener according to his or her own values and biases.

Informal communications, too, play their part. "The grapevine" was mentioned by 40% of our parent sample as one way in which they received information about their child's school.

Throughout this book, we have seen examples of the interconnectedness of various aspects of the schools we studied. In chapter 3, we found that although the teachers didn't generally have very much contact with their principals, still the principals' behavior, as perceived by the teachers, had a great deal to do with the teachers' overall job satisfaction. In chapter 4, we found evidence that students' satisfaction with their school as work place was closely tied to their perceptions of its adequacy as a social environment. And chapter 6 described how, in the classrooms we studied, many aspects of class climate were interrelated and connected to other things as well--student satisfaction, teaching practices, perceived teacher affect, observed time on task, track level, student gender and to some extent student ethnicity, and the teacher's satisfaction with his or her work, for a start.

We can agree, I think, on the complexity of the school and on the ecological interconnectedness of all of its parts. Perhaps we can also agree, with Sarason, that even an insider can never fully understand the culture of a school in all of its dimensions. As a result of such understanding, educators should make every effort to avoid initiating change in schools without taking the potential systemic consequences into account. In effect, before a change is initiated--especially a major one, originating at the district level--the educational equivalent of an "environmental impact study" should be made.

Multiple Realities

Another feature of schools which makes them complicated to understand is the "Rashomon effect:" essentially, the story one hears depends on who's telling the tale. Recent psychological studies show that a group of people who witness an incident will rarely agree on what actually happened, a phenomenon long understood by writers of mystery novels.

One might also think of the seven blind men and the elephant; each had a different idea of what an elephant "was," because he "saw" only a small part of it. Principals have been known to say that the teachers "don't have the complete picture," as a way of explaining why they don't involve teachers more in school decision-making. But I'd be willing to bet that most principals have a limited view themselves. Likewise, students see the school from their own place within it, and parents see it through the eyes of their children, through television and newspaper reports, and through the grapevine. Even parents who are actively involved with the school through the PTA or even volunteer service in the school only see parts of the complete system.

A number of interesting examples of differing perceptions emerged from our exploration of the data in chapters 5 and 6. We found some evidence to suggest that what the teachers thought they were doing in their classrooms wasn't necessarily what the students perceived them to be doing, nor was it was what the trained observers reported them to be doing.

Students, for instance, generally reported that the cognitive level of most classroom activities was pretty low, while teachers tended to report that they used activities at all cognitive levels, including the highest ones of analysis, synthesis, and evaluation. Students said that what they mostly did was memorize information for later recall. Samples of tests given by teachers (provided to us by the teachers themselves) tended to support the students' view, for these tests nearly always required recall skills and rarely, if ever, asked for synthesis.

Similarly, while teachers told us they believed that praising students was extremely important, and probably felt that they did a fair amount of it, our observers reported that the 525 teachers whose classes they observed almost never praised their students, either individually or as a group. The origin of this discrepancy may lie in the way in which teachers sometimes learn that a particular practice--such as praise, or open-ended questioning--is desirable pedagogically, but they don't learn how to do these things; they don't have opportunities, in their training programs, to practice them.[2]

This phenomenon of multiple realities can be found in all human social systems, to be sure, not only in schools. A question one might pose, however, is whether the organizational characteristics of a social system tend to minimize or to maximize the degree of perceptual fragmentation found in that system. The answer to this question would probably be yes. We found that the organization of the high schools we studied, for example, separates teacher from teacher, student from student, and administrators from both teachers and students. Our society's requirements that a high school provide a diversity of programs ensures both higher levels of organizational complexity and a greater variety of perceptions about what schools are like, what they are for, and what goes on in them.

Tracking as an organizational characteristic is a case in point. As we found in chapter 6, students in classes identified as "low" track had a very different set of schooling experiences than did students in classes identified as "high" track. Likewise, teachers of high-track classes have very different experiences from teachers of low-track classes, and the seniority/ status hierarchy often found in American high schools prevents principals from assigning all teachers an approximately equal number of both, even if it occurs to them that such shared responsibility for all students would be desirable.

The college/non-college dichotomy is another example of an organizational characteristic that guarantees that students will have differing perceptions of school. As we were able to show in over half of the schools we studied, once slotted into a "general" curriculum (i.e., non-college preparatory), students almost never encountered peers who were in college preparatory classes, and vice versa.

Earlier in our history, the idea of a commonly shared schooling experience predominated. Assimilation and unification were national goals and the common school movement reflected this. The common schools were elementary schools, of course, not secondary schools. And to a great extent, public elementary elementary schools still do provide Americans with a shared educational experience. But the special mission of the secondary school--to prepare young people for the world of work, or for higher education--made a certain amount of diversity inevitable.

The question, however, is not whether diversity is inevitable, but rather how much of it is desirable. I maintain that the comprehensive high school has, perhaps, become too fragmented an institution. The largest ones in particular--over 2,000 students, say--while they might once have made sense economically, have proven to be less than successful in human terms.

In chapter 3, for example, we found that the teachers in our sample indicated higher job satisfaction in schools which had fewer problems, and these tended to be the smaller schools.

In chapter 4, we discovered linkages between school size, student participation in a variety of extracurricular activities, student satisfaction with various aspects of schooling, and the "grade" which students gave their school.

And finally, in chapter 6, we found some evidence to show that as a rule students got less individual attention from their teachers at the larger schools.

A research study specifically designed to test differences between large and small schools would, I suspect, be likely to provide far more definitive support for my contention that a school of fewer than 1,500 students is a healthier learning environment for young people. As it happens, just such a study was done some time ago by Roger Barker and his colleagues. They found that students in smaller schools are likely to be more fully involved in the life of their school, and are likely to feel more responsibility toward their school, than are students in larger schools. Larger schools are much more likely to have sizable populations of students who are, more or less, "outsiders"-- who feel no sense of responsibility for or involvement with their school.[3]

Consolidation of schools proceeded during the 1960s and 70s despite this evidence, however. For one thing, James Conant advocated larger schools, and his message reached the general public,[4] while news of the Barker studies did not. For another thing, consolidation was viewed as financially desirable. That is, it was argued that it is less expensive to operate one large high school than two or three smaller ones. No doubt there is some truth to this, but the economic advantages could not then and cannot now be seen to outweigh the social, psychological, and pedagogical disadvantages of large, consolidated schools.

Thirdly, large consolidated schools and districts were viewed by educational administrators as being easier to manage. Centralization of authority meant there would be less chance that individual schools would be doing their own thing, and that was seen as desirable.

And finally, the movement to close smaller, outlying schools and send students to a large, new centrally-located high school was in tune with the national mood of the post-WW II years. Growth was the order of the day, and big was better. In effect, schools responded to the national momentum; once again, we see how our schools mirror our society.

The present era of decline--in school enrollments, as well as in national economic growth--is unprecedented in our national experience, and throws us into a confusion with which we are poorly equipped to cope. It may be that smaller high schools will suddenly be "discovered" to have real advantages over large ones. If so, this too will be a reflection of societal forces, just as the move to bigness was. It will, however, have the advantage of being closer to the truth: smaller schools do seem to be healthier learning environments for young people.

In arguing for smaller high schools, I am not suggesting a return to the "enclave" system which existed in the 40s, 50s, and early 60s. The "neighborhood school," serving an ethnically and/or socioeconomically homogeneous community, is not what is needed now. Like it or not, we are a multicultural society and all of our children will continue to need to learn to live and work with children who are different from themselves.

In chapter 6, I made a case for dismantling the tracking system and replacing it with a deliberate policy of heterogeneous grouping. Each classroom would have a range of student abilities, and no formal or informal system would be used to separate students or to grant certain knowledge and skills to some but not to others. My support for heterogeneous schools is a logical extension of my support for heterogeneous classrooms.

I will pursue this discussion at some length towards the end of this chapter, in the section on policy recommendations. My purpose in this section has been merely to suggest that the comprehensive high school is an enormously complex organism, and that by separating students and giving them different experiences we are adding to the confusion by ensuring that very few people in our society will agree either on what goes on in schools or on what schools are for. Lacking such agreement as to purposes, our schools will continue to flounder, trying to be all things to all people and satisfying almost no one. Change and improvement efforts will be more likely to bog down in the complexities of the ecosystem, unless the system itself is simplified.

*   *   *

In chapter 1, I observed that working with the data from A Study of Schooling was a little like exploring a large forest. Decisions had to be made at every step: which direction to go, what to look at carefully and what to pass by. The choice was made to focus on two types of questions. The first three questions have been addressed in chapters 3, 4, 5, and 6: What are the frustrations and satisfactions of teaching? How do schools shape students' behavior? and What goes on in classrooms? In effect, these three questions provided the basic structural framework of this book.

Four additional questions, however, also emerged from the data presented in chapters 3 through 6. No less intrinsic to the Study, these four questions reflect the cumulative and overlapping nature of much of the Study data: How could teachers be better prepared? Are all schools basically alike? What are the chances of improving high schools? And what policy changes would help make such improvement possible?

Answers to all seven questions emerge directly from the findings that have been presented in this book. It is time, now, to review these findings in terms of the seven questions.

I.

What are the frustrations and satisfactions of teaching?

The job itself is exhausting. Most of the teachers in our sample dealt with 120-150 students each day. They tried, during five class periods of about 45-50 minutes each, to present information, teach skills, evaluate progress, and do what they could to engage their students in the learning process.

The output of psychic energy needed to confront over one hundred students every day in a caring, enthusiastic, and professionally competent way is tremendous. No one who has not been a teacher can really imagine the energy it takes to focus on the varying needs of a classroom of teenagers. Within the space of just a few minutes, one student may need an explanation, another may need a word of praise, and another may need to be reprimanded. At virtually the same time, a messenger may appear at the door with a note from the guidance office and the P.A. system may come to life with an announcement about placement testing or cheerleader tryouts. Despite all this, we found that teachers actually managed to devote 40-42 minutes of each class, on the average to instruction. Much of this consisted of lecture-style presentation by the teacher or question-and-answer interaction directed by the teacher. In other words, the teacher is "on stage" nearly all the time. In fact, we found that teachers out-talked all students by a ratio of three to one. After about fifty minutes of this, there is a break of three or four minutes as classes change. Then another class troops in, and the whole thing begins again.

Furthermore, we found, it was not possible for most teachers to avoid taking schoolwork home at night and on weekends. The high school teachers in our sample estimated that they spent about 50-60 hours a week on their work, on the average. This did not include other professional duties such as attendance at staff meetings, in-service activities, PTA, and so on. Nor did it include the extra duties often expected of teachers, such as chaperoning dances, selling football tickets, and supervising clubs or other after-school activities.

All things considered, it is hardly surprising that we found such a neutral atmosphere in the classes we observed. I believe that Joyce Wright's conjecture about the emotionally "flat" tone of these classrooms is very close to the truth:

> To respond to students with a great deal of feeling, be it positive or negative, requires a lot of energy. Perhaps it is too much to expect one individual to constantly respond at a heightened level to large numbers of students six hours a day, five days a week.[5]

In order to do the job at all, even the most conscientious high school teachers must conserve their energy, parceling it out in moderate doses so as to get through each day and each week, and still feel able to face the next day and the next week.

There is no doubt in my mind that high school teachers could benefit greatly from sabbatical leaves similar to those provided for college teachers. Certainly, they have no less a need to re-charge their batteries. A combination of smaller classes, slightly lighter teaching loads (four classes a day, say, instead of five), and one year of paid sabbatical leave for every seven years of service would go a long way towards making high school teaching a more attractive career. Combined with more selective admissions policies at teacher training institutions and certain changes in teacher training programs, the long-range result would be better teaching in our high schools and better learning experiences for our young people.

Considering the demands of high school teaching and the great expenditures of energy required, it is reassuring that as many as two-thirds of the teachers we sampled indicated that if they had it to do over, they would again choose teaching as a career. Obviously, these teachers got a good deal of satisfaction from their work despite the physical and emotional demands connected with it. What makes for job satisfaction in high school teaching?

The autonomy enjoyed by most high school teachers in their own classrooms is one big source of satisfaction. In effect, the high school teacher is the ruler of that kingdom--three walls and a window, thirty desks and a chalkboard--and is in control of what happens there. Indeed, the teachers in our study did indicate a high degree of satisfaction with the amount of control they felt they had over various aspects of their work lives.

What else makes teachers feel happy with their work? In the schools we studied, teacher job satisfaction was related to the number and intensity of problems that the teachers perceived to exist at their school. Those schools which had a lot of serious problems were those at which teacher job satisfaction was lower, and as a rule these tended to be the larger schools.*

---

* School size correlated with teacher composite school problems score .70.

Another aspect of the teaching career which one might expect to have a bearing on the overall job satisfaction of teachers is the quality of staff relationships. In general, the teachers in our sample seemed to feel fairly good about their colleagues. Two schools at which this was not the case were Newport and Rosemont--both large, urban schools with many problems and low teacher job satisfaction.

Even in a study of this size, it is not possible to examine everything. One area that we did not tackle was the life of the teachers' lounge. I would hypothe-size that, when teachers have a period free from the pressure of the classroom, a cup of coffee and a few minutes of relaxation in the teachers' lounge are almost a psychological necessity. I would further speculate--and here I have some indirect support from our data--that conversations in the teachers' lounge, if they were to be recorded and categorized over a period of time, would be found to be about mostly non-school topics (with the possible exception of the constantly fascinating subject of problem students). That this may be so is suggested by our finding that the teachers in our sample reported knowing very little about their fellow teachers' behavior with students, their job competence, or their educational beliefs. We know, too, that teachers rarely if ever have occa-sion to observe each other's teaching, so that the average teacher has no basis upon which to estimate a colleague's job competence or to know about his or her behavior with students.

What all this suggests is that our finding that staff relations were generally regarded as satisfactory by the teachers at most of our schools must be quali-fied. My guess is that most high school teachers really don't know each other very well. They tend to assume that their colleagues are just about as compe-tent as they are themselves, and that in the absence of any evidence to the contrary they share a feeling of common cause: "We're all in this together, doing the best we can."

The third major influence on the job satisfaction of high school teachers seem to be the type of leader-ship provided by the school administration, and in particular by the principal. In this area of our findings there were enormous differences between the thirteen schools.

What sort of leadership earns a positive response from teachers? The principal who was perceived by the teachers in our Study as providing good leadership allowed his staff considerable freedom of action, and was open to new ideas. He was supportive and encouraging, and the teachers felt that he trusted them and respected their judgment. Basically democratic in his leadership style rather than authoritarian or laissez-faire, he often sought out the teachers' ideas, and consulted with them before making any decision that would affect them. The teachers felt included in the school's decision-making process, and agreed that "the administrators and teachers collaborate in making this school run effectively." Staff meetings were not seen as a waste of time, but when they were called, were viewed by teachers as being about moderately important or very important matters.

Sarason has some intriguing things to say about the limitations on what a principal can do. Two are of interest here. First of all, a principal is constrained to some extent by the expectations and norms of the superordinate system; that is, the school district. He is rewarded for maintaining the status quo. However--and this, I think, is fascinating--the principal himself may impose limits on his own actions which are not strictly necessary. In effect, the principal's belief about what "the system" will allow is central to the amount of freedom, participation, and innovation he will support in his school:

> The tendency to anticipate trouble in relation
> to the system is characteristic of many princi-
> pals and one of the most frequent and strong
> obstacles to trying what they conceive to be an
> atypical procedure.[6]

In other words, the principal's conception of what the system will allow, whether this conception is in fact right or wrong, determines how that principal performs his role. It seems that the principals at Palisades, Crestview, and Dennison, who were well-liked by their teachers for many of the reasons listed earlier, must have been able to conceive of the system as one which would tolerate considerable innovation, teacher participation in decision-making, and freedom of action for teachers.

The principals at Vista, Atwater, and Bradford, on the other hand, were extremely unpopular with their teachers. The teachers at those schools felt that their principal was not open to new ideas, allowed them little freedom of action, treated them in an authoritarian manner and made decisions unilaterally. I would be prepared to hypothesize that these three men might well have had narrow conceptions of what the system would tolerate. They might have been the type to hide behind the higher authority of the superintendent, the Board of Education, or the policy manual.

The Study of Schooling data bank contains a considerable body of information from and about the principals who were involved in the Study, enough to fill another book. My hypothesis must remain just that, an informed speculation, until such time as another researcher goes further into the principal data than I have time or space to do here.

What I do consider important is the finding that the teachers in our Study responded most positively to an open, democratic leadership style very much like McGregor's "Theory Y" leadership,[7] and that such a style seems to require a fairly open-ended set of assumptions about what is possible to do within the system.

A question that this discussion raises, of course, is: what type of principal is most likely to emerge from the Education Administration programs of our colleges and universities? Are we getting real leaders, or are we getting mostly administrators/managers? At most of the high schools we studied, the teachers perceived their principals as being more like administrators. It is my belief, too, that true leadership in a high school principal is rather rare in our educational system. I'm not even sure that real leadership,[8] with its tendency to challenge the status quo, is wanted. Most school systems seem to prefer middle-management personnel who aren't going to rock the boat.

As far as teachers' lives are concerned, we can conclude that the principal plays an important role in shaping the school's work environment. He does this whether or not he actually has frequent contact with his teachers.

We know from the literature on leadership that teacher satisfaction with the principal may well be related to the kinds of expectations the teachers have.[9] Our data showed that many teachers wanted more contact with and help from their principal than they were getting. In particular, many seemed to want their principal to offer more helpful supervision and support of the type that would assist them in solving classroom problems and in improving their teaching. That they didn't usually get this type of help from their principal is likely to have contributed to their feeling that he was primarily an administrator rather than an instructional leader. That the teachers, on the average, felt that they should be more involved in school decision-making than they were may also have contributed to this view.

These, then, are the elements of job satisfaction for teachers: the presence or absence of serious school problems, the quality of staff relationships, and the nature of the leadership provided by the principal. Other factors also contribute, of course. For example, we found that teachers felt very frustrated by what they perceived as lack of student interest in learning. In a few schools they were very unhappy about the inadequacy of equipment, learning materials, and supplies. Overcrowded classrooms added further pressure to the lives of teachers in some of our schools.

Sometimes, teachers tell me that when the pressure really builds there isn't much that one can do but laugh--or cry. Teaching is a stimulating, complex, demanding and exhausting profession. Many things intrude upon the teaching and learning process. But somehow teachers carry on, and students do learn. I salute the teacher I met once, who one day in the middle of a class pushed a chair against the wall, leaped upon it, and tore the P.A. speaker down. It had interrupted once too often with distracting and unnecessary announcements. For me, this story says a lot about what life is like for high school teachers, on weekdays between 8:00 in the morning and 3:00 in the afternoon.

How do schools shape students' behavior?

Considered as a habitat, the American high school has certain regular features which give it a distinctive character. One is its uniformity. Within the schools we studied, most of the spaces in which instruction took place were the same size and shape, and contained similar furnishings. This was true whether the school was an old-fashioned four-story brick edifice or a modern, one-story "finger-type" building. The opportunity to bring students together in smaller or larger groups was therefore severely limited by the absence of a variety of classroom sizes.

By the time they reach high school, of course, students are thoroughly accustomed to this environment, so much so that anything different--lecture rooms seating sixty, seminar rooms designed for six, open space between classes, or a conventional classroom containing several different kinds of furniture in several different work stations, for example--would be unsettling to many, if not most, students.

Another regularity of the high school environment is its control orientation. The school building, the school day, and the school program--all are designed to keep students under control: (1) only enough minutes between classes for students to get from one room to another, only enough time at mid-day to funnel everyone through the cafeteria and out again; (2) rules which prohibit students from venturing off the school grounds from 8:00 to 3:00 without permission from the proper authority; (3) teaching practices and classroom management techniques which keep students seated and, usually, quiet. These are only a few of the more obvious examples.

Social psychologists have commented on the tendency of people to assume that, on the whole, the way things are is the way they ought to be. During the late 1960's a rather unusual wave of discontent swept through American high schools and colleges and for awhile it looked as if some changes were here to stay. Students wanted more freedom, and to be included in school decision-making processes. But the thirteen high schools we studied in 1977 were strikingly similar

334

to those I attended in the late 1950's: the ferment of the 60's had subsided, and once again the regularities of high school life were more or less taken for granted by the students themselves. Above all, we found a fairly positive acceptance by students of the many ways in which the school managed to control them. In fact, most of the 7,677 students in our sample seemed fairly happy with their school experiences. They were a captive audience, but most of them didn't seem to mind.

Evidently our society values obedience and passivity very highly at this point in its development. For regardless of what we say about the importance of originality, independence, and responsible self-direction, we do not provide our young people with a schooling environment which allows them to develop such behaviors.

A third regularity of the high school environment is the separation of students into tracks. I have already discussed this at some length in chapter 6. What deserves further comment here is the extent to which the students themselves have come to accept the tracking system as right and proper. The most insidious effect of tracking, in my opinion, is the psychological one for both "high" and "low" track students. Low-track students have, by the time they reach high school, come to accept an image of themselves as inferior, and sometimes may even give up without even trying, because they've come to believe they'll inevitably fail. High-track students, on the other hand, have developed a healthy self-confidence and a feeling that success is possible. A certain smugness may go along with this sense of being one of the advantaged of the world, and I believe this smugness is just as harmful to society as the poorer students' sense of failure.

Above all, we have created a setting in which students come to think of their peers in terms of categories. Unlike the teachers, who feel "we're all in this together," students are more likely to gather into cliques based on perceptions of "us" and "them." How many high school students miss forming valuable friendships because school norms keep them separated? A good many, I expect. And the social consequences of this separation are harmful, especially in a multicultural society such as ours in which mutual understanding, respect, and cooperation are so important. Archie

Bunker was funny on TV, but a nation of Archie Bunkers is not a laughing matter.

If a school "feels" different to students depending on which track level they're in, it also feels different to boys than it does to girls. In chapter 4 I discussed our finding that, on the average, the girls in our sample were more involved in the life of their schools than were boys. They were more active in extracurricular programs, and their attitudes towards attending school were more positive. In chapter 6 we found that girls felt happier with their classroom experiences than did boys. Girls more often perceived their teachers to be enthusiastic, concerned, and professionally competent while, on the average, boys tended to see the same teachers as more authoritarian and punitive, and less helpful.

These were the perceptions of the students of both sexes. Are they true? Do teachers, in reality, treat boys and girls so very differently? We did find that male teachers, as a group, were more control-oriented and traditional in their educational beliefs while female teachers' responses to the educational beliefs scales reflected more empathy for students. But these findings relate to the sex of the teacher, not that of the students. It would require further analysis of our data to explore the question of differential treatment of boys and girls by teachers of different sexes. It could be done, however, by identifying those classes taught by men and those taught by women, and by comparing the perceptions of boys taught by women to those of girls taught by women, and the perceptions of girls taught by men to those of boys taught by men.

Even so, we would still only have sets of student perceptions. These would need to be supplemented with observation data if we were to approach an answer to the question of whether teachers really do treat boys and girls differently. The observation instrument we used, however, did not capture this degree of detail in classroom interaction, since it did not provide for the coding of teacher behavior by student gender. Another observation tool--perhaps a more ethnographic methodology--would be needed. Such a study would be an interesting and valuable extension of what the Study of Schooling was able to discover about gender differences in student experiences of schooling.

336

In chapter 1, when I first raised the question of what life is like for students in high schools, one of the things I was curious about was the degree to which American teenagers assume that the reason for going to school is economic: to get a "good"--that is, well-paying--job. A number of student responses discussed in chapter 4 suggest that this was, indeed, a pervasive assumption among the students in our sample.

For one thing, when asked what was most important for them, more students selected the Vocational function of schooling ("to get a better job") than any of the other three functions--Intellectual, Personal, or Social. Also, about nine out of every ten of the students in our sample felt that high school students should have job experience as part of their school program. The same percentage agreed that "it is worth going to school because it will help me in the future."

When we asked students to tell us what was "the most important thing you've learned in this class so far this year," we received a good many answers such as "Nothing, because it won't help me in the career I've chosen," or "What I'm learning will come in useful later because I'll need to know it when I become a--(whatever the student listed)."

Nor were the students in our sample atypical in their belief in the market value of schooling and their desire for an even closer relationship between their high school programs and practical preparation for the world of work. 71% of the approximately 20,000 members of the high school class of 1972 who are participating in the National Longitudinal Study and 70% of the 28,000 members of the class of 1980 who are participating in the High School and Beyond Study agreed that their high schools "should have placed more emphasis on vocational and technical programs."[10]

I have said it before--in chapter 4--and I'll say it again: the belief that the reason a person goes to school is to be able to get a good job and earn more money as an adult has robbed our society of two important values. First of all, it deprives young people of the feeling that what they are doing now is important. All the rewards are seen to be somewhere in the future. Secondly, it deprives society of the understanding that learning has value in itself and not just as a saleable commodity. This greatly reduces the range of knowledge

that is considered worth having, and creates a population of narrowly-educated citizens. While it is true
that the information explosion of the 20th century has
made it virtually impossible for anyone to attain the
classical ideal of broad knowledge in many areas,
surely the attitude that "I don't want to know it if it
doesn't apply directly to my own daily life and work"
is willful ignorance masquerading as realism.

    The call for "relevance" in the curriculum during
the late 1960's and early 1970's was disturbing in this
respect as well.   "Relevance," after all, sounds like
a good thing. The effect when this ideas is put into
practice, however, is to further fragment the curriculum, to further narrow the range of each individual
student's knowledge and understanding, and ultimately
to create a nation of citizens who have very little in
common with each other. In short, a nation of people
who really believe that "doing your own thing" is what
it's all about. I will return to this theme a little
later, in proposing a common general education for all
young people through the 10th grade.

                        III.

What goes on in classrooms?

Form and Function

    We have already discussed the control orientation
of schools and classrooms, and the passive behaviors
expected of students. The physical structure of the
classroom does its bit to enforce this passivity, as
well. I do not know if form follows function or
function follows form, but there is no doubt in my mind
that the physical characteristics of the high school
classroom are related to what happens--and does not
happen--in it. This issue has been briefly touched
upon in chapters 3 and 5.

    The 525 classrooms we studied were, physically,
much the same: a room large enough to accommodate 20 to
30 people adequately, with desks or tables arranged in
rows. The floors were wood or tile. There were
chalkboards and bulletin boards on three of the four

                        338

walls; the fourth wall was usually a bank of windows. A closet and some shelves were also standard. Finally, the teacher's desk was placed either in the front, facing the students, or in the back, so the teacher could keep an eye on the students from behind (this strategy puts the students at a psychological disadvantage, since they cannot see what the teacher is doing).

Now, let's examine each of these descriptors separately. (1) The size of the room itself if "large enough to accommodate 20 to 30 people adequately" only if those 20-30 people are behaving in certain ways. The standard high school classroom is not large enough for 30 people who are square dancing, fencing, or practicing karate. More realistically, often it is not even large enough for six small groups to carry on problem-solving discussions without being distracted. The typical high school classroom is just about right, however, for 20-30 people who are watching a film, listening to a speaker, taking a test, or reading a book; especially since all these activities require that the people be seated, which brings us to the next point, and non-interactive, which is yet another issue.

(2) Whether the room is furnished with individual desks or with tables large enough for two to six people, there is a place for every person to sit down. Not a cushion or a couch, mind you, but a chair. Furthermore, often students are assigned to a certain chair and are told they may use no other. Moving around the room is thus discouraged, and the range of possible learning activities is further narrowed to those things that can be done while seated in a chair.

(3) The desks or tables, we found, were usually arranged in rows, facing in one direction. This arrangement reduces the amount of interaction possible among students (though students are ingenious at circumventing this). Those in the front of the room can see only those to each side of them and the teacher. Those in the back of the room can see the teacher--and the backs of their classmates' heads.

Frontal presentation to the whole group was the teaching method most often used by the teachers in our sample. Was this because the desks were all facing the front of the room? But the desks were moveable: the teacher could have used a non-frontal method, small groups for example, easily enough. No, teachers don't lecture because the seats all face one way, though in the past, when the seats were bolted to the floor, that may have been true. In this case, form follows function: the seats all face the same way <u>so</u> <u>that</u> the teacher can lecture.

The rationale for this heavy reliance on frontal teaching is as follows: "I, as a teacher, have certain knowledge that my students need. Because my students are at a certain grade level and a certain track level, I can safely assume that almost all of them need to learn the same thing from me. True, a few probably know it, and others may never learn it, but <u>most</u> of them need to learn it and can learn it. I must reach the majority with my teaching. Besides, if I'm talking to the whole class at once and can see all their faces, it's a lot easier for me to stay in control and keep them all quiet."

Aha! There's that hidden agenda again: control. This emphasis on containing students is not new, of course. A historian of education could, no doubt, trace it right back to the early days of schooling in America, when children were regarded by society as little animals in need of taming. This legacy is still with us, determining the decisions of school boards and architects as they have continued to design high schools full of standard classrooms such as those described here. It is with us, as well, in the assumptions of teachers in newer open- or flexible-space schools, who yearn for traditional, closed-off classrooms, and plead for the construction of permanent walls. And it is with us in the assumptions of principals, parents, teachers--in fact, most of us--that a quiet room is a room where learning is taking place, and a noisy room is a room where nothing constructive can possibly be happening.

The physical environment of the high school classroom reinforces the passive behavior of students and facilitates the containment and control of students. This is one answer to the question, What goes on in classrooms?

The Emperor Has No Clothes

The next answer to that question is the pedagogical equivalent of the concept of negative space: in looking at a phenomenon, we notice what isn't there. In looking at our 525 high school classrooms, we couldn't help but notice that there was little or no individualization of instruction* taking place in them. This finding was most discouraging in view of the general agreement within the profession that some individualization helps student learning. In addition, much attention has been focused on techniques of individualization in the past ten to fifteen years in the literature, in conferences, in research studies, and in in-service workshops.

Why has individualization not taken hold at the high school level? One big reason is the control orientation just discussed. Teachers learn how to manage a whole class group, and this learning doesn't only take place in college teacher preparation programs, but begins long before, when the future teacher is a student him/herself. They do not, as a rule, master alternative patterns of classroom management in their teacher preparation programs. Like all of us, teachers are most comfortable with what is familiar and in this case, a big part of feeling comfortable is feeling in control.

Closely related to containment and control, as we have seen, are the physical arrangements which make whole-class, frontal teaching easy and make alternative teaching practices difficult. In fact, what we must face is the reality that individualized teaching

---

* "Individualization" does not mean relating to students only one at a time. It means diagnosis to determine varying levels of student learning need, followed by within-class grouping and different assignments for different groups of students with similar needs. Sometimes presentation to the whole class is appropriate, but much more teacher time is likely to be spent in moving between groups as they proceed with their assignments. For some learning, dividing the class in half is appropriate. For other learning, smaller groups might be better. There may be one or two students who need special, individual help. One can see how normal assumptions about "being in control" would need to be changed before a teacher could effectively manage an individualized classroom such as this.

practices and the classroom management techniques compatible with individualization are <u>incompatible</u> with the standard physical arrangement of <u>most high</u> school classrooms. Something's got to give. Either we abandon our rows of desks facing front and find ways to give our young people learning experiences better suited to their actual needs, or we keep our rows of desks and our lecture notes, and stop pretending that we're "individualizing" instruction. We can't have it both ways.

A third reason why individualization of instruction hasn't taken hold at the high school level is because the mythology of tracking allows us to believe that all the students at a given grade level and within a given track in fact have the same learning needs. I have referred to this in chapter 6 as the myth of the "teachably homogeneous group." It is fallacious not only because students in a given class may <u>not</u> need to know the same information (some may already know it well) but because, even if they <u>do</u> all need basically the same information, they are unlikely to all learn it in the same way or at the same speed. As any experienced teacher knows, not all students learn well from books; students may have very different learning styles and speeds. One who grasps a concept quickly but is unable to explain it to someone else the next day is certainly not a better learner, though faster, than one who grasps the concept slowly, after days of pondering and questioning. We do mistakenly tend to confuse quickness with intelligence.

Beyond the Basics

We have noted that, in the classrooms we studied, the "basics"--reading, writing, computation and citizenship--were very much a part of the content being taught. We have also seen that the <u>methods</u> of instruction used were traditional: presentation to the whole group, followed by practice and evaluation; and that the classrooms were definitely teacher-directed. These are the elements of what Rosenshine has called "direct instruction."[11] Some research indicates that direct instruction may be effective when basic skills mastery is the goal but much less effective when mastery of critical thinking skills and the enhancement of creativity are the goals.[12]

The question we must face, therefore, is: do we value critical thinking and creativity enough, as student learning goals, to make a place for them in our classrooms? Doing so should not require additional time, because learning activities can be constructed so as to combine both basic skills development and critical thinking skills development--debates, for example, or the writing of persuasive essays. No, it's <u>not</u> a question of taking time away from the basics to devote to other worthwhile goals. It <u>is</u> a matter of re-examining our assumptions about learning activities.

Nor is it a question of abandoning direct instruction. Direct instruction is appropriate for some learning goals and it certainly was the most familiar and comfortable teaching style for the 525 high school teachers we observed. It's actually a matter of mastering additional teaching styles, of having a repertoire of different techniques and the ability (and confidence) to use each type appropriately. In the eyes of the students we sampled, you may recall, one of the dimensions of good teaching was being "willing to try different ways of doing things."

If we are to go beyond the basics, then, to provide a well-rounded educational experience for our young people, we will have to supplement our existing direct-instruction approaches with alternative teaching strategies, including some techniques of individualization. And, inevitably, we will have to learn to move the furniture around as the learning activities require, rather than allowing rows of desks to determine learning activities.

On the other hand, we have also seen how physically and psychologically exhausting high school teaching can be. We know that high school teachers face as many as 150 students a day, sometimes in overcrowded conditions or with inadequate supplies of teaching materials. We've hypothesized that the affective tone of the high school classroom is predominantly neutral, or bland, because teachers simply can't respond with a great deal of emotion--whether positive or negative--to 150 students. "Getting the information across" is sometimes all one can reasonably expect.

I further hypothesize that the use of direct instruction is a way of keeping the lid on--there's that concern for control again--and that there isn't a

343

lot of energy (or patience) left over for trying alternative teaching strategies.

How, then, <u>can</u> we go "beyond the basics?" Various suggestions have emerged in the chapters of this book. None of them are, in and of themselves, <u>the</u> solution. For one thing, our findings suggest that as a rule, teacher satisfaction is greater in smaller schools than in very large ones and that student satisfaction is likely to be higher in schools where teacher satisfaction is also high. In short, happier teachers do tend to produce happier students. So perhaps we should welcome the decline in school enrollments as an opportunity to achieve some of the advantages of smaller, more closely-knit learning communities.

Furthermore, the pressures of high school teaching could be relieved somewhat by lowering the teacher-pupil ratio to a legal maximum of 20:1 and by lightening the teaching load from five classes a day to four. The high school teacher would then encounter no more than 80 students a day, instead of 150. The energy thus released could be constructively directed towards improving teaching practices, giving each student more personal attention, trying new learning activities, and so forth. It should also not escape our notice that a room containing 20 people is more flexible than the same room containing 30 people. A wider variety of classroom activity is possible when a room is less crowded.

We cannot expect teachers to make changes in their customary ways of doing things unless we are prepared to meet them halfway. Classrooms are the way they are, after all, because teachers strive to do the best they can within a complex network of interconnected factors, including physical constraints, policies which limit innovation, long-standing assumptions about what is possible--or even desirable--and simple force of habit, too. Sarason reminds us that we tend to <u>tell</u> teachers how they should think and act, without realizing the extent to which we may be asking them to un-learn and to re-learn, and without being sensitive to the feel-ings and ideas of the teachers themselves.[12] My experience and, I believe, that of many other school people at all levels, suggests that improvements not actively desired by the teachers themselves are likely to disappear after a couple of years, if not sooner.

344

I have said that we must be prepared to meet teachers halfway, and I've discussed a number of ways in which this might be done. In return, we would want teachers to take some significant steps towards improving the teaching-learning process. This brings us to our fourth question:

IV.

How could teachers be better prepared?

Our findings provide a useful set of guidelines for the improvement of teaching practices. These efforts should take place in both the schools themselves, among teachers who are already on the job, and in colleges and university departments of education, among those who are preparing the teachers of the future.

The data reported in chapters 5 and 6 suggest fourteen points at which teaching could be improved. Twelve of these can be addressed in both pre-service and in-service teacher training programs; the last two can only be tackled by teachers who are already on the job. All fourteen are well worth working on and, in view of our findings, paying attention to these skill areas may well lead to noticeable changes in student attitudes and in classroom climate generally. A dedicated and conscientious teacher might use some of the fourteen points as the basis of a professional growth effort. A principal interested in upgrading the quality of teaching at his or her high school would do well to make these fourteen points the basis of an ongoing faculty in-service plan. And a college of education faculty interested in evaluating its present programs might consider using our findings as a yardstick: how well do its past and present graduates perform in the fourteen areas in which the teachers in our sample* were weak? The list below shows our fourteen "improvable" areas:

1. using pre-tests
2. managing small groups
3. working with mixed ability classes

---

* A representative, though admittedly not a statistically generalizable, sample.

4. involving students in some classroom decisions
   5. using a wider variety of learning materials and
      activities
   6. giving clear instructions and explanations
   7. asking more open-ended questions
   8. giving more frequent feedback
   9. giving more praise and encouragement
  10. using computer-scorable objective tests, and
      giving more essay-question assignments
  11. using self-awareness tools
  12. learning to help and be helped by colleagues
  13. increasing the amount of class time spent on
      instruction
  14. showing no favoritism; being fair

1. Using pre-tests

The reader will recall that we found teachers using
very little in the way of diagnostic testing (chapter
6). This was part of the larger finding that efforts
at individualization were almost nonexistent. If we
are genuinely serious about teaching each child as
effectively as possible, however, a new school year, a
new semester, or a new unit of study should begin with
some form of pre-test to determine what the students
already know and areas in which their knowledge or
their skills are weak. "Diagnosis" sounds awesome, but
pre-testing really doesn't need to be a complicated
matter. It's simply a way for teachers to gather some
information which will help them plan for more effective teaching. The time spent on pre-testing--whether
a day or a week--is really time saved in the long run,
since the chances of re-teaching what students already
know (or, for that matter, introducing something for
which they're not yet ready) are greatly diminished.

Some pre-testing doesn't even require the development of new instruments. Spanish II students may be
given the Spanish I final exam on the first day of
class, for example. In this way the teacher can
ascertain how much the students have retained from the
previous year's work, and which skills need reviewing
or even re-teaching.

A slightly different approach would be to give the
midterm or the final exam for a course on the first day
of class. This should show how many students may
already know some of what the teacher had planned to

introduce as new content. If a few students already have more advanced knowledge or skills, they might form one of the natural in-class groupings for which different learning activities would be planned.

Being able to express themselves clearly in writing is a weak area for many high school students, and this should be of concern to teachers of all subject areas. A useful pre-test to see how articulate the students can be on paper, which could be done on the first day of class or at the beginning of a new unit, would be a simple essay question requiring a well thought-out answer. The substance of the question would deal with some aspect of the course content, whether it be math, science, social studies, French, music, art, home economics, industrial arts, or any other course. These one-page essays will reveal much about what the student knows about the subject as well as information about his or her composition and thinking skills.

Teachers will be able to envision other useful ways of getting information, in the first few days of class, about what students already know--or do not know. What is needed is that we all come to think in terms of pre-testing as the natural starting-point for teaching.

2. Managing small groups

Students, like all of us, get set in their ways. Once the school year is under way, trying to get a class that is accustomed to frontal presentation to begin working cooperatively in small groups is probably a lost cause. However, if small group processes are established as the norm right from the first day of class, students can adjust to that way of doing things as easily as they can to any other. It requires only clear explanation of the expectations and consistent reinforcement, by the teacher, of the desired new behaviors. I have seen second-graders quietly going about their business in a small group (or multi-task) setting--some getting out their folders, some listening to a tape, some working from their books, some having a skill session with the teacher, some helping each other on an assignment--and I see no reason to doubt that high schoolers can master these behaviors just as well as eight-year olds can. We do know that the high school students in our sample, on the average, said they liked working in small groups but did not do so often.

Such adjustments may well be more difficult for the teachers than for the students, given the traditional patterns of classroom management we found to exist almost universally in the schools we studied. Starting the school year with a classroom that is divided into learning stations, mastering a management system for keeping track of student work, and learning to work with students individually and in small groups--all of these involve un-learning and re-learning. A lot of self-confidence and a certain amount of willingness to risk is necessary if a teacher is to venture into these unfamiliar waters.

Colleges of education could make a real contribution by training prospective teachers to manage the multi-task classroom and by placing student teachers in schools where they will be encouraged to practice the skills they have learned. Unfortunately, the instructional mode in the college classroom is also traditional. The effect on the prospective teacher is disconcerting: he or she is told to do something different but is not <u>shown how</u> it can, in fact, be done. Really effective use of small group teaching methods must be demonstrated by the professors of education if the cycle of "I teach as I was taught" is ever to be broken.

3. Working with mixed-ability classes

Having mastered the use of pre-tests and the management of the small group mode, a teacher should be well-equipped with the skills--and the confidence--necessary to teach mixed-ability classes. In the future, teachers and prospective teachers will be expected to work with a wider range of students. The mainstreaming of students with learning disabilities contributes to this increasing heterogeneity. So does the cultural diversity resulting from the influx of immigrants and refugees from South and Central America and Southeast Asia. Some California school districts now have as high as 80 percent non-English-speaking student populations. These students, who may be very bright indeed, are set back by having to learn a new language and a new culture all at once, not to mention coping with the emotional adjustment to being uprooted from a familiar

348

environment and set down in an alien one. Such young-sters obviously need special help. Lockstep curricula, based on a single syllabus, will no longer meet all our needs. A perceptual shift and a related change of attitude will be required: the myth of the teachably homogeneous group will have to be laid to rest once and for all.

4. Involving students in some classroom decisions

We found that, in the "happiest" classrooms--that is, those in which student satisfaction scores were high--students were willing to rely on the teacher's judgment. In the "unhappy" classrooms, by contrast, students were very interested in being more involved in classroom decisions. Other factors contributed to the dissatisfaction, of course, and simply allowing students to make a few choices would probably not turn an unhappy classroom into a happy one. The complexity of classroom climate is clearly evident in the data presented in chapter 6.

The small group, or multi-task, mode of classroom management does allow for a good deal of student decision-making, self-regulation and individual respon-sibility. Teachers who are unwilling or unable to manage small group teaching styles might give some thought to ways in which they could introduce more opportunities for student decision and choice into their traditional classrooms. Using a wider variety of learning materials and activities offers some possibil-ities in this regard.

5. Using a wider variety of learning materials and activities

Data reported in chapter five showed a rather meager array of learning materials (mostly textbooks and worksheets) and activities (mostly listening to the teacher and writing answers to questions) being used in the classroom we studied. Teachers generally agreed that many other kinds of materials and activities would be useful for student learning, but that they didn't use them. Unfortunately, we did not ask them to tell us why they didn't use those other materials and activities. A study which attempted to find the answer to that question would be a useful extension of our efforts. In the meantime, we can only speculate as to the reasons for the widespread reliance on such a limited number of teaching tools.

Limited budgets no doubt affect the purchase and use of good supplementary materials such as newspapers, magazines, learning kits, and educational games. Cumbersome borrowing procedures sometimes limit the use of audiovisual materials--for example, in some school districts it is necessary for teachers to order films from the district film library months ahead of time. Unless the teacher has kept the class on a rigid timetable, when the film arrives it may or may not be pertinent to what is then being studied. Many good teachers, I suspect, forgo the use of film in their classes for this reason.

Force of habit may be another reason why such a limited range of materials and activities are used in high school classes. It seldom occurs to book selection committees to order ten copies of three different books instead of thirty copies of one book. If the syllabus requires a unit on a certain topic--plant photosynthesis, for example, or the voyages of discovery--it is most common to find all students using the same book on the subject and very uncommon to find groups of students reading different books on the same subject. (The different books might be written at different reading difficulty levels, or might offer differing perspectives on the topic being studied). It costs little more to purchase three sets of ten than one set of thirty, but force of habit interferes so that most of us don't even recognize book ordering procedures as an opportunity to get a wider array of learning materials into the classroom.

A fourth reason why many teachers do not use some kinds of materials and activities is simply that they don't know how: in their college training, they were not taught how to use videotape as a teaching/learning tool. They were not taught how to use computer games in their subject areas; never found out how simple it can be to arrange for a guest speaker; never learned how to introduce students to role-playing. In the absence of know-how and the confidence that goes with it, teachers rely on force of habit and generally stick to what's familiar.

Finally, of course, there's that same old theme again: fear of losing control of the class. I suspect that this fear lies behind the reluctance of many teachers to allow students to plan some of their own learning experiences. As a result, skits, debates, simulations and other "active" activities are fairly rare in high school classrooms.

To find explanations for the narrow range of materials and activities used in our schools is not to excuse the situation. Finding ways to widen that narrow range, however, would be quite a challenge. As we've noted earlier in this chapter, introducing change into one part of the system can--and, in schools, often does--have repercussions throughout the system. Nevertheless, if one agrees that students can learn well from all kinds of materials and activities, and if evidence suggests that student satisfaction would be greater and class climate more positive if a wider array of learning experiences were available, it seems well worth trying.

6. Giving clear instructions and explanations

We found that the students in our sample associated teacher concern with teacher clarity. That is, they seemed to feel that a teacher who gave clear directions and understandable explanations was a teacher who really cared--about the quality of his or her teaching, and about the students, too. In fact, teacher clarity and knowledge of objectives were the two sets of teaching practices that were most closely linked with teacher concern in the minds of the students. To get an idea of what actual behaviors are involved, it is instructive to look at some of the individual items that were in these two scales:

Teacher Clarity

The teacher gives clear directions.
The teacher uses words I can understand.
The students understand what the teacher is talking about.
I understand what the teacher is talking about.

Knowledge of Objectives

We know exactly what we have to get done in this class.
We know why the things we are learning in this class are important.
Students know the goals of this class.
Our teacher gives us good reasons for learning in this class.

Teachers don't always begin a new unit with a clear statement of why the material is important to learn, but this would be a fairly easy thing to start doing. Being more clear when giving directions and explanations might be a little more difficult (most of us believe we are reasonably clear already) but, judging by our findings, any real improvement in clarity would be much appreciated by students. They would be likely to view it as an increase in caring behavior on the part of the teacher.

7. Asking more open-ended questions

We found a striking absence of open-ended questions in the classrooms we studied. For some reason, asking open-ended questions doesn't come easily to most high school teachers. I suspect it may be because, to a teacher, waiting for the students to think and then to articulate their thoughts feels like a pause or a drop in the momentum of the class. There seems to be an almost instinctive drive to keep things moving, and an anxiety that if a pause lasts too long, the class may get out of control.

There is also the element of unpredictability which goes with open-ended questions. What will students say? Will I be able to respond adequately? What if one asks me a question in return, and I don't know the answer? What if one raises a touchy topic? This unpredictability, like a drop in the momentum, may cause a teacher to feel that he or she is losing control of the situation.

Asking direct, or "closed," questions—questions to which there is one right answer—is a way of keeping things moving and avoiding unpredictable incidents both at the same time. Of all the thousands of FMI (Five-Minute Interaction) frames coded during the observation of our 525 high school classrooms, slightly over five percent of them were direct questions asked by the teacher. Just one-half of one percent of them were open questions. On the other hand, over 28% of them were explanation or instruction. In other words, telling was something teachers were observed to do often; questioning of any kind was less frequent and open questions were practically nonexistent.

Educators have known for a long time that learning is both more meaningful and more likely to be permanent when the learner has an opportunity to make it his/her own through both active involvement and reflection. Parroting back memorized answers isn't real learning and it certainly isn't <u>education</u> in the original sense of the term--a "drawing-out" of comprehension and understanding.

We don't always practice what we know to be sound pedagogy, however, and open questions are an excellent example of this. Nor is much time spent, in teacher preparation programs, on developing this skill. I believe, however, that it <u>can</u> be developed; <u>and</u> that the anxieties related to classroom management can and should be confronted directly. If teachers practice open questioning strategies until they feel comfortable with them and if, at the same time, they can come to understand the pressures which tend to <u>discourage</u> the use of open questions in the classroom, they should be well equipped to add this teaching technique to their repertoire.

8. Giving more feedback

In chapter 6, I suggested that teachers be taught to use computer-scorable objective tests because this would free them from hand-scoring and allow more time for them to read and respond to essay question answers. I will return to this point shortly, but just now it seems appropriate to point out that computer-scorable tests have an additional advantage: they can be <u>quickly</u> done. Test results can be back to the students in a day or two. We all learned in our educational psychology courses that learning is likely to be more permanent and meaningful if appropriate feedback is received quickly. The following scenario could become common practice in the years ahead: a class takes a test on, say, a Tuesday. Answers to the objective part of it are entered on computer-scorable answer sheets, and answers to the essay questions are done on regular notebook paper. The teacher collects all the tests, turning the computer-scorable answer sheets in to the school or district computer center with appropriately filled-out programming cards, and takes the essay questions home. That evening, time formerly spent on scoring objective tests can be devoted to reading and responding to the essay questions. Next day or the day after, when students' grades from both sections of the test have been entered in the grade book, the test results can be given back to the students and discussed in class. The rapidity of the computer scoring plus the use of more essay questions means that students will likely be getting more feedback, more rapidly, than ever before.

Quickness and quantity of feedback do not, however, necessarily mean quality. The completeness and thoroughness with which teachers respond to essay questions is extremely important. The conscientious teacher, given the time to do a good job, will provide the student with much, much more information on a test or assignment paper than simply a grade and assorted editorial corrections of spelling and and grammar mistakes. Ideally, a teacher would try to respond to the ideas and to the effectiveness with which they are articulated as well. This type of feedback is time consuming to give but very important to the quality of the learning that takes place.

9. Giving more essay-question assignments

I have already discussed the potential saving of time offered by the use of computer-scorable objective tests, and the related likelihood that one constructive result of using this technology would be that students could receive more feedback, more frequently. But this emphasis on increasing the amount of feedback and decreasing the turn-around time needed for grading tests is only one side of the evaluation issue. More important, in my opinion, is the potential for improving the quality of evaluation itself, through the use of many more essay questions than are now commonly used by teachers. These are rarely used because there isn't time left to read them carefully enough after the "main part" of the test--the objective questions--has been scored. But if a machine is scoring the objective questions, the teacher can concentrate on the essays.

And we do know that many, though not all, essay questions require a student to use higher-level cognitive skills: analysis, synthesis, and/or evaluation. They require that the students find their own words for their thoughts and ideas. As we saw in chapter 5, in the thirteen schools we studied, students reported that they seldom were asked to explain what they were

354

learning in their own words. This was true in all
subject areas. We also saw that objective tests
predominated and essay question tests were rarely used.
Thus, the students in our sample were getting lots of
practice in recalling information, but very little in
actually thinking and explaining.

I believed the quality of learning would be improved if lots of essay questions formed a regular part of
evaluation in all subject areas, and I would like to
see this belief tested in a rigorously-designed study.

10. Giving more praise and encouragement

Our observation data revealed that, in our 525
observed classrooms, teachers were seen to be giving
"acknowledgement, praise, or encouragement" only 2.4%
of the time. That means that in a class period 50
minutes long, one might expect to find, on the average,
only 1.2 minutes of acknowledgement, praise, or encouragement. That's not much, especially in view of what
is known about the motivating effects of praise. A
systematic effort to give more encouragement and praise
would be a worthwhile personal improvement goal for any
high school teacher. I also believe that more attention should be given to the development of this kind of
behavior during the student teacher semester.

11. Using self-awareness tools

The secondary methods courses offered in most
college and university departments of education rarely
include much training in how to be aware of oneself in
one's role as a teacher. By "awareness" in this
context, I mean several things:

-- sensitivity to one's own reasons for wanting to
   become a teacher;

-- cognizance of one's strengths and weaknesses in
   the classroom;

-- a willingness to surface and examine one's own
   assumptions about students, about learning, and
   about the purposes of schooling;

-- understanding one's own values in relation to schooling; and

-- recognizing one's own biases.

The need for self-awareness-building in the teacher preparation curriculum has been a concern of mine for some time.[14] The data from the Study of Schooling have done nothing to diminish that concern and, in fact, have strengthened it. For the Study data showed clearly that the teachers in our sample were inconsistent and often contradictory in their educational beliefs. Further, there was often a discrepancy between their stated beliefs and what they actually did in their classes.* Proper and sufficient attention to self-awareness-building skills during the teacher preparation program would, I feel, go a long way towards eliminating some of these inconsistencies and discrepancies. Teachers need to be conscious of why they do what they do in class, and how their behavior is grounded in values and/or habits. Sometimes teachers aren't even aware of some of the things they do while teaching. An instrument such as our Class Climate Inventory could be used by a teacher to obtain a profile of his or her teaching practices as seen by the students; this would be one way to start becoming more aware of oneself as a teacher. Other such tools exist; an important part of teacher pre-service and in-service would be to train teachers in their use.

12. Learning to help and be helped by colleagues

Clinical supervision is also a tool that, when well done, can be enormously helpful in helping a teacher in our sample see himself or herself clearly. Our data showed that the teachers in our sample did not observe each other's classes, but that they would like to have had opportunities to do so. There's no particular mystique about teachers observing each other and then discussing strategies for improvement, but it isn't customarily done in American public high schools.

Sometimes the observation cycle (pre-conference, observation, post-conference) is taught in teacher preparation programs and practiced during the student-

_____
* See, for example, the discussion of praise-giving in chapter 6.

356

teaching semester. But this is usually part of the formal relationship between the trainee and the professor who is his or her supervisor during the student teaching term. When the trainee takes his or her first full-time teaching job, this support stops because, as we have seen in our data (chapter 3), high school principals seldom if ever provide helping supervision.

Unfortunately, the norms already in place in most high schools seem to discourage new teachers from turning to other teachers for such help. Advice is sought--and given--to be sure. But rarely do teachers use the steps of the observation cycle to help, and be helped by, their colleagues.

Part of the problem, too, is the teachers' work load and the school's schedule. It's not always possible to find a colleague who is free to visit that one particular class you'd like to have some help with. This problem could be alleviated somewhat if teacher work loads were altered from five classes and one planning period to a more realistic and reasonable four classes and two planning periods, as was suggested earlier in this chapter.

Finally, teachers already established in the school who are not familiar with the peer observation cycle need in-service which will introduce the process in a non-threatening way and give them opportunities to practice it with each other.

13. Increasing the amount of time spent on instruction

The results of our Study showed a clear relationship between student satisfaction, positive class climate, good teaching practices, and the amount of class time spent on instruction (as opposed to routines, behavior, or socializing). Of course, spending more time on instruction isn't going to improve the other variables automatically, but it is a starting-place. At the same time, attention must also be given to the improvement of specific teaching practices such as clarity, feedback, praise, and so forth.

14. Showing no favoritism; being fair

It's hard not to prefer some students to others, but on the whole it is generally understood that one shouldn't show one's preferences. The students in our sample make a connection between overt favoritism and other negative teacher attributes such as authoritarianism and punitiveness. Young people place enormous value on whether or not a person is fair. In the school context, one aspect of fairness involves treating all students according to the same set of criteria, neither having favorites nor "picking on" certain students.

Teachers may not even be aware of the little ways in which they show extra partiality to or dislike of some students. Using an instrument such as our Class Climate Inventory would reveal whether the students perceive a teacher as showing favoritism. If they do, the teacher needs to do some self-study in order to identify exactly how his or her preferences for (or dislike of) certain students is revealed in his or her classroom behavior. A colleague may be able to help after observing the class two or three times. It may not be easy to change these patterns, grounded as they probably are in the teacher's most fundamental attitudes toward and feelings about young people. But for a teacher who is interested in making continuous improvement professionally, "being fair" is an excellent personal goal.

*   *   *

These fourteen points suggest a program for improving teacher effectiveness which is both data-based and realistic. Simply recognizing their validity--or even making a commitment to work on one or more of them--is not enough to guarantee that such goals will be reached. In some cases fairly profound changes in behavior are required (as, for example, decreasing use of the lecture method and increasing the use of other teaching methods and grouping patterns). In other cases, new equipment or new services at the school district level are required (e.g., facilities for quick computer scoring of objective tests). In all cases, funds for released time and high-quality in-service training, as well as for ongoing support and supervision, will be needed if increased teacher effectiveness is to be a serious goal for our high schools.

V.

Are all schools basically alike?

In chapter 1, I referred to one of the paradoxes of schooling: the fact that American schools are very much alike, but are at the same time very different. The findings reported in subsequent chapters have, if anything, reaffirmed this paradox. As far as the regularities of schooling are concerned (the physical uniformity of classrooms; the overall control orientation of policy, program, and pedagogy; the general similarity of curriculum; and the practice of tracking, among others), all thirteen of the high schools we studied were, indeed, basically very much alike.

And yet each one was also unique, different from the others in dozens of big and little ways. The cumulative effect of these differences gave each school its particular personality; we shall re-visit our thirteen schools in a moment.

Some readers might be inclined to say that the similarities obviously outweigh the differences, since they have to do with the deepest structures and assumptions of schooling. I'm not so sure. As long as one is solely concerned with <u>describing</u> schools, it may be true that the commonalities are most important. As soon as one becomes concerned with the processes involved in <u>improving</u> schools, however, the differences become equally important. For the key to changing a school lies in the particular configuration of forces that give <u>that</u> school its unique personality.[15] That is why a change strategy that works at one school may not work at another, and why changes mandated at the district or the state level will be implemented with varying degrees of success in the schools to which those mandates apply. If one understands the unique personality of a school, however--if one can feel its pulse, so to speak--one may be successful in changing even the deep structure. Part of understanding the school would be the knowledge of the processes by which the school maintains the delicate balance of its interrelated parts, and recognition of the effects that a change in one part would have on the others; this is the point with which I opened this chapter, as the reader will recall.

359

To give an example: supposing a school district adopted a policy that all classes should henceforth be heterogeneously grouped rather than tracked. The degree to which any given school would be able to successfully implement this policy would depend on the extent to which the principal would be able and willing to help his teachers to learn the new sets of skills they would need in order to work comfortably and effectively with mixed-ability groups, among other things. It could also depend on the quality of staff relationships, the rigidity of the existing tracking system, the potential reactions of parents, the number and intensity of school problems perceived by the teachers, the existence or non-existence of open communication and mechanisms for shared decision-making, and much, much more. These are the areas in which each school is different from every other, and these are the areas within which a school's power to change is determined.

The thirteen schools revisited

Little Dennison came close to being the kind of school educators dream about. The teachers at Dennison found the work environment satisfying on all eleven dimensions of the Work Environment Inventory. They had very positive feelings about their principal, an energetic young man who taught classes as well as taking care of administrative business for the school. Dennison teachers viewed their school as having few problems, and the school rated high on the composite teacher satisfaction index. The curriculum was innovative, providing the staff with a good deal of professional challenge within a supportive environment. From the teachers' point of view, the only real drawback to working at Dennison Secondary School was its isolation--the nearest sizable town was 70 miles away. Several commented on this, and on the lack of recreational facilities in a rural village of only 350 people. Annual teacher turnover was quite high even though so many other aspects of the job were very good. Continuity, therefore, could have been a problem at Dennison.

Dennison students, like their teachers, were very satisfied with their school and gave it a higher grade than did students at any other high school in the Study. They were very involved in extracurricular

360

activities--no other high school in the Study had a comparably high level of student participation after school.

The personality of Dennison Secondary must have been very much shaped by its small size (61 students in grades 7-12) and its rural location, but the quality of the leadership provided by its administration also had a great deal to do with the busy, cheerful ambience of this school.

Woodlake High was also rated one of the "more satisfying" schools by its teaching staff. Woodlake teachers viewed their school as having few problems. The school building was brand-new in 1977, and had pods for each subject area with teacher work areas in the center of each pod. The school had all the latest and most modern equipment, which must have been very satisfying for the teachers.

The stability of the administration--the principal had been at Woodlake for 20 years--provided continuity through the move to the new school building. The Woodlake teachers seemed happy with their principal, and felt that he allowed them to exert a good deal of influence in school decision-making.

Woodlake students, like their teachers, were very satisfied with their school. As compared to the other schools in the Study, Woodlake High had a higher percentage of what I have called, in chapter 6, "happy" classrooms--that is, classes in which students reported good teaching practices, positive peer interaction, and warm teacher affect. Many Woodlake students were also very involved with the school outside of class time, participating in special-interest clubs and school or community service activities.

The Woodlake community was the site of a large U.S. Navy air base. The existence of this facility greatly affected Woodlake High in a number of ways. For one thing, many teachers and students were from Navy families; for another, the school district qualified for special, extra federal funding for buildings, equipment, and materials.

The Woodlake High curriculum was more or less standard, much like that found in American high schools from coast to coast. It did, however, include Marine

Biology, Oceanography, and Naval ROTC, all reflecting the needs and interests of the community of which the school was a part.

Euclid High was more than four times larger than Dennison but even so, it was a small school (262 students in grades 9-12). As at Dennison and Woodlake, Euclid teachers viewed their school as having few problems, and the school rated high on the composite teacher satisfaction index. The Euclid community (pop. 4,392) was large enough to sustain some recreational facilities; Euclid teachers did not complain about the isolation and lack of social life, and annual teacher turnover was quite low.

The Euclid curriculum was fairly standard, but a quarter-course schedule allowed the school to offer a wider range of courses than one might have expected to find at a small school. The full range of agriculture courses provided at Euclid High reflected the needs and interests of the surrounding community.

Euclid students seemed quite satisfied with most aspects of their school experience, although they were not happy with the school's guidance counselor. As at Dennison and Woodlake, Euclid students were very involved in extracurricular activities.

Medium-sized Palisades High, located in a lovely, affluent suburb of a southeastern city, was perhaps one of the more complex high schools we studied. As far as integration was concerned, it was a showcase school which had managed to adjust to the desegregation process with little obvious friction. This may have been partly due to the fact that both the local white students and the bused-in black students were primarily from upper-middle class, education-oriented families.

The faculty of 31 white and 28 nonwhite teachers was one of the highest-paid teaching staffs in our sample. They classed Palisades High as a "moderately satisfying" place to work. While feeling that the school had some problems, the Palisades teachers didn't rate any of those problems as major (chapter 3, table 3.2). They seemed to like and respect their new principal.

The Palisades students in our sample reported high satisfaction with their school. As a group, they were

362

very education conscious. The largest percentage of the sample chose the intellectual function of schooling as the function most important to them, and district officials estimated that 65% of Palisades High School students go on to four-year colleges or universities.

Atwater High School was another small school--450 students in grades 10-12. Located in a middle class suburban community, Atwater High's "personality" was shaped to some extent by the rather low educational aspirations of its student body, most of whom wanted either to go to a trade school or junior college (33%) or to just finish high school and go no further (30%). Not surprisingly, the largest percentage of our student sample at Atwater High chose the vocational function as the function that was most important to them. This work orientation may have been at least partly due to the existence, in the community, of a good deal of local light industry. The relatively low educational attainment of many of the students' parents, too, may have had a lot to do with it (only 12% of the parent sample had completed college, while over half had gone no further than high school themselves).

Atwater teachers didn't view their school as having any major problems, although there was a good deal of negative feeling about the principal (see Atwater case study, chapter 3). On the whole, the Atwater teachers we sampled seemed to feel that theirs was a moderately satisfying school in which to work, and the year before the Study, no teachers had either left or joined the faculty. The general impression as far as the educational program was concerned is one of strong teachers doing good work with a fairly traditional curriculum. The change potential at Atwater, however, would be severely limited by the teachers' reluctance to cooperate with a principal whom they viewed as an adversary rather than an ally.

Crestview High was a medium-sized suburban school located in a predominantly working-class community. The Crestview teachers found their school a moderately satisfying place to work, despite what they perceived as low student and parent interest in schooling. In fact, both parent educational achievement and student educational aspirations were low, and the largest percentage of Crestview students in our sample chose the vocational function as the one that was most important to them.

363

Student absenteeism was fairly high (11-13%) at Crestview, and students reported a good deal of alcohol use among their peers. Interestingly, alcohol use was identified by Crestview students as a major problem, while Crestview teachers rated it as only a minor problem.

Crestview teachers were very happy with their principal and seemed to get along quite well with each other, too. They had just begun a teacher-advisor program, in an effort to keep a closer watch on student progress and problems.

Crestview's curriculum was standard, the major subjects were tracked, students normally took six classes and one study hall per day, and teachers worked alone. Pedagogically speaking, the Crestview program exemplified many of the patterns we found to be pervasive--frontal teaching of standard subject matter in traditional, "egg carton" classrooms.

These, then, were the "happier" schools, as far as we could tell: first Dennison, Woodlake, and Euclid; then Palisades, Atwater, and Crestview. The potential for healthy change and improvement at these schools was probably fairly good. The rest--Vista, Rosemont, Newport, Manchester, Bradford, Laurel, and Fairfield-- were all in their different ways much less satisfying places for teachers and students alike.

Though located not far from Crestview, Vista High was quite different. One of the largest schools in the Study (2,312), Vista seemed to have a good many problems and in fact, as far as the teachers were concerned, the size of the school was one of its biggest problems. Student misbehavior was another problem which Vista teachers rated as being major. Vista teachers were also rather unhappy with their principal; they perceived him as distant and either unable or unwilling to provide real leadership. The quarter-course schedule at Vista was a demanding one, and teacher turnover was fairly high--about 23% yearly. In spite of all this, the Vista teachers in our sample rated their school as a moderately satisfying place to work.

Vista students reported that both alcohol and drug use were serious problems among students at Vista. The educational mission of the school was somewhat unfocused--the largest percentage of sampled students chose the vocational function as the function of schooling that was most important to them, and the district estimated that less than half of the Vista High students typically went on to college. A very telling detail, in my opinion, was the rather high incidence of vandalism at Vista High School.

Rosemont High was evidently a frustrating work place for many of its teachers. Rosemont emerged as a "less satisfying" school, with a high composite problems score. The teachers at Rosemont viewed lack of parent interest and student language difficulties as major problems. The student language difficulties were real, since for many students, Spanish was their mother tongue. Lack of parent interest, however, is harder to pin down. Although the teachers considered it a major problem, our data in fact show a high degree of parent involvement at Rosemont, as compared to that found at the other twelve high schools we studied. This is especially remarkable in view of the fact that nearly 80% of the Rosemont parents in our sample had not graduated from high school themselves.

Student attitudes were rather good at Rosemont, and in a way it is difficult to see why the teachers were so frustrated there. The largest percentage of students in the sample chose the intellectual function of schooling as the function most important to them. Many Rosemont students chose "good student attitudes," "the classes I'm taking," or "variety of class offerings" as the one best thing about Rosemont High. And smart students were seen by many as the most popular students at Rosemont, a phenomenon which occurred at no other high school in the Study. A high degree of student satisfaction is also suggested by the fact that over 84% agreed "this school gives students a good education." By far the largest percentage of Rosemont students felt that "how the school is organized" was the school's biggest problem (37%), while only 17% and 16%, respectively, felt that the biggest problems were drug and alcohol use or student misbehavior, the two most common responses at most of the other schools. Teachers, too, did not feel that drug or alcohol use and student misbehavior were major problems at Rosemont High.

The school was located in a beautiful new building and the students evidently were quite proud of it: for a high school of that size (2,702), vandalism was relatively rare.

A large part of Newport High School's uniqueness was due to the incredible heterogeneity of the Newport community: as many as 58 different nationalities and 36 different languages are to be found in the Newport district. It's not surprising that Newport teachers identified student language problems as one of the major problems at that school. In addition, the Newport community is very mobile, far more so than any of the other twelve communities we studied. Student transiency is a regular fact of life there.

Newport High was surrounded by the usual kinds of big-city problems--crowded living conditions, poor housing, traffic congestion, drug abuse, and crime--and these would affect the school's personality as inevitably as rural isolation affected the personality of Dennison Secondary School.

Newport High teachers viewed their school as having many problems. Those they identified as major, in addition to student language problems, were school size (2,508) and lack of student interest in learning. Vandalism, too, was seen as a problem by many Newport teachers. Others felt that inadequate resources were a big problem.

Negative scores on the four staff relationship scales of the Work Environment Inventory suggest that working relationships between the teachers at Newport High were not harmonious. All in all, it doesn't come as a surprise to learn that Newport was rated "less satisfying" by the teachers who worked there.

Newport students, like their teachers, were dissatisfied with their school. Over half of the students sampled identified drug use as a problem at Newport. Perhaps sensing the degree of teacher dissatisfaction that evidently existed at their school, almost half (47%) of the Newport students agreed that "many teachers at this school don't care about students." One out of every ten students in the Newport sample chose "Nothing" in response to the question, "What is the one best thing about this school?" This suggests a fairly high percentage of marginal students at Newport, who felt neither involved with the school nor motivated to behave responsibly toward it.

Manchester High School was located in a middle class section of a large midwestern city. The community was predominantly black and the student body of Manchester High was almost exclusively black. The faculty, however, was 53% white (including all eleven guidance counselors). The school building was large and gloomy, and looked more like a factory than a school.

Manchester teachers gave their school a high composite problems score and identified many major problems: student misbehavior, lack of student interest, school size (3,006), lack of parent interest, and inadequate resources. They also felt that vandalism and student violence were problems at Manchester High. The Manchester community had recently defeated a school bond issue and in 1977 the teachers were having to make do with far fewer resources than they were accustomed to having. They had also been given a longer teaching day, and were unhappy about that. The Manchester faculty was the oldest in the Study; the average number of years of teaching experience was 15.7. Many of those teachers must have felt that things had been much better "in the old days," so it isn't surprising the Manchester was classified as a "less satisfying" school on the composite teacher satisfaction index.

Manchester students were not particularly satisfied with the school, either. Almost half (48%) felt that "many teachers at this school don't care about students," and a whopping 75% disagreed that "people at this school can be trusted." When asked to identify the one best thing about Manchester High, the largest percentage chose "my friends" (as was true at every other high school in the Study), but the second and third largest percentages were for "nothing" (19%) and "sports" (12%). One-fifth of the students sampled considered gang members to be the most popular students at Manchester High.

Nevertheless, Manchester students were fairly education-conscious. 44% selected the intellectual function of schooling as the most important to them, and over half expected to go on to some form of higher education. One gets the impression that there was great unrealized potential in the Manchester situation,

367

but that it was stifled by the negativity of the teachers.

Bradford High was also rated one of the "less satisfying" schools by its teaching staff. Bradford teachers viewed their school as having many serious problems, among them student apathy, lack of parental interest and support, and inadequate resources. They were quite negative about their principal and felt that he just sort of let the school drift along, and had done so for 14 years. Not surprisingly, staff morale was very low at Bradford.

Bradford students weren't exactly the most highly motivated young people one might hope to find in a school. The community offered many opportunities for them to enter the work force right after high school, and that is what many of their parents had done. The largest percentage of Bradford students chose the vocational function as the one that was most important to them. 60% of the students sampled at Bradford identified drug use as a major problem; student participation in extracurricular activities was very low; and vandalism was fairly high. Despite these indicators of a student population which was not much interested in education, many Bradford students also identified poor teaching as a major problem, and nearly half of them felt that "many teachers at this school don't care about students."* It seems that at Bradford High School, teacher dissatisfaction and student dissatisfaction fed each other, perpetuating a depressing cycle which the principal was unable to turn around. Indeed, one wonders if he was even aware of it.

Bradford High's personality was also influenced by the community's anxiety about blacks. The possibility of metropolitan busing or of more and more black families moving into the Bradford area kept the white, blue-collar inhabitants of Bradford very much on edge during the 1970s. Seventy percent of the students in the Bradford sample viewed their peers as prejudiced, and one-third felt that the teachers were also prejudiced. Life must have been difficult indeed for the few (8%) black students who did attend Bradford High School.

---

* See Bradford case study in chapter 4.

Thus far, all of our most unhappy schools have been fairly large, from Bradford with 1,350 students to Manchester with 3,006. Laurel was our only small unhappy school (271). Laurel teachers viewed their school as having some serious problems. Student apathy and lack of parent interest they considered to be major problems; they were also unhappy with what they considered to be a "do-nothing" principal. The median salary at Laurel in 1977 was lower, and teacher turnover was higher, than at any other high school in the Study. Many teachers had to commute long distances to teach in rural Laurel. They never formed attachments to the Laurel community, and as soon as they could, they found work closer to home.

The dissatisfaction of the Laurel staff found expression in the classroom and was reflected in the unhappiness of the students: our class climate data showed that little Laurel had a rather remarkably high percentage of what I have termed "unhappy" classrooms. Laurel students were likely to view their teachers as authoritarian and punitive, their classmates as apathetic, and their classes as unsettled.* Forty-two percent of the students sampled at Laurel agreed that "many teachers at this school don't care about students."

Laurel had the highest estimated dropout rate in the Study, and a very low percentage of students who planned on going on to some form of higher education. Interestingly, while Laurel High had many problems, drug and alcohol use was not one of them. Prejudice, however, was. Laurel schools had been desegregated just a few years before the Study and the entire community was still very nervous about it.

Fairfield High School was also rated as one of the "less satisfying" schools by its teaching staff. Fairfield teachers viewed their school as having many problems; student misbehavior and inadequate resources topped the list. Vandalism was also seen as a problem, and indeed the district estimate for annual vandalism costs was higher for Fairfield than for any other high school in the Study.

---

* See chapter 6, part I: Exploring Class Climate/by school.

Fairfield's personality was partly shaped by an ongoing power struggle between the administration and the teacher who was in charge of the extensive vocational program. The vocational program was housed in a separate building and the Vocational Director treated it--and its teaching staff--as his exclusive domain. The situation was aggravated by the fact that the principal was new, while the Vocational Director had been around for some time. Our data show that the Fairfield teachers liked their new principal very much; even so, because of the frustrations of dealing with the Vocational Director and with the Board, the principal was already thinking of moving on. Rapid administrative turnover often, I have observed, makes the problems of an unhappy school even worse than they already are.

Starting salaries at Fairfield High were the lowest in the Study, and teacher turnover was estimated at a high 30% annually. As a result, the teaching staff at Fairfield was comparatively young and inexperienced.

Fairfield students, like their teachers, were dissatisfied with their school. 41% of the students sampled felt that many of the teachers at Fairfield didn't care about students. Students identified both drug and alcohol use as major problems at Fairfield. Racial prejudice was identified as a minor problem and interestingly enough, this response didn't come only from the Mexican-American students. Approximately the same percentage of Anglo students also agreed that there was some student and teacher prejudice at Fairfield High School.

The students at Fairfield were divided into two distinct groups, vocational and academic (hands vs. heads again), and different curriculums were provided for each group. The result was almost like having two entirely separate student bodies.

The Fairfield community, too, was composed of separate elements: farmers and ranchers on one hand, and suburban tract-house dwellers employed at one of two nearby Air Force bases, on the other. The military families were transient, while the farming families were relatively stable. Fairfield was a poor community, and the school was poor as well. Two-thirds of the parent sample had only a high school education themselves; just 8% were college graduates.

These, then, were our thirteen high schools. Each had its own unique character, shaped by its history, the nature of the community of which it was a part, and internal factors such as teacher-administrator relationships, the number and intensity of school problems, and the quality of class climate in most of the classrooms. I have reviewed these schools roughly in order, from what seem from our data to be the most successful schools, to what seem to be the most unhappy schools. Time and again in our findings, Fairfield High School emerges at the bottom of the heap, followed closely by Laurel and Bradford. Manchester, Newport, Rosemont, and Vista were schools where conditions were more negative than positive, but which seemed to have some potential for improvement. Crestview, Atwater, and Palisades were happy places, on the whole. Finally, Euclid, Woodlake, and Dennison seemed to be almost ideal environments for teaching and learning.

But whether a school was a happy or an unhappy place, each one was first and foremost itself, a complex ecological habitat in which many factors interacted to produce that particular school at that particular point in time. The answer to question five must, therefore, be both yes and no. Schools are basically alike when it comes to fundamentals, but they are very different when it comes to the special blend of characteristics which give each one a distinct personality, and it is these characteristics which must be fully understood by anyone who hopes to make some changes in a school.

VI.

What are the chances of improving high schools?

I have suggested that we think of schools as having two levels of characteristics, the deep structure and the unique personality. All of the high schools we studied shared the characteristics which I have termed "deep structure." These include the pervasive control orientation found in every aspect of schooling; the general similarity of curriculum and of teaching practices; a pervasive resistance to change; and the practice of tracking, whether formal or informal.

At the other level, each of our thirteen schools was very different from the others. The characteristics at this level include the type of principal leadership; the number, intensity, and type of problems which exist at the school; the quality of staff interaction; the nature of the school's relationship to the community in which it is located; and the existence or non-existence of open communication and shared decision-making.

It is my belief that a school's power to change is determined by the configuration of characteristics which make up its unique personality. Supposing, for example, that a school staff decides to work together to improve the quality of staff interaction. The teachers decide that they want to increase cooperation and sharing among themselves. Whether this change goal is relatively easy or fairly difficult to achieve depends on the quality of communication which already exists among the teachers; the intensity of other school problems which also claim the teachers' time, attention, and energy; and the nature of the relationship between the teachers and the principal. In a school where teaching materials and supplies are scarce and where communication between teachers is poor, cooperation and sharing may be a goal that will be very difficult to achieve. Hoarding, rather than sharing, would be the norm. However, in a school where there is healthy, open communication and where the principal actively works with teachers to help them identify and solve problems, the chances of dealing constructively with the issue of hoarding and of improving cooperation and sharing are much better. This is what I mean when I say that a school's power to change is determined by the configuration of characteristics which make up its unique personality.

Goals for change can be set at either level. However, it is important to realize that a change in one or more aspects of a school's unique personality can leave the deep structure unchanged, as Figure 1 suggests. For example, teachers may work together to improve the quality of staff interaction, but this will not necessarily affect the curriculum, teaching practices, or the basic assumption that students must be kept under control.

On the other hand, a change cannot be made in any aspect of the deep structure without affecting some

372

aspects of the unique personality layer as well. It is as if one must go through the unique personality layer in order to reach the deep structure; in fact, it may be necessary to postpone change efforts at the deeper level until certain changes at the unique personality level have been changed. Changing from a system of tracking to a system of heterogeneous grouping, for instance, is unlikely to succeed unless (1) the teachers have first been helped to acquire the skills needed for teaching mixed-ability groups, and (2) the parents have been thoroughly informed of the reasons for the change, and are willing to support it. Thus, it would be necessary to work on teaching practices, open communication, and the school-community relationship--all aspects of a school's unique personality--if a change in the school's tracking practices were to be successful.

Figure 1

A change in the unique personality characteristics of a school may leave the deep structure characteristics unchanged

Unique * Personality	change in quality of staff interaction
Deep Structure	no change in any aspect of the deep structure

Key: * = primary change target

At the beginning of this chapter, I discussed the idea, from systems theory, that a change in one part of a system may have repercussions in many other parts. I also suggested that an ecological system such as a school will attempt to re-establish its equilibrium following such a change. What I am suggesting now is that there may be a directionality to change efforts which must be taken into account if those efforts are to have a hope of success.

In proposing that changes at the unique personality level probably need to precede changes at the deeper level, I am not implying that changes in the deep structure are more worthwhile or more important, only that they are far more difficult to achieve. They disturb a school's equilibrium far more profoundly and, because the organism is so complex, they run a much greater risk of failing. The elements of schooling which I have termed "deep structure" are rooted in society's values and assumptions about what is desirable and appropriate educational experience for young people. These elements (such as tracking, for example) are part of the conventional wisdom about schooling, and come to be accepted without question.

It is unlikely, therefore, that a school staff would consider tackling a fundamental change at the deep structure level. But if they did, they would really have their work cut out for them. Let's say that the teachers at a medium-sized high school decide to work on using a wider variety of learning activities and materials in their teaching. In effect, they have agreed to try and get away from the predominant pattern of lecture/question/test. Even reaching agreement on this goal would be difficult, considering the deeply-entrenched norm of classroom autonomy which exists in American schooling. But suppose that a staff did set such a goal for itself; what barriers to change would influence their efforts? To some extent, they would have to overcome their own training, which prepared them primarily to lecture. They would have to be emotionally willing to take some risks trying unfamiliar activities and involving students in new ways in the classrooms. They would encounter resistance from the students themselves, perhaps, or from parents who believe that lecturing is the right way to teach, because that's how they were taught. Perhaps the teachers would have to do an inventory of all the learning materials in the school, and set up a system to ensure that the materials were available as needed to those teachers planning to use them. Possibly they would have to work with the principal, the PTA, or a district committee to locate funds for a wider variety of learning materials (newspapers, films, computer terminals, and so on). They would have to locate consultants capable of providing the in-service

374

training which they themselves would need in order to learn and practice the new teaching methods and activities. These are just a few of the pressures which might accompany such a change effort. On the whole, it's much easier to give up and go back to the old, familiar, tried-and-true pattern: teachers talk, students listen and then write. In my experience, most change efforts begin to backslide in about the third year of implementation. A change that cannot survive the "year three crisis" is likely to have been a change that was tackled without sufficient attention to all the systemic pressures and consequences. Changes at the deep structure level are more difficult to achieve because of their fundamental challenge to the status quo and because of the complexity of their connectedness to all the other aspects of schooling.

Such changes as do occur in our high schools, then, are more likely to be at the more accessible level of the school's unique personality. Improving staff interaction, solving school problems, building mechanisms for shared decision-making, and all the other possible goals for improvement of the school at the unique personality level are extremely worthwhile. They can go a long way towards making the individual school a happier and more productive place, and that is all to the good.

American secondary education as an institution, however, will not improve significantly as long as changes are made only at this level, in individual schools. Changes in elements of the deep structure, shared by all schools, would also have to occur, and these require the kind of substantial support that can come only from policy changes. This, then, brings us to our seventh and final question:

VII.

What policy changes would help to make school improvement possible?

Changes in the combination of characteristics which form a school's unique personality are the proper concern and responsibility of those directly involved with that particular school--its administration, its teaching and support staffs, its students and, to some

extent, the parents of its students. Support and
encouragement, it is to be hoped, would be forthcoming
from higher levels--specifically, from the Board of
Education and the School District offices. But the
initiative as well as the follow-through for change
efforts at the unique personality level must come from
within the school itself. This is basically what we
mean when we say that the proper unit of change is the
single school.

The notion of two levels of school characteristics,
however, one of which is highly resistant to change in
the single school setting, requires that we define the
responsibilities of the superordinate system with
regard to the dynamics of educational change. Simply
put, single school change efforts at the deep structure
level are likely to fail unless they have the <u>official-
ly sanctioned support</u> of the education establishment
within which the school is embedded. This means that
policy changes are needed if elements of the deep
structure are to be altered.

In many cases, local Board of Education or school
district policies may need to be changed. For example,
a school district may decide to mandate use of a
teacher-advisor program in all of its secondary
schools, or adopt an open campus policy, or develop a
calendar which includes released time for teacher
in-service. In other cases, the policy changes must be
made at the state level--in the legislature or the
State Department of Education. It is generally the
state, for example, that sets policy concerning financial support for education, textbook adoption, and
maximum pupil-teacher ratio.

Certain elements of the deep structure are so
entrenched in the conventional wisdom and vested
interests that nothing short of legislative action
could change them. The "rightness" of curriculum
differentiation and of tracking are cases in point.
Despite all the evidence that these educational structures and practices actually fragment our society along
class lines and diminish the learning experiences of
young people, we carry on, trying to force the high
school to be all things to all people and pretending
that we are doing the right thing by pigeonholing
youngsters sometimes as early as 7th grade. It is time
to take a fresh look at what our high schools could and
should be. I believe it may be time to think seriously

about making that "radical change" that Conant said might be necessary if the comprehensive high school concept fails to work for our society.

Presumably the purpose of educational research is to provide information for decision-making at all levels of the educational enterprise. One of the purposes of A Study of Schooling was to describe a sample of real schools in such detail that policy issues would be raised for consideration by school people, the public, and educational policy makers. The various policy issues which have emerged in the chapters of this book can be grouped into four general categories: pre-service training of administrators; upgrading the quality of teaching; curriculum; and the custodial role of the school. Obviously, there are many areas of overlap, and one category does not emerge as more important than the others. Nor could many of these suggested changes be made in isolation--the reader will realize by now that the improvement process is nothing if not systemic, and that one change effort leads naturally to others.

Figure 2

Elements of the deep structure are so well entrenched that a single school cannot change them without the support of higher authority

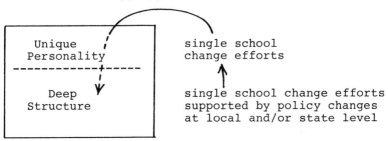

Curriculum

It seems to me that, using our findings, policymakers could begin to build quite a strong case for scaling down the high school. Distinct educational and social advantages seem to be possible when a high school is not too large: I would suggest that a maximum of 1,000 become what we think of as the ideal high school size. Existing buildings constructed to accommodate more can be put to use as community centers. A school district might even consider selling its largest high school (creative entrepreneurs could turn it into a popular shopping mall or arts and crafts center) and moving the high school students to a smaller building--perhaps an empty junior high school, thus reversing the trend of the past 20 years.

The organizational complexity of the high schools we studied was due in large measure to the combining of the comprehensive high school idea with the cumbersome system of tracking. The resulting differentiation of curriculum creates an educative institution which is fragmented and which contributes much to the increasing fragmentation of our society. People are separated in school, quite early on, and experience little which would tend to bring them together in later life. Class divisions in our culture seem to be getting deeper, and our system of secondary schooling contributes to this.

Let's consider a possible alternative. Supposing we separate the high school years into junior secondary and senior secondary phases. In 9th and 10th grade, all students would experience a common curriculum. There would be no tracking; all classes would consist of mixed-ability groups. Within classes, however, teachers would group and re-group as necessary according to student progress, interests, and abilities. A variety of learning materials and activities would also be utilized, and remedial help, as well as more rigorous work for gifted students, would be available as needed.

All 9th and 10th grade students would take the same courses during a 30-period week which would include work in language arts, math, science, social studies, the arts, physical education, and a foreign language. During the course of a week, each student would also spend two periods with his or her advisory group and two periods in a special course on career awareness and study skills.

This junior secondary program would go a long way towards building more real educational equity into our system. Students who would once have been lumped together into average or low-track classes would instead be in mixed-ability classes, receiving (as our data have shown) more instruction of a better quality than they would have gotten under the tracking system. Within-class individualization would ensure that quick learners would not get bored and slow learners would not be left behind--as we shall see in the section on improving the quality of teaching, class sizes would be smaller and the nature of teaching would change some-what. Best of all, our young people would experience learning together with others of their own age who have, perhaps, different backgrounds and values as well as different plans for the future. Friendships could exist across class lines in a way that is, under the present system, rare indeed. Ultimately, our society should become more rather than less tolerant of its own inevitable--and healthy--diversity.

A strong transitional guidance program in the 10th grade would prepare students to make the choice of which curriculum to enter for the remainder of their high school years. 11th and 12th grades would be the time for specialization and preparation for entering the world of work and full adulthood. Indeed, the senior secondary program would be so different from the junior secondary program that it might very well be housed in an entirely different location. Students entering the 11th grade would choose from a variety of vocational preparation programs and two college prepa-ration programs, general college preparation and advanced placement. The choice would be theirs, and they would be ready for it because of their experiences in their advisory group and their career awareness course in 9th and 10th grade.

Some cities might even decide to offer specialized senior secondary schools, such as Science High School or the High School for the Performing Arts, or an American Crafts High School offering training in vocational areas such as weaving and textiles, pottery, stained glass, leathercrafting and woodwork. A Human Services High School, with training programs in social sciences, child care, and hospital occupations would be another possibility. It's exciting to think of the wide variety of programs that could be offered in such a senior secondary arrangement.

It goes without saying that students should be prepared, by 11th grade, to accept responsibility for their behavior and for their choices. The senior secondary schools would operate with open campus policies, with each student coming and going according to his or her own class schedule.

To summarize: I am proposing a common curriculum and mixed-ability grouping for the junior secondary school (grades 9 and 10) and a rather specialized, vocationally-oriented senior secondary program for grades 11 and 12. Clearly, deep structure changes such as these would require policy decisions at every level--local, state, and even national.

Upgrading the Quality of Teaching

This critical area can be subdivided into pre-service and in-service categories. Changes in teacher training (pre-service) programs would include the following:

(1) Withdrawal of some institutions of higher education from the whole business of teacher preparation. This would enable the remaining institutions to become more selective in their standards[13] for admission to teacher training programs.

(2) Establishment of a new norm for professors of education: they should be expected to model the teaching behaviors they wish their teacher trainees to master and to use. Above all, they should be able to use a variety of materials and activities in their courses, to avoid an over-reliance on lecturing, to use lots of open questions, to test using the essay-question format, and so on.

(3) Development of a teacher preparation program based on the fourteen skill areas discussed earlier in this chapter.

(4) Expansion of the Foundations requirement to include one semester each of history, philosophy, and sociology of education. It is in these courses that students preparing to be teachers should learn the skills and habits of

380

self-awareness which form the essential coun-
terbalance to the more mechanical aspects of
learning to teach--the "whys" to go with the
"hows."

Eventually we may see fewer discrepancies,
of the type our Study data revealed, between
teacher belief and teacher action. Ideally,
teachers should be able to clearly explain what
they do in the classroom and why they do it.

(5) Placement of student teachers in schools where
teachers work together and where a variety of
teaching modes and styles are in use. There is
always a tension between the ideal and the real
in this area of teacher preparation, though:
one might argue that it is futile to prepare
new teachers to work cooperatively if they are
going into schools where faculty members do not
behave that way. But the cycle must be broken
somewhere. Following the necessary policy
decisions, schools of education and public
schools will need to work towards these deep
structure changes simultaneously--and interac-
tively. I can envision an arrangement, for
example, in which a school of education estab-
lishes a working relationship with specific
high schools that are actively involved in the
kinds of change processes I have been proposing; student teachers would be placed only in
those schools.

These five areas of policy change in teacher
training would put deep structure changes in the
quality of teaching within reach of individual schools
and school districts. But they could not occur in
isolation. Related changes in the nature of the
teaching career itself would have to take place at more
or less the same time:

(1) State legislatures should lower the maximum
pupil-teacher ratio to 20:1, and provide
funding for salaries accordingly. Our data
show a clear relationship between class size
and time spent on instruction, and classroom
space will be more flexible to the extent that
it is less crowded, thus allowing teachers to
use a greater variety of learning activities
and grouping patterns.

(2) School districts, with the support of the state department of education, should reduce the teacher class load to four teaching periods a day. Of the other two periods, one would be for planning--preparing lessons, grading papers, and the like--and the other would be a "helping" period (three days a week, during this period, the teacher would meet with his or her advisee group; the other two days the teacher would be expected to work with, help, or be helped by other teachers--team planning, observing or being observed, and so forth). The amount of energy released by reducing the actual teaching load to four periods a day could mean a real boost for classroom climate and, as we have seen, there is evidence to support the old saying that "happy teachers make for happy students."

(3) Districts, working together with teachers' associations, should adopt annual calendars (and budgets) which allow plenty of released time for in-service training. The professional growth and continuous improvement of teachers is a worthwhile investment for any community to make, in spite of its rather intangible nature. Results will be seen in staff morale, quality of teaching, and ultimately in student attitudes and the quality of learning as well. 190 or 195-day contracts should be considered--180 days of instruction and 10 to 15 in-service days spread throughout the school year.

(4) For the same reasons, states and districts should adopt--and provide ample financial support for--sabbatical leave policies which allow teachers one semester of paid leave for every seven semesters of service. District guidelines would of course have to be developed, but travel, writing, taking more college courses, and volunteer work in an area relevant to the teacher's field of specialization would be appropriate uses of the sabbatical leave.

(5) High school teaching needs to become a respected profession. Quality control and appropriate incentives are both important aspects of this issue. In our society at the present time, it is difficult to raise a family on a teacher's

382

salary. As we found, most male high school teachers held second jobs for some portion of the school year, and most married female teachers were providing their family's second income. States will have to provide higher pay scales for teachers, and these should be approximately similar in all school districts statewide.

(6) Someone needs to be available to help teachers work on improving their classroom performance. Ideally, each school would have a principal or a vice-principal who is both willing and able to function as an instructional leader. Until such time as a school district can find and hire such personnel, however, a worthwhile investment would be the hiring of a staff development specialist. Such a person would constitute a "support staff" for teachers. Districts should provide one staff development specialist for every two high schools in the district, and these personnel would spend all their time in the two schools, not in the district office.

(7) Districts interested in helping teachers to upgrade the quality of classroom testing and evaluation should provide computer-scoring services for teachers, along with appropriate in-service training to ensure that the teachers know how to use the service. Follow-up to check that they are, in fact, using it would be part of the role of the staff development specialist.

(8) Hiring policies directly affect the work environment of a school and are therefore also connected to staff morale and the quality of teaching. District personnel offices should be on the lookout for applicants who seem to have what John Dewey called "the power to go on growing." This would include the ability and willingness to set professional self-improvement goals, to work cooperatively with other teachers, to observe and be observed in classroom situations, and to use a wide variety of learning activities and materials, teaching styles, and grouping patterns in the classroom. Insofar as possible, evidence of divergent

thinking and creativity would also be desirable.

(9) School and district policies should provide for more teacher involvement in decision-making than is presently common. The teachers are the keystone of the enterprise, after all, and their perceptions are as important as those of administrators to full understanding of school processes and problems. On their part, teachers should be ready to shoulder a larger share of responsibility for school and district decisions, and this means additional time spent in committee work and meetings. Data presented in chapter 3 suggests several areas of decision-making in which teachers could well become more involved.

To summarize: a number of modifications in teacher preparation and in the nature of teaching as a professional occupation would have to occur if the quality of the teaching-learning process at the deep structure level is to be significantly improved. What's more, these cannot be tackled piecemeal; most of them are inter-connected, and should be considered as part of a comprehensive, system-wide change program. Each of them would require one or more policy changes at the local, state, or--in the case of the accreditation of teacher training programs--regional agency level.

Administrator Training

The third general category of policy issues to emerge from the research findings presented in this book has to do with aspects of administrator training.

Our Study is not the first--and will not be the last--to demonstrate that the principal is a key person in the school. We saw strong linkages between the type of leadership that was (or was not) provided by the principal and the work environment and general morale of the teachers (see, for example the Atwater case study in chapter three and the Bradford case study in chapter four).[16] We also found that, in general, the principals of the schools we studied were regarded by their teachers as being primarily administrators, concerned with maintaining the status quo. The principal of Dennison Secondary was the only one in our sample who seemed to be providing genuine leadership for school improvement. (One is tempted to regard the small size of the school and the comparative isolation of the community as buffers which allowed the Dennison principal to function in this way.)

Sarason has documented the process by which principals advance through the ranks, learning conforming behavior as they do so, and the pressures which are exerted--once they reach the principalship--by the superordinate system, to ensure continued conformity and convergent behavior.[17] Callahan, too, described the ways in which educational administration has come to be a matter of management rather than of leadership.[18] If the social and institutional forces described so well by Sarason and Callahan are in fact what has shaped the present generation of high school principals, it's little wonder that twelve of the thirteen principals in our Study fell into the administrator/manager mold. They would have adjusted themselves as necessary on their way up the ladder. This state of affairs is certainly part of the deep structure of schooling as a whole, and major policy changes would be necessary in order to turn it around:

(1) The criteria which determine who gets admitted to administrator credentialing programs might well be reconsidered. At the present time, there is little or no screening; in many institutions--though not all--anyone with the price of tuition can get into the program.

(2) The substance of such programs should not be limited to school law, school finance, collective bargaining, and administrative theory in the abstract. It ought to include both the theory and the practice of instructional leadership skills and helping supervision. No would-be high school principal (or district superintendent) should be granted an administrative credential until he or she has demonstrated leadership capabilities such as the ability to motivate others, to involve teachers in decision-making, to communicate effectively, to establish appropriate problem-solving and curriculum improvement procedures, to provide helping supervision using the clinical supervision model, and to create a climate of mutual trust.

385

(3) As long as a principal's job security is dependent upon "satisfying the higher-ups," an untenable situation will exist within the school--the principal's allegiance will inevitably lie with the superordinate system and a gulf will separate that principal from his or her teachers. Real teamwork is not possible in this kind of a climate--the "us versus them" mentality always gets in the way. Policy changes to reduce this dichotomy should be seriously contemplated by district superintendents and school boards. The ultimate goals, after all, are positive student attitudes and effective student learning, and we now know that happy teachers and a healthy school climate (both of which are affected by the quality of leadership provided by the principal, which in turn may well be determined at least partly by the extent to which the principal sees himself or herself as an advocate and partner of the teachers rather than as their opponent) have a great deal to do with both of these goals. For a start, I would suggest that school districts make the job security of their principals dependent upon their getting good ratings from their teachers, in an evaluation process which would take place every second or third year.

Control Orientation/Custodial Role of the School

The containment and control of young people in school forms the basic core around which all other educational purposes adjust themselves. We pay lip service to the idea of instilling a sense of responsibility in teenagers, but we do not provide them with many real opportunities to actually practice responsible behavior. We expect them to be obedient, yes; but being obedient isn't quite the same thing as acting responsibly. The difference lies in the fact that obedience--and even cooperation--involves following orders or acceding to the wishes of someone else, while responsibility implies acting appropriately and maturely on one's own initiative. This is something we tend to assume that teenagers are incapable of doing, and we have designed our high schools accordingly.

386

(1) As a matter of policy, I would suggest that the monitored study hall be eliminated from the school schedule. The library is available for students who wish to spend extra time studying or doing homework.

(2) All senior secondary schools should operate on an open campus policy. Indeed, if they were to function as I have already outlined, an open campus policy would be unavoidable.

(3) Every student should be well known to at least one adult in the school. In chapter 4 we saw how human potential may be wasted when high-risk students are not identified and helped. The teacher-advisor system is the best way I know of to ensure that no more of our teenagers slip through the cracks of the system and are lost to us. The student's advisory group is his or her emotional home base within the school. It also enables the teachers to keep a closer watch on each student's academic progress, and to nip potential problems in the bud, before they become unmanageable. School districts would do well to eliminate the generally meaningless home room period and install the much more comprehensive teacher-advisor system at both the junior and senior secondary levels. As a matter of policy, every teacher in the school (including coaches and librarians) would have an advisee group of from ten to fifteen students which meets two or three periods a week. The advisee period is sacrosanct and should not be interrupted by anyone for any reason short of a real emergency. The teachers will need in-service training a year in advance to prepare for this new role; the district would, of course, allow for this in planning and budgeting.

(4) The data presented in this book suggest that schools which have not lost sight of their educative mission are, on the whole, happier environments for students and teachers alike. Perhaps it should be a matter of policy as well as of philosophy that the purpose of the junior secondary school (grades 9 and 10) is general education, and that expectations are kept fairly high.

In heterogeneously grouped, individualized classes every student regardless of his or her ability is helped and encouraged to perform not just adequately, but at the best level of which they are capable. Teachers and students share the responsibility for making sure that this happens, and each student's advisor keeps track of the situation as well.

In the senior secondary school, the student would take a larger share of the responsibility for his or her learning, although each student would still have an advisor to turn to if needed. Since the purpose of the senior secondary school would be primarily vocational rather than academic, presumably a student's motivation to do well would be more intrinsic than it might otherwise have been.

These, then, are the four areas of policy issues raised by the data presented in this book. I have tried to suggest policy changes which seem logical in light of our findings, but I have barely scratched the surface. I offer these suggestions as, simply, a starting-point for discussion. What is clear, I feel, is that high schools as they are--as we found the ones we studied in depth--are not good enough. We cannot afford to move on into the 21st century getting just "more of the same." Changes at both levels--the unique personality level and the deep structure level--will be necessary, and these changes will involve all of us: legislators, teacher educators, boards of education, school district personnel, administrators, teachers, parents, and students. The most important theme of this book, though, is that these changes will not be easy, and that their consequences will be systemic. In an organization as complex as a school, a decision to try doing something differently can never exist in isolation.

*   *   *

Looking to the Future

In the fall of 1957, I was a high school sophomore. One of the facts of my life that year was Mr. Blaustein, the biology teacher. Mr. Blaustein's style was forceful, dramatic, and a little bit sarcastic. We

388

were afraid of the sarcasm but intrigued and entertain-
ed by the drama, and when Mr. Blaustein talked, we
listened. Mr. Blaustein lectured a lot. Once in
awhile we did experiments, but most of the time we
listened and took notes. That was the expectation in
biology, as it was the expectation in all of the
required courses--English, math, and social studies,
too.

A quarter of a century has passed, and I am now
involved in teacher training and staff development. My
work often includes the supervision of teachers.
Recently I sat in a sophomore biology class and listened to a lecture on photosynthesis. The teacher wasn't
like Mr. Blaustein--he lacked Mr. Blaustein's sarcasm--
but the teaching practices I saw, and most of the
content as well, were no different. The teacher
lectured, and the students listened and took notes.
Once in a while a student would ask for clarification
of a point. The morning sun filtered in through the
dusty science room windows, the threat of an impending
test on cell structure had subdued the class, and the
teacher across the hall could be heard, lecturing to
his class. It took very little effort to imagine
myself back in Mr. Blaustein's class so many years ago.
Nothing was really different.

A Study of Schooling findings presented in this
book reveal 13 American high schools that were not, in
1977, much different from high schools in the 1950s.
The system of secondary schooling in this country
evolved between 1850 and 1950, roughly, and then it
stopped. The whole network--school district structures, lines of authority, the curriculum, and so
on--solidified in a form which our society, by and
large, found acceptable. Public notions of what the
high school should not be* joined with vested interests
to discourage further change and innovation.

This "steady state" period which began in the 1950s
has had, thus far, three major phases. The criticism
of the late '50s and early '60s constituted the first
phase. This was followed by the improvement efforts of
the late '60s and early '70s. The late '70s and early

---

* I do not mean to suggest that the public has ever reached a
consensus as to what the high school should be, but I do think
there is general agreement as to what is should not be.

'80s, by contrast, have been a period of disillusion and withdrawal of support for public schooling. Alternative schools, voucher plans, and the flight to private schools are some of the forms which this withdrawal has taken.

In the schools themselves, morale declines. It becomes more difficult to attract good young people into teaching, as Schlechty and Vance have document-ed.[19] In any case, there aren't many job openings for new teachers, as the school-age population declines and many districts decide to close some existing schools. Teachers already in place hang onto their jobs despite the low morale, and the median age of the profession increases year by year. If it weren't for a promising new emphasis on staff development and professional growth programs, the overall impression would be one of more or less unrelieved stagnation.

This is exacerbated by the negative images of school conveyed to the public by the mass media, which notoriously neglect the small daily and weekly triumphs of hard-working teachers and focus instead on school problems and conflicts.

The political climate, too, is part of the problem. In referring to LBJ, historian Lawrence Cremin has noted the incredible power that the office of the Presidency now exerts over "the nature and purposes of public education."[20] This is true also of the Reagan administration. Its systematic dismantling of federal education agencies and the decision to spend tax dollars on military hardware rather than on education and research (partners in the search for knowledge and understanding) are changing the way Americans think about schooling. As a society, we seem to have lost sight of our earlier vision of the vital importance of schools to the health of the nation. One rarely hears discussion, these days, of the greater good or of what constitutes an individual's social responsibility. No longer do I hear voices echoing Dewey, that

> ...what the best and wisest parent wants for his own child, that must the community want for all of its children. Any other ideal for our schools is narrow and unlovely; acted upon, it destroys our democracy.
> (The School and Society, 1899)

Economic hard times don't help matters, either. Duke and Meckel have documented the effects of fiscal retrenchment on a high school in San Jose, California and the story is being repeated in school districts across the country with increasing frequency.[21] The world economy, and ours with it, seems to be in a downward spiral which is unlike any that has been experienced before. The possible collapse of the international banking system hangs like a cloud over the 1980s.

At such a time, just when flexibility and innovation might help to turn things around, it seems that people cling even more adamantly to what they have. Power, privilege, or affluence--as John Gardner has observed, "Vested interests may be found wherever a man acquires a shirt for his back or rights and privileges he would be reluctant to lose."[22] In an organization, maintenance workers can have a vested interest in the status quo, just as the president can. In a school, the teachers may have a vested interest in the way things are which prompts them to defend their rights and privileges in all sorts of ways, from passive resistance to strikes. For example, autonomy in the classroom is one of the things teachers cherish. Indeed, it is one of the reasons many people are attracted to teaching as a career. Changes which they perceive as threats to that autonomy--such as team teaching and peer observation--are met with passive resistance. Other vested interests, such as pay scales and working hours, become targets of negotiation and sometimes are the basis of strikes. The relative merits of teacher strikes are not at issue here; what interests me is the nature of vested interests, and the fact that these may exist at all levels of an organization--or a society.

And a democratic form of organization is by no means immune to this consequence. Indeed, the more democratic it is the more vividly the vested interests of its members will be reflected in the policy of the organization. Thus a stagnant democratic organization may be particularly resistant to change.[23]

Over a hundred years ago, Abraham Lincoln urged the people of our nation to, in effect, set aside their vested interests for the common good: "...the occasion is piled high with difficulty and we must rise with the occasion. As our case is new, so we must think anew and act anew. We must disenthrall ourselves...." What I fear is that now, in these difficult times of the waning 20th century, we will simply not be able to "disenthrall ourselves" enough. Our society has been resilient in the past, but resilience is a characteristic of youth and our society has aged quickly in its brief existence. "So stubborn are the defenses of a mature society against change that shock treatment is often required to bring about renewal. A nation will postpone critically important social changes until war or depression forces the issue. Many a business firm has had to go through bankruptcy before initiating obviously necessary reforms."[24]

And what about our high schools? There's no doubt that vested interests are at stake. There's no denying that high schools have changed little in the past 35 years. And there's ample evidence that the years ahead will be critical ones for secondary education. Will we continue along our present path, or will we find the capacity, the vision and, indeed, the selflessness required to help in the rejuvenation and reconstruction of schooling?

Scenario I: More of the Same

We could just let things slide. We could do our jobs, ask no questions, collect our pay checks, and indulge in depression or bitterness about the decline of support for public schooling. Things would go on more or less as they "always" have (at least within the lifetimes of most of us) and probably everyone, school people and the public alike, would be pretty comfortable.

Meanwhile, like a fox stealing into a chicken coop, the computer revolution is gathering momentum. When its full impact is realized, feathers will fly. The nature of secondary schooling could be profoundly altered. True, some educators have enrolled in computer literacy courses in an effort to stay abreast of the coming changes in information processing and retrieval. Some high schools (unfortunately, usually the most affluent) have managed to purchase computer hard- and software, and to hire trained teachers; these relatively few schools are able to offer computer literacy

392

classes for their students.[25] Such students will leave high school with a tremendous advantage over most of their peers, who either did not have the luck to attend a school with computer education facilities, or the foresight to benefit from attendance at a school that did.

In 1950, relatively few households had a television set; ten years later, few were without one. As this book goes to press, relatively few households have home computers, but it may take even less than ten years for home computers to become as much a part of our lives as television has become. And when that happens (and when communications satellites containing the libraries of the world orbit the earth, making all of human knowledge accessible to those who have the equipment needed to tap into it) why would students need to go to school? Home learning centers could be so complete that the only thing missing from the educational experience would be peer group interaction. Student/teacher interaction will be possible. Lectures will be possible. Learning programs to develop and test all kinds of intellectual skills will be available. A student could practice conversational Spanish, dissect a frog, solve algebra problems, learn a recipe and prepare the dish for dinner, read a novel and reflect upon its author's intentions and techniques, and study the battle strategies used in the Civil War on a typical "school day" at home.

Schools as they presently exist might serve very different functions than they do now. They might be materials distribution centers, for one thing. A student would go there to get a frog, and to check out dissection equipment or a microscope. Periodically, the student would report to school for tutorial sessions, small group discussions, or a conference with his or her advisor. The use of space in a school building would change, as well. Only a few classrooms of various sizes would be needed for special events not possible on the home system. Instead, teachers would need office space, and the facilities necessary to interact with students via a combination of computer, video-telephone, and ETV (educational TV) hookups.

I could go on imagining this scenario--in truth, I do not know enough about computers yet to speculate knowledgeably as to their potential impact. But I believe they will change our lives, and I also believe, as Humpty Dumpty said, that "...the question is, which is to be the master." It is possible to envision a world in which ordinary people are very much not the masters, even of their own lives. But is is also possible to imagine a world in which computer technology is wisely used for the greater good, kept within reasonable bounds by wise leadership and, as necessary, by public outrage when technology abuse does occur.

Scenario II: One Vision of the Possible

Earlier in this chapter I outlined an alternative scenario for secondary education (grades 9-12) which would preserve the best elements of the comprehensive high school while at the same time ensuring a greater degree of commonly-experienced general education than is possible under the present system. The high school years would be divided into junior and senior secondary phases. All students in the junior secondary school (grades 9 and 10) would take a common curriculum consisting of language arts, math and computer literacy, science, social studies, a second language, the arts, physical education, career awareness/study skills, and advisory group. At this level, there would be no tracking; all classes would consist of mixed-ability groups. Teachers would, however, use within-class grouping and re-grouping to provide appropriate learning experiences for students of differing needs and abilities in each class. A variety of learning activities and materials would be utilized, and remedial help would be available as needed.

A strong transitional guidance program in the 10th grade would prepare students to make a good choice as to which curriculum to enter in 11th grade. The senior secondary phase--11th and 12th grades--would be the time for specialization and preparation for entering the world of work and full adulthood. Students entering 11th grade would choose from among a variety of vocational preparation programs and two college-preparatory programs: general college prep and advanced placement. Work-study programs would be available as appropriate.

I hope it is clear that I am not calling for the demise of the comprehensive high school. I fully agree with Daniel Tanner that splitting up the secondary school along what would amount to social class lines--

that is, separating high achievers from low achievers, and the college-bound from the laborers--would "only lead to an even more divided society."[26] In fact, what I am proposing would keep young people together, sharing a common schooling experience, far longer than is now the case. In some school systems, the "heads-hands," "slow-fast" separation[27] of students begins in 7th grade, or even earlier. I am suggesting that this not take place until 11th grade, and then only after careful preparation for the decision has been made.

The return to an emphasis on high-quality general education through 10th grade could be tremendously important for our society. Individual differences would be taken into consideration and planned for in each class, so no student would be either held back or left behind. At the same time, all young people would acquire a common set of learnings. Even more importantly, they would be together, learning to communicate and to get along despite differences in family background, values, interests, opinions, and plans for the future. Indeed, understanding of a variety of viewpoints is one of the citizen's primary tasks in a democracy, and this can only be achieved if teenagers have substantial contact with a variety of people, both within and beyond their peer group. It is important that, insofar as it is possible, school populations as well as classroom groups be socially and economically heterogeneous.

At the senior secondary level, students would elect a pre-career path which would separate them, at least during class time, from their peers according to the type of training necessary for the career or career cluster they choose to enter. Under the present system, this separation takes place much earlier (as we have seen, it can be in place by the end of elementary school and certainly exists in the junior high and middle schools) and it is based on a variety of factors, none of which have much to do with thoughtful, informed career choice on the student's part.

Teacher pre-service and in-service training, a re-thinking of our incentive and reward systems in public education, and a restructuring of the teacher's work load would be critical to the success of a change such as the 9-10/11-12 split high school I am

395

proposing. These have already been discussed and need be only briefly summarized here:

1) Present and future teachers would need to develop competence in the 14 areas of teacher effectiveness which were discussed at length earlier in this chapter. These include the use of pre-tests and small group activities, interdisciplinary approaches to subject matter, managing mixed-ability classes, using more essay tests and using computer-scored objective tests, utilizing a broader array of learning activities and materials, and so forth. Pre-service teacher training would need to be restructured so as to include these competencies, and school districts would have to provide systematic in-service opportunities for existing faculties to acquire this retraining.

2) Substantial salary increases for teachers who not only demonstrate mastery of the necessary skills but who actually use them consistently in their teaching would provide the incentives and rewards needed to attract and keep the best teachers within the new framework for high schools. In addition, one semester of paid sabbatical leave would be offered for every seven semesters of service.

3) The typical teacher work load would consist of four class periods, one advisory period, and one or two planning periods daily. Maximum allowable class size would be twenty students.

That's my vision of the revitalization of the American high school. All of the suggested changes emerge logically from the Study of Schooling findings presented in this book. Some are deep structure changes requiring major policy decisions at federal, state, and local levels. Others are changes specific to each individual school. These will require the concentrated, cooperative effort of teachers, administrators, and non-teaching school staff such as guidance counselors, librarians, and district consultants. Parents, other citizens, and students should be involved as appropriate.

The complexity of the task must not be underestimated. Many times, in this book, we have seen examples of how organically connected all the parts of the high

396

school are to each other, and how a change in one part can affect the other parts. Nevertheless, I believe the changes proposed are both realistic and achievable. It would be a challenge to be a part of such a rejuvenation of the high school. It would be deeply satisfying. And I think it would be fun.

CHAPTER VII, NOTES AND REFERENCES

1. The Culture of the School and the Problem of Change by Seymour B. Sarason. (Boston: Allyn and Bacon, 1971).

2. The Scientific Basis of the Art of Teaching by N.L. Gage. (Teachers College Press, 1978):44-45.

3. Big School, Small School: High School Size and Student Behavior by Roger G. Barker and Paul V. Gump, (Palo Alto: Stanford University Press, 1964).

4. Robert L. Hampel, "The American High School Today: James Bryant Conant's Reservations and Reconsiderations," Phi Delta Kappan (May, 1983):607-612.

5. Joyce Wright, Teaching and Learning, (Technical Report No. 18, 1980), p. 56.

6. Sarason, op. cit., p. 139.

7. The Human Side of Enterprise by Douglas McGregor, (New York: McGraw-Hill, 1961).

8. Kenneth A. Tye, "The Times They Are A-Changin' for School Principals," Thrust, Association of California School Administrators, (November, 1977).

9. The Management of Organizational Behavior by Paul Hersey and Kenneth Blanchard. (Englewood Cliffs, NJ: Prentice-Hall, 1977).

10. National Longitudinal Study of the Class of 1972, NCES, 1974; op. cit., High School and Beyond, NCES, 1981; op. cit.

11. Rosenshine, B.V. "Content, Time, and Direct Instruction" Research on Teaching: Concepts, Findings, and Implications (Berkeley: McCutchan) 1979.

12. Horowitz, R.A. "Psychological Effects of the Open Classroom" Review of Educational Research 49(I): 71-85, 1979. Peterson, Penelope L. "Direct Instruction: Effective for What and For Whom?" Educational Leadership 37(I):46-48, 1979.

13. Teacher Preparation: Exploration of an Alternative Model. Unpublished doctoral dissertation, B.J. Benham. Texas Tech University, 1977.

14. Paul Heckman, Exploring the Concept of School Renewal: Cultural Differences and Similarities Between More and Less Renewing Schools, (Technical Report No. 33, 1982).

15. Fred M. Hechinger, "The Decline in Teacher Status," San Francisco Chronicle, This World Section, p. 19 (August 8, 1982).

16. Richard Daly, A Causal Analysis of Satisfaction, Performance, Work Environment and Leadership in Secondary School, (Technical Report No. 31, 1981).

17. Sarason, op. cit.

18. The Cult of Efficiency by Raymond Callahan. (Chicago: University of Chicago Press, 1962).

19. "The Distribution of Academic Ability in the Teaching Force: Policy Implications," by Victor S. Vance and Phillip C. Schlecty. Phi Delta Kappan (September, 1982):22-27.

20. The Genius of American Education by Lawrence Cremin (New York: Vintage, 1965):97.

21. "The Slow Death of a Public High School," by Daniel Duke and Adrienne Meckel. Phi Delta Kappan (June, 1980):674-677.

22. Self-Renewal: The Individual and the Innovative Society by John W. Gardner. (New York: Harper and Row, 1963. Perennial Library paperback edition, 1971) p. 65.

23. Gardner, ibid., p. 65.

24. Ibid., p. 54.

25. "The Computer Age in Education," Phi Delta Kappan (January, 1982).

26. "Splitting Up the School System: Are Comprehensive High Schools Doomed?" by Daniel Tanner. Phi Delta Kappan (October, 1979):92-97.

27. The Junior High: School in Search of a Mission by Kenneth A. Tye (Lanham, MD: University Press of America, 1985).